GROSS MISCONDUCT

HITTING FROM BEHIND

Sandra Young Kolbuc, M.Sc., RMFT, CCC
& Tracy Stark, Mother

 FriesenPress

One Printers Way
Altona, MB R0G 0B0
Canada

www.friesenpress.com

ISBN
978-1-03-910403-7 (Hardcover)
978-1-03-910402-0 (Paperback)
978-1-03-910404-4 (eBook)

1. BIOGRAPHY & AUTOBIOGRAPHY, PERSONAL MEMOIRS

Distributed to the trade by The Ingram Book Company

DISCLAIMER

THE CONTENT OF THE BOOK IS EXTREMELY DISQUIETING IN SHARING THE experience of a mother finding her two young boys murdered. The book is raw and it is real and we discourage anyone from reading the book if they think they may be totally disturbed by its contents.

Interactive dialogue in therapy session is taken from the sum total of many therapeutic interactions between the therapist and the client. We take no responsibility for any discrepancies that may arise in the recollections of others in any of these or other included events.

The therapeutic information provided in this book is included in the telling of the story but should not be considered as a source of therapeutic advice for the reader. The publication is meant as a source of valuable information for the reader. However it is not meant as a substitute for direct expert assistance. If such a level of assistance is required the services of a competent professional should be sought.

The authors have made every effort to ensure the information in this book is correct at press time and while the publication is designed to provide accurate information in regard to the subject matter covered, the authors assume no responsibility for errors, inaccuracies, omissions, or any other inconsistencies herein and hereby disclaim any liability to any party for any loss, damage or disruption caused by such errors or omissions, whether such errors or omission result from negligence, accident or any other cause.

Sandra Young Kolbuc & Tracy Stark

A Mother's Love

This Book Is

DEDICATED TO THE MEMORY
of
Ryder Patryk (2003-2016) & Radek Stryker (2005-2016)

The R&R Heart Image

TABLE OF CONTENTS

Preface

WHAT DO YOU DO WHEN ONE COLD WINTER DAY IN DECEMBER OF 2016, the trajectory of your life changes in a way you could never have imagined? What do you do when your primary purpose, your most important and most sacred role in life, is snuffed out by the horrific actions of the biological father of your children?

When my husband Brent and I discovered the bodies of my two sons, Radek and Ryder, in the home of my ex-husband just six days before Christmas, my life was forever changed. In the weeks and months that followed, the tentacles of the unbelievable trauma, grief, and loss attempted to rip my entire life from me. Like most who lose a child, or in my case two beautiful children, I struggled to get out of bed every morning and put one foot in front of the other.

I was simply trying to survive the incredible sorrow and handle the daunting rage that coursed through my body each day. But capturing an audience and getting my story into the minds of those who could make the changes needed so another child did not die at the hands of a controlling, angry parent was nowhere on my radar. I had the words. F*ck, I had a lot of words.

Shortly after my boys died, through what I now term both synchronicity and circumstance, a woman well-versed in treating trauma became my counsellor. After we spent some time together, she suggested that writing, and then, in session, processing what I had written, might be helpful in my healing. Such proved to be true.

After over two years of travelling together on the rocky road of trauma and grief, I asked Sandra Young Kolbuc, my counselling therapist, to join me in writing my story and that of my precious boys and to tell my story through her eyes as well as mine. When she agreed to write with me, the telling of the story began to take shape with information shared in my counselling sessions, my Facebook posts and texts and email exchanges between us where I answered further questions she posed to me outside our sessions.

My writing journey, with my therapist by my side, guiding me in this process, has given me the strength and courage to share my narrative with a larger audience. It is in the hopes that those who read it, or hear it, if they recognize themselves in my story, will be moved to action and work to generate real change within themselves to create a more positive dynamic for their children. My greatest intention is to bring awareness to the importance of changing laws, procedures, and circumstances that failed to protect two blameless children caught in the cross hairs of an angry, revengeful father bent on coercive control.

Since being a childless mother has become my reality, I have come to believe that the actions of a rage-filled, controlling ex-husband could have been averted if the legal and provincial systems had had appropriate protocols in place. If those in positions of influence had spoken up loudly and clearly in the best interest of two innocent children, my hockey-playing sons could still be putting on their hockey gear, racing down the ice surface, shooting pucks, scoring goals, and simply loving life. Instead, today, they reside in two urns sitting reverently in the spaces that were once their bedrooms.

As I think now of what happened, I contend there must be a review of laws regarding custody and access to men who continue to display abusive and disrespectful actions to their ex-wives. As well, it is totally unacceptable to grant those privileges to those ex-partners who create fear in their children or put those children at risk either emotionally, mentally, or physically while in their care. Displaying hate-filled behaviours toward a former spouse in front of the very children caught in the middle of custody anfd access battles is also beyond reprehensible.

I am not saying that mothers are always innocent of such wrongdoings. They certainly are not. Filicide statistics show that mothers kill, maim, and abuse their children, often younger children and most often as a result of postpartum depression, another mental illness, or an unwanted pregnancies. There is also evidence of women tormenting their ex-husbands with their own need for control and revenge.

However, if people read the research regarding filicide by men, they'll find far too many instances of fathers killing their children to get back at their ex-wives. In my case, my children became those victims. When their father was angry at me, he so often took it out on my boys. How sick is that? How very sick.

Since my boys died, I have heard from many parents legally bound to share custody of their children with an angry ex-spouse. Many can relate to my experience of the continual pain and aggravation caused by a former partner in sharing the parenting of a child or children after ending a relationship. Such conflict has been shown to affect innocent children not only in the present moment but also long term in their lives.

This story focuses on my relationship with my ex-husband, my previous battles regarding the custody and access of my children, and the events leading up to and following the deaths of my boys. It is the story of my healing walk with my therapist to find peace and purpose, meaning and mastery in my life since the date of December 19, 2016, was indelibly tattooed on my soul. It is also my devoted purpose to share with the world the privilege of being the mother of two incredible sons, Radek Stryker and Ryder Patryk, forever known as **R&R.** This is not only my story but their story as well

Some may read this and think, *Wow! What is the "other side" of the story?* Well, the "other side" blew off his own head after taking a loaded shotgun to my sleeping children. That is the other side of the story.

Gross Misconduct: Hitting from Behind … … … … … A Mother's Love Story is not only a recounting of devastation and loss. It details, as well, the power of love in one's restorative journey to a degree of sanity after such an experience. It is my story of being a woman who loved, absolutely loved, being a mom. It is the story of a woman who is continually surrounded by the love of both friends and strangers alike. It is a story of such love emanating from citizens known and unknown to me in the two small hockey-centric communities of Spruce Grove and Whitecourt, Alberta, in support of a grieving family. It is the outcry of those horrified by what happened on a cold December night in a small city, in a small suburb, just down the block, in a house like any other.

As I continue to move forward to find peace in my soul and reckoning for my boys, many have walked beside me as the reality of the death of my sons resonated in my bones. More than anything, other than their return to earth, what I want for my boys is to know that although their lives were short, they made and will continue to make a difference in the lives of other mothers and children caught in systems built to support them but which wretchedly fail to do so.

The book is, as well, a reflection of the love and kindness of many throughout the entire world who continue to be there for my husband Brent and me in our quest to keep ever before us a beacon of hope. Hope that sharing my experience will make a profound difference in the lives of others and liberate other women from the potential trauma of such a scene as my husband and I came upon the morning of December 19, 2016.

May hearing my story also help families caught in the craziness of separation and divorce to recognize that all too often, children are the victims of parents who fail to do their own work when rage, resentment, jealousy, addictions, or control become their way of walking in the world. Tragically, such became my children's reality.

The story is at times very harsh and very raw, and you, the reader, may need courage to read it. Hopefully you are that brave. May you be inspired to find your voice about things that matter in your life or in the lives of others afraid to find theirs. I invite you to join me in a quest to stand for safety and justice for all children, children just like Radek and Ryder, my **R&R.**

Tracy Stark, Mother

***

As Muriel Rukeyser (1913–1980), American poet and political activist, most famous for her poems about equality, feminism, and social justice, is reported to have said: "What if one woman told the truth about her life? The world would split open."

Followed by ... "The universe is made up of stories, not of atoms."[1] With grit and grace, great love and grizzly tenacity, let the telling of a mother's love story ... begin.

Sandra Young Kolbuc, Counselling Therapist

NOTE TO READERS:

Emails and texts are designated in the following manner:
TRS to SYK: Tracy Ross Stark/Sandra Young Kolbuc and vice versa
TRS to CGM: Tracy Ross Stark/Corry Gene MacDougall and vice versa

---

1   https://www.goodreads.com Muriel Rukeyser Quotes (Author of *The Life of Poetry*)

Chapter 1

MANIC MONDAY

IT WAS MONDAY MORNING, DECEMBER 19, 2016. IT HAD BEEN TRACY'S weekend with her boys, Radek, aged eleven, and Ryder, aged thirteen. Her sons would be celebrating Christmas with their dad this year as, per the court order, it was his turn for Christmas. On December 29th, Tracy would again get the boys in her care for the remainder of the school holidays.

Since September, Radek and Ryder had been living with their biological father in Spruce Grove, a little more than an hour away from their hometown of Whitecourt, Alberta. Tracy had agreed to the new arrangement in order to give the boys a chance to play a more competitive level of hockey in the larger centre.

The past weekend, Tracy and her second husband, Brent, had had their own holiday celebration with her boys in the new duplex Tracy had rented in Spruce Grove. She had missed her sons far more than she ever thought she would when she'd made the decision to allow them to live with their dad. While she still maintained primary custody, having the boys in her care every second weekend wasn't cutting it. As well, she was disturbed by information the boys had shared with her two weeks prior, regarding their experiences in living with their dad for the last three months. Their first month had been great but then, things had changed dramatically.

After hearing what was going on for her sons, Tracy and Brent decided Tracy would rent a duplex in Spruce Grove to be more involved with the day-to-day life of the boys and to be close by if they needed her. It was there that Tracy and Brent had spent the pre-holiday weekend with the boys.

Sunday evening, Brent, Tracy, and Radek drove with Ryder to his hockey game. They were excited to watch their up-and-coming hockey player from the stands. Tracy shared her Merry Christmas wishes and goodbye hugs with her older son outside the Millwoods Recreation Centre before he headed to the dressing room to change for his upcoming game. Ryder said he loved her and would call her after the game. She waved to him as they left the arena between the second and third periods to head to Whitecourt.

After loading up the boys' suitcases into the back of Corry's truck, Tracy turned to hug Radek goodbye in the parking lot. The young boy teared up as she drew him close. She held him away from her and asked, "What's wrong, Radek?"

He responded haltingly, "I'm just gonna miss you, Mom."

Tracy hugged her younger son tightly as the tears fell from his eyes. "You don't have to go with your dad, Radek," she said. "You can come home with me."

Radek shook his head and insisted he had to go with his dad. He worked hard at controlling his tears, and his mother's arms held him close until he felt he was good to go. One last hug and then he headed back inside the arena to sit with his dad.

As Tracy and Brent began to head to Whitecourt, Tracy started thinking of Radek's reaction when they had said goodbye. She was concerned with Radek being so upset and turned to her husband and said, "We need to stay in Spruce Grove tonight, Brent. I want to be close by in case the kids need me."

Brent shrugged and headed the truck toward the duplex. Tracy's mind was full of all the things she needed to do to get the boys back permanently in her care.

Later, in a counselling session, Tracy, shared her thought process of that evening with me, her counselling therapist. "I remained calm as we drove to the duplex. I thought about the texting between me and Corry those last two days, knowing in my mind, that since he had refused my offer of shared custody, I was taking my kids back. I knew parenting young boys could be challenging but, in my mind Corry's home had become unsafe for my kids. I was becoming more and more determined that Corry would never get them in his care again. I would find a way to remove them from his home despite him telling me he now has primary residence and the boys wanted to stay with him. That was bullsh*t! I was biding my time. We would go with the original plan of the boys spending Christmas with Dad and his family. I reminded myself that they would be around people who loved them. Everything would be okay. I have given the boys explicit instructions not to talk about the duplex or anything related to moving to Spruce Grove that might set their dad off."

She reassured herself. *Me and Brent will pick them up on December 29th. I'll have time to get everything in place to follow the plan I have lining up in my head. Everything will be okay.*

***

The next morning, as Brent started to pack up for their trip home to Whitecourt, he called out to his wife, "Hey Tracy. Did Ryder call last night after the game?"

Tracy replied, "No, he didn't, which doesn't surprise me, but I haven't heard from Radek this morning, and that's not like him. He's usually called by now."

She picked up her cell phone and called her younger son. No answer. Then she tried Ryder's number. Again, no answer. The kids' phones both went straight to voice mail.

"I'll bet Corry took their phones away," she said. "I will be so glad when they are out of that damn house."

She texted Corry. "Did you take the kids' phones away?" No response. She sent a second text: "If you don't call me back within half an hour, Corry, I'm going to call the police." No response.

Waiting for Brent, she started to pace, wondering if she was overreacting. Once she knew school was in, she called the boys' school. The receptionist informed her that both boys had been marked absent. She must have sensed the panic in Tracy's voice as she asked, "Are you the mom?"

Tracy began to tear up and said, "Yes, I am."

Brent turned to look at her as she thanked the woman on the other end of the phone and hung up.

She grabbed her bag, moving quickly as she said, "Let's go, Brent. Something isn't right. They aren't at school. I want to get over to Corry's house right away."

Within minutes, they were on the road. As they sped toward Corry's place, Brent turned to Tracy and said, "Well, Trac, maybe Corry is just being a d*ck. He's done this before."

Tracy continued texting Corry. "Called the kids' school. They are not there." She waited impatiently for his reply. Again, no response.

Again, she hit the buttons. "Coward! Guess you have forgotten that my court order is police-enforced from the last time you pulled this sh*t."

The Hollow, Eerie Cry of Reality

They pulled up to the front of the house. It was dark except for a light in an upper room. Brent parked on the street, blocking the driveway.

There was no hint of danger, except for the uneasiness in Tracy's gut. This was just Corry being his controlling self. She ran quickly up to the front door and rang the doorbell as she peered in the tall, frosted window. She thought, *Maybe Corry is just keeping them home this morning.* There was a strange silence. No dog barking. Too quiet.

Both of Corry's vehicles were parked outside. His work truck was on the street beside the house and his blue personal truck was in the driveway along with a trailer holding two sleds.

Later, in recounting that fateful morning in a future email, Tracy sent the following recollection of that horrendous day to me, her counselling therapist.

> TRS to SYK: I rang the doorbell. I looked up the stairs and down the stairs and saw nothing unusual. I could see Radek's tall black and red CCM hockey bag at the bottom of the stairs. However, my heart began to race. Something didn't seem right. I continued to bang on the door and rang the doorbell like a crazy woman. I looked in the window one last time, and something told me to look down at the landing. That's when I saw the bare legs of a child. I changed the angle of my view. It was RYDER! Thinking ... *that's a strange place for him to be.* His legs were in a fetal position with his one hand between his legs. Then I seen what looked like blood smeared on his legs. After all my banging on the door and ringing of the doorbell, he wasn't moving.
>
> OMG! My breath left my body. My guts twisted violently. Then it hit me. My RYDER was dead! I remember screaming into the gloominess of the morning sky. Brent, standing on the foot rail of his vehicle called out, asking me what was going on. I yelled to him, "I think the boys are dead!"
>
> Brent insisted I come back and sit in the vehicle where I watched as he approached the door of Corry's house. He was looking in the window and then, shrugging his shoulders, looked back at me, and yelled: "I don't see any-thing Tracy."
>
> I got out of the truck and ran back to him and looked again in the window, thinking to myself, '*Have I lost my mind?*' I had not. Lying there in front of me,

behind the glass, was my older son. I backed up and pointed to Ryder lying on the floor.

Then Brent seen what I seen and shouted at me to get back in the vehicle as he put his shoulder to the locked door, attempting to break in.

A neighbour saw what Brent was doing and yelled at us, "Why the hell are you trying to break into my best friend's house?"

I screamed at him, "Your f*#ing best friend just killed my kid!!" I soon learned his best friend owned the house, which Corry was renting. Corry MacDougall, the man who had murdered his own children, was not his best friend.

Brent dialed 911.

The winter air was filled with the hollow, eerie cries of a mother experiencing the worst possible scenario imaginable.

Later, in a counselling session, Tracy recounted her experience by sharing more of what she had written.

I could not stop screaming. This was unf**king real! Ryder was dead! Where was my Radek? The neighbour thought he and Brent might be able to get in the back door. They raced to the back of the house and upon opening the door, Corry's boxer dog came flying out. Brent suddenly realized that Corry might be still inside, alive! People began coming out of their homes, standing on their front steps to see what was going on. Someone else, witnessing the unthinkable scene unfolding in their neighbourhood, called 911 as well.

The SWAT team arrived on the scene within minutes. Coming from every direction, the officers swarmed around Corry's house like yellow- jackets on a hive. One team member, wearing jeans and a police jacket with a lanyard identifying him as the crime scene investigator, came up to me and told me to remain in my vehicle as his team took charge of the crime scene. I sat in the truck, horrified at what was unfolding before my eyes. As I watched the two officers beat down the front door that opened to where my baby's lifeless body lay, I saw Ryder wearing only a blue shirt. He was naked from the waist down. As the police officers entered the home, Ryder's body just remained there for all the world to see. I started screaming wildly for them to cover him up. I remember yelling "He's naked. He's cold! And … he's mine!"

More officers entered the house via the side gate, which led to the back yard. Corry's dog had obviously borne witness to a horrific chain of events and was totally traumatized. Someone tended to the terrified animal. He was whimpering uncontrollably. The well-being of the dog bothered me, but I was not allowed to leave the truck. Later, I wondered what had happened to him as he was my kids' dog and he was completely unsettled.

This horror movie was becoming my reality. I couldn't click the remote and shut it off. It was real. I began to rock back and forth on the front seat of the truck and recall thinking, *What about Radek? Where is my baby? Oh my God. This can't be happening*! I was shaking uncontrollably. The investigator returned to where I was sitting sideways in Brent's vehicle with the door open. He approached me and confirmed there were three dead in the home. An adult and two children. My Radek had been found dead in his father's bed. I was

inconsolable. Not that anyone other than Brent tried to calm me down. My heart was beating out of my chest.

A female member of SWAT came to speak with me. "How are you?" asked the officer.

I looked at her and blurted out. "Not so good, Officer. I've just found out my kids are dead!"

The woman showed not a seed of empathy. I suppose what one might say was that her demeanour was "extremely professional." She looked rather surprised at my reaction. My God! Was there no RCMP script as to what were appropriate and inappropriate questions or procedures to follow from one of Canada's Finest who should have some definitive idea from her training as to how to deal with a woman who has just been told her children were dead or how to deal with a mother totally in shock with what she had witnessed, with what she has just been told?

I felt like I was having a horrible nightmare. This couldn't be real. There was not an ounce of compassion from anyone on the SWAT team. They were on task, focused on doing their job, which obviously did not include tending to a mother locked in the traumatic responses of what she had seen, what she was experiencing.

I was sure that coming upon what the officers found when they entered Corry's house was not easy, but what did they think it was like for me, the boys' mother, sitting in a truck a few feet away from my sons, unable to go to them, hold them, rock them, cry over their bodies? However, the SWAT team had their positions to play as a part of their team and I was obviously just in the way.

In her recollection of the event, at a future session, Tracy shared, "I squeezed my eyes shut and opened them again. This couldn't be true! I could not stop shaking until suddenly, a calmness descended upon me. Then nothing seemed to be registering. I was in another zone."

Months later, Tracy understood that what had happened to her at that time was called dissociation.[2] She had been in such a totally traumatized state; her nervous system had been totally overwhelmed. Too much! Too fast! In order to manage what was happening, she had briefly checked out as the investigation went on. Her email continued.

> TRS to SYK: When Brent arrived back at the truck, I suddenly snapped back to reality. He attempted to calm me, but I would not be calmed. I desperately wanted to see my kids. To hold them. To rock them. To push their hair back from their foreheads and say everything would be all right even though I knew it wouldn't!
>
> I remember Brent, through his own tears, holding on to me and saying, "No Tracy. No! It would do you no good to see them as they are right now. No!"
>
> I freaked, thinking of what my boys had been through with someone they thought they could trust—THEIR F*#KING DAD for God's sakes! My world, as I knew it, was falling apart. The police officers remained distant. There was little attention paid by the officers to the depth of what me and Brent were experiencing. We were both in shock as we were told we were to report immediately to the RCMP Offices in Stony Plain where statements from each of us would be taken.

Suspects

We left the scene knowing nothing, not even how my kids had been killed. Everyone involved seemed totally impersonal. I felt perceived as someone guilty of a crime. That is exactly how I was treated. In retrospect, I wonder if there is not a protocol that would have been kinder and more therapeutic for a mother who had just seen her child lying on the floor, covered in blood, not moving, and

---

2   Dissociation: Has its roots in the brain's opioid system, which secretes endorphins to blunt strong, painful feelings allowing a temporary break whereby an individual can be physically present but psychologically unreachable, tuning out and becoming amnestic to the whole traumatic experience. (CFTRE.com)

naked from the waist down. A woman who had just been told that her second son was also dead.

Brent and I left the scene where my babies had taken their last breaths. It was so very hard to leave them in that house, but we had been told we were to follow a police cruiser to the Stony Plain Detachment.

Once there, a police officer escorted us into the building. I was taken to one room and Brent to another and just like in the movies, the investigator introduced himself, pulled out his hand-held recorder, and started questioning me. That was when I realized I was a suspect.

When the questions were over, the investigator shut off his recorder and got up to leave the room. As his hand rested on the door handle, he looked back at me and asked, "What school did your boys attend?"

I replied, "Greystone."

He asked, "What grades were they in?"

"Grade six and eight."

Very matter of fact he said, "My daughter probably knew them." He turned and left the room.

I think, *My God, Officer. Is that that the best you got? You have kids and yet lack any hint of understanding of what I might be going through? These are my babies for God's sake! What the hell?*

The Closet

Shortly after the investigator left, I was escorted to a room across the hall. Someone brought me a Tim Horton's coffee. It was reportedly from a neighbour. The "coffee guy" was probably the poor man I had screamed at when he came running across the street, saying it was his best friend's front door we were beating on! Even though I was not a coffee drinker, this was the most caring action I had received all morning. That kind gesture meant so much to me because no one in uniform had shown me a hint of compassion. Anything could have been better than what I had experienced thus far. No one seems to know what to do in this current situation.

I sat in a small, windowless room. Then, two women were brought in, and I was told they were from Victims' Services. They introduced themselves. So now the three of us were sitting in a room the size of a closet. They did not say anything.

I looked at them blankly and asked them why they were there.

One said, "We are here to make sure you are okay."

I asked them if they had kids.

They both answered, "Yes," and looked down, obviously holding back their own tears.

I remember saying, "How could this happen? How could their dad kill them?"

There was no response from either of them. I was the only one talking. They just stared at me, obviously at a loss for words.

The female officer who had been at the scene and whom we had followed to the detachment came to the door.

I asked if I could use the washroom.

She paused, then said, "Well normally we don't allow the public to use the washroom but I will let you."

OMG! Really? This officer had to weigh the pros and cons of allowing a totally traumatized mother to use a washroom? It was almost as though she wanted me to know she was doing me a big favour by letting me use her precious washroom! But why was I surprised? She was the same officer who had rubbed me the wrong way at the crime scene.

The officer accompanied me to the "off limits" washroom. A colleague of the officer in the washroom started joking with my "companion" as the officer waited for me. It was like … life just continued as per normal in everyone else's world!

My world, on the other hand, was totally cratering as the reality of what had happened penetrated my very core. Inside I was shattering into a million pieces. I was coming totally unglued.

Once I used the washroom, the female officer escorted me back to the cubbyhole, where the two women were waiting for me. Nothing had changed. I texted Brent, as again the women and I sat in silence.

"Where are you?" I texted.

He replied: "Just finished being questioned. I'm in the parking lot with Joey and Jenneka."

I texted back, "Come get me!"

The women sitting with me were obviously well-intentioned, wonderful, caring women, but I was falling apart. I saw no purpose in staying in this situation. I was filled with undeniable rage. But who was I to rage at? My f*#king coward of an ex-husband had taken his own life too!

The Circle of Love

As Brent and I exited the police station, our phones were already lit up with messages from friends and family, who had already heard the news. Then, exiting their vehicles outside the RCMP station, their arms open wide to smother us with their love and concern, were Carla and Brett, Jenneka and Joey, four of our dear friends along with Jenneka and Joey's little three-year-old daughter, Khyle. All were as broken as I was.

I collapsed into their arms as they formed a shield around me and Brent as if to protect us from all that was going on. The comfort of their hugs reminded me of the good, kind, and loving people in my world. My friends and family, who would help me make it through the next breath, the next five minutes, the next hour, and the one after that and the one after that … and …

As we released each other, I asked everyone to follow us to my new place in Spruce Grove. My family was already on their way from Edson. I called my parents with directions to the duplex. As we pulled up to my new home, I saw that Wayfair had delivered the kids' new beds, which lay there in unopened boxes propped up against the garage door. *Oh my God! Please! Please! Please! Give me the strength to get through this!*

We went into the duplex and sat in quiet, shocked conversation until my parents and brothers arrived. Everyone was in pieces. I received the tightest hugs that I had ever felt from my mother and my dad. To see my dad so devastated hurt my heart even more than I could ever have imagined. Much more.

My dad had never shown much emotion, but that day he just continued to hug me. With tears flowing freely from his eyes, he said, "I don't know how to fix this for you, Tracy."

I could feel his body trembling as he continued to embrace me. Maybe it was just my body trembling. Maybe it was both of us locked in this unbelievable nightmare.

When he released me, I looked around and said, "I can't be here. I want to go home. Home to my safe place. Away from here."

Everyone agreed that we should head to Whitecourt. Again, I was suddenly calm. Brent asked my brother to drive my Range Rover and I jumped in with Brent. We were both locked in the trauma of what had happened. I desperately needed his strength and he too needed mine. We were a team. We would get through this together.

We drove in silence, engulfed in our own thoughts with some form of "I can't believe this is happening" coupled with bouts of crying. No! This couldn't be real. It just couldn't! The shocking reality of what I had just witnessed was beginning to permeate my whole body. I was again shaking.

On the hour and a half drive home, the media did not stop calling. Were they serious? Could they just not give us time to absorb the horrific scene of which we had been a part?

I wanted to strike out at something. Anything. I was in total shock. The media did not stop calling and calling. No way. Brent finally said a few words to them ending with, "A coward of a father shot his boys and then shot himself."

Their persistence was unbelievable. They wanted a story. I got that. It was all about the story, but couldn't they please just leave us alone? For God's sake, we had just found our kids murdered by their biological father, my ex-husband. Couldn't they respect the state we were in? How could they be so insensitive to what was going on in my gut? In my heart? In my soul?"

CBC News

Two Boys, 11 and 13, Killed in Spruce Grove Murder-Suicide[3]

Mother and stepfather called 911 when they arrived to take children home for the holidays

ANDREA ROSS, CBC NEWS, DECEMBER 19, 2016

A mother found her two young boys dead in a Spruce Grove, Alta., home in an apparent murder-suicide at the hands of their father, the boys' stepfather says.

The boys, age 11 and 13, were found dead in the home Monday morning when their mother and stepfather arrived to take them home to Whitecourt for the holidays, the boys' stepfather, Brent Stark, told CBC News.

"We both showed up to the home and a coward of a father took his life and his two boys' lives," Stark said.

RCMP confirmed three people were found dead after police responded to a 911 call at 2 Haney Ct. in the Hilldowns neighbourhood of Spruce Grove, west of Edmonton, around 10:30 a.m.

Police said they aren't looking for anyone in relation to the deaths, and don't have anyone in custody. They have not released the names of the deceased. Autopsies are scheduled for Tuesday morning.

Sgt. Jack Poitras wouldn't say if RCMP are investigating the incident as a murder-suicide.

"I don't want to speculate," Poitras said. "It speaks volumes when we are not looking for anyone in regards to this at this time."

The boys' stepfather said Radek and Ryder MacDougall were killed in the home by their father, Corry MacDougall, who then took his own life.

Stark said he arrived at the home around 9:30 a.m. with his wife, Tracy, the mother of the boys.

The couple called 911 after knocking on the front door window.

---

3   Andrea Ross, "Two Boys, 11 and 13, Killed in Spruce Grove Murder-Suicide," *CBC News*, December 19, 2016, https://www.cbc.ca/news/canada/edmonton/two-boys-11-and-13-killed-in-spruce-grove-murder-suicide-1.3904439

"You go knock on a door and you see the legs of one of your boys laying on the ground, things don't go too well from there," Stark said.

The family will now spend the holidays planning their funeral, he said.

Stark said the boys played hockey in Spruce Grove.

"Great kids, young boys, good-looking boys," Stark said.

"Big hearts, that's all you can say. Great kids growing up, they're on top of the world and some f--king coward took it from them."

'Just Completely Disturbing'

Mike Lodge lives two doors away from the home where the boys and their father were found dead.

He was coming home around 10:20 Monday morning when he saw the couple pounding on the door of the home.

"She was just completely distraught — destroyed," he said. *"Crying, scream-ing very loudly, pounding on the door. She was talking to somebody either on the phone or to her husband, I'm assuming, that she was with. Just continuing to try to get inside the home, I guess."*

Lodge said he saw the woman's partner trying to kick the door in. A neigh-bour from across the street asked why they were trying to get into the home, he said.

"She said … 'He killed my babies,'" Lodge said. *"And she started screaming at him, at the neighbour, and the neighbour walked away, because she actually said, 'Look in the door, you can see my baby dead on the floor.'"*

Lodge said he called 911 and police officers showed up at the home shortly after.

He said the man who lived in the home had been renting it for a year and a half or two years.

On Monday evening, the Christmas tree remained lit in the home, visible through the back windows.

Lodge, who has two children of his own, said he could see it from his yard.

"It's just completely disturbing to think that anything like this could happen," Lodge said.

"The fact that there's a mother out there with two slain children … that she's not going to get to see and definitely not going to spend the holidays with, is just a horrible, horrible fact."

Months after the event, in a subsequent email, Tracy recounted her experience of the rest of that despicable day.

TRS to SYK: I was already having flashbacks of the scene me and Brent had come upon when we looked into Corry's house. My body continued to shake uncontrollably. How many times had I seen my ex-husband go from 0 to 100 in anger when we were together? He would have that look. Dark eyes, black as coal. Crazy eyes filled with rage. I had often called them "the eyes of the DEVIL." I wondered over and over, *Did my boys witness those eyes that night?*

I still could not believe Corry capable of such an unspeakable act. I kept blinking, attempting to sort through what must have happened to my boys. My thoughts were racing. Obviously Radek had been scared and had been sleeping with his dad as he was found in Corry's bed. Ryder, at some point, must have gotten away from his father and made it to the front door where he would eventually take his last breath. On the other hand, he must have confronted his dad and grabbed the hot barrel of the shotgun, which would explain the burns on Ryder's hands that the police officer had noted. His father was still much broader than Ryder and must have overpowered my boy with a loaded shotgun in his hands. It would have been a totally unfair fight. OMG! OMG! Please God. Let me wake up from this craziness! My face was in my hands. I wanted to throw up. Agitation filled my body.

I called out to Brent over and over. "Brent! Please tell me it's not real!! PLEASE! PLEASE! Tell me it's not real." He continued to focus on the road ahead, his eyes brimming with tears of rage as his hands gripped the steering wheel. I knew he was filled with fury at Corry for what he had done. He could not stop the tape playing over and over in his head. *How could a man actually do this to his children? How?*

We pulled into our driveway. Brent's daughter, Alesha, met us at the house. I exited the vehicle and embraced my stepdaughter with a tight hug before walking briskly inside, crossing the floor to the liquor cabinet, setting a glass on the counter, and pouring myself a shot of whisky. With shaking hands, I quickly downed it, hoping to calm my nerves. My anxiety was overflowing. I could not stop shaking. It was impossible to contain the activation in the confines of my body. I could barely hold a glass! This couldn't be real! It just couldn't!

The house began to fill up with friends devastated by the news blaring from every radio and TV station in Alberta. Everyone wanted to hear what had happened. Our cell phones would not stop ringing or beeping, but we did not want to turn them off. We needed to feel that support. We needed that contact. Friends and family, horrified that this had actually happened, continued to gather at the house to provide their hugs, their tears, and their loving kindness through this madness.

The Tattoo

In the midst of all the commotion, a call from the Whitecourt RCMP Station came in to Brent's cell phone. Someone on the line was asking us to identify Corry's body through pictures the police had taken of a tattoo on Corry's arm.

What? It was already after four p.m. The officer on the phone said they were unable to remove the bodies of the boys from the house until their father's body had been identified. I was incensed. My babies were still in that f*#king house, hours after their bodies had been discovered. What was wrong with this picture? I had given the detective who interviewed me at the RCMP station cell phone numbers of my ex-husband's father, his father's wife, and his brother, and we were the ones being asked to identifying the monster's body?

Two Whitecourt officers showed up at our front door. One had a picture of a tattoo of my boys' names intertwined in a picture of a bike chain on an arm. They wanted me and Brent to identify Corry through this tattoo. They asked us to view the photo separately.

Brent went first. My body started vibrating when the officer was showing Brent the picture. To hell with that! I crossed the floor of our entranceway to take a look. Corry was wearing the black t-shirt with HONDA printed in red; a shirt that he had worn back when we were still married. I leaned in and said, "Yup. That's the f*#king loser. Now go take my babies out of that house!"

The police officers looked at me with deep sadness in their eyes. They bloody well should! We should never have had to identify Corry's body. That was his family's responsibility. Not mine! Not Brent's! Then, on the way out, they asked me the name of my children's dentist! I have no idea how I ever survived that day.

After receiving her email of June 15, 2017, where she had detailed her experience of the day the boys died, I immediately replied:

SYK to TRS: But you did, Tracy. Somehow you did survive! You made it through that day. Please take time to breathe that in! Let's take some time to process this.

I quickly grabbed my iPhone and called her. We breathed. We titrated.[4] We resourced. We released. Then, I spoke. "As I said before, Tracy, when your boys died, the Creator blew the breath of your sons into your being and that breath has given you the strength to handle whatever comes your way, and you have and you are and you will midst all of whatever is going on for you right now. Feel their essence inside of you, Tracy. Right now, in this moment. Breathe it in!"

We take our time. Gradually, she begins to settle.

---

4   Titration is a skill set that involves managing the speed of processing trauma so as not to retraumatize the client. It is an act of working with only a tiny piece of the client's experience in order to allow the client to process and integrate past trauma successfully.

Chapter 2

REMEMBERING THE BOYS

Whitecourt Candlelight Vigil
December 20, 2016

Sandra Young Kolbuc, Counselling Therapist

ON THE TUESDAY EVENING, FOLLOWING THE TRAGEDY OF DECEMBER 19TH, I walked with my daughter and her husband and my two little granddaughters from their home, a couple of blocks away from that of the Starks, to the first of the candlelight vigils honouring Radek and Ryder. It was a cold winter night made colder by the intensity of what was happening. I was, as were the rest of our community, totally devastated by what had happened the previous day. Many walked reverently into the silence of the night until they found places in front of the home of a deeply grieving family to stand with hundreds of other supporters from our community. People kept coming out of the houses, out of the trucks and the cars, walking reverently from the vehicles, pulling their own children on sleds or holding tightly to their mittened hands, all coming together in support of a broken-hearted family.

Brent's girls, Alesha and Shelbey, stood beside their dad and Tracy. The hockey boys from Radek and Ryder's 2015–16 hockey year were there in Whitecourt Wolverine team jackets and jerseys huddling together, some openly crying. Others were stoic because they had somehow already learned … *real men don't cry!* So many young lives had been changed by the reality of the horrific death of their friends.

The crowd kept getting bigger and bigger by the minute, spilling over into the snow-covered lawns of the homes in the neighbourhood. Everyone seemed to be wanting to reach out with love and compassion to the Stark family.

A series of speeches, laced with emotion, filled the air as one after another, the speakers attempted to radiate a degree of hope and understanding of life's challenges and in remembering the boys. I stood near the back of the crowd wrapped in my own thoughts as I watched members of the crowd aching for Tracy, a woman I hardly knew, though like many mothers in the gathering, identifying with her tremendous pain. I thought of how difficult this must have been for Tracy and Brent as the full reality of what had transpired in the last thirty-six hours began to truly sink in.

Brent's massive shoulders cradled his wife as she attempted to thank everyone for coming. Her voice was strained and weak as she spoke haltingly, with deep tender-heartedness for the boys' friends and their families. She was to share with me later that her entire focus that evening had been on speaking to the boys' many friends, who were lining the streets, struggling to "be men."

She spoke quietly but directly to her audience. "It's hard enough for an adult to try to understand. All these kids don't have an answer. Nor do we." She paused, grasping for the words and the courage to continue. "I just know Ryder and Radek are looking down on us and they are going to give me and everyone else who is here the strength to get through this. I just want to thank you all for being here and supporting and loving us and loving them. Never forget them." Her voice broke as she finished uttering her gutsy words.

Our communal aching hearts meshed with hers in deep sadness for the Stark family, their friends and those of the boys and for our community of Whitecourt, touched so deeply by the tragedy.

Soon, floating lanterns were released into the dark sky, carrying the loving energy of the crowd up to the boys. Everyone in the crowd seemed to want to share their love and concern for this brutalized couple. Brent and Tracy held each other close as they offered thanks to everyone for their support. When the vigil ended, no one moved. We all stood there mesmerized and still in shock over the unbelievable reason we were there supporting the Stark family. How had this happened? How could it have happened?

Brent & Tracy at the Whitecourt Vigil

I breathed in. I couldn't see my son Joseph and my grandson Gavin in the fullness of the crowd, and hoped Joseph had done okay herding his team of young hockey players from the arena to the vigil. Joe had coached both Radek and Ryder in their progression as Wolverines and had always had a strong connection with his players. Like everyone, he was devastated by the news of what had transpired. He too had known Corry as a friend.

I had done a brief therapy session with my grandson that day to ensure he was doing okay, as he had been a teammate of the boys. The session had been challenging, because, in typical male fashion, although only twelve years old, he kept his feelings inside like so many of the other young boys. They were each impacted by the tragedy in their own way and frightened that such could happen to their friends—that a dad would actually kill his sons.

The silence of the night enveloped us as Whitecourt mourned the loss of Ryder and Radek. The boys had been born in Edmonton but had lived all but the last four months of their brief lives in our community. I could sense the sorrow of our small town in the faces of all those old enough to know what had happened that December 19, 2016.

Corry too had been an integral part of our community as a young teen and as an adult. As I watched the lanterns being released into the night sky, the words of a song kept playing in my head. Maybe it was looking up and watching the sky ablaze with the beauty of the lights moving higher and higher into the darkness. Maybe it was just my therapeutic stance of wanting to be there for the others enveloped by the sadness in the night air, wanting to help all those in the crowd to ache a little less. It was the refrain from a song that I had learned and adapted in honouring others who had died. As I watched the lanterns go higher and higher until they extinguished in the night sky midst the stars above, the song with my slight variation making it comply with the death of two not three continued to play in my head. The lyrics from "Three Stars"[5] were simple.

> Look up in the sky
> Up toward the north
> There are *'two'* new stars
> Brightly shining forth
> They're shining so bright
> From the heavens above.
> Gee we're gonna miss you
> Everybody sends their love.

Within my soul, I knew that someday I would share that verse with Tracy Stark. Little did we know that night that Radek and Ryder were to become **R&R,** our forever immortalized Wolverines not just in Whitecourt but across the globe, out at sea, and beyond the stars. Gone but never forgotten. Forever in our hearts …

The Longest Day

Much later, in a future email, Tracy shared the happenings of the day between the Whitecourt and the Spruce Grove vigils:

TRS to SYK: On Wednesday, Brent and I made the most challenging trek of my life—a trip to Park Memorial Funeral Home in Mayerthorpe, 30 km away, in order to make arrangements for the boys' funeral service. This trip would prove to be beyond what I ever thought I could handle. I wanted to have my sons cremated, so that they could stay with me forever in our home. When we arrived at the funeral home, I asked Fran, the funeral director, if my boys were there.

She said solemnly, "Yes Tracy. Ryder and Radek are resting in our care."

We followed her to her office and the process I had never imaged would be a part of my life, began. Fran was skilled at her craft and extremely gentle in her

---

5   "Three Stars": A song written and recorded by Tommy Dee with Carol Kay and first released in April 1959 as a tribute to the three popstars Buddy Holly, Ritchie Valens, and J.P. Richardson (The Big Bopper), who died in a small plane crash following a concert in February 1959.

approach as we discussed the arrangements we had to make for my sons. How I needed her loving kindness to make it through the decisions we had to make... However, more than anything on earth I just wanted some private time with my boys prior to the cremation. I asked Fran if I could have some time alone with Ryder and Radek.

I felt the empathy present in Fran's eyes as she looked at me and said softly: 'Unfortunately Tracy, you can't see them now ... because of their injuries."

OMG! I just fell apart. I knew what had happened to them but hearing her say that tore my heart in two as the reality of why we were there blasted apart my avoiding the truth of what was now my life. Brent and I just clung to each other right there in the funeral home and sobbed. I could no longer fight against the actuality of my boys' deaths. Somehow, again, I managed to survive what I was experiencing and our responsibilities continued.

Fran escorted us to a little room filled with caskets and urns. My true compassion goes out to any parent who has had the experience of picking out an eternal holding place for their child because it has to be one of the most difficult tasks any parent ever had to do. I had to select urns in which to put my children? Why? Why the f*#k was I here having to do the unthinkable? My heart began to race. Why??? Because their dad had done the unthinkable.

Brent was my rock. As we were finishing up, Fran asked me to select the clothing I wanted the kids to wear when they were cremated. It was brutal. She said she would come by our home later than evening to retrieve the boys' outfits. We headed back home in silence.

As was usual, when we returned to our house, we had a welcoming crew waiting to provide us with their love in every possible manner. As the day went on, the house filled up with more and more people. Brent and I excused ourselves and went to pick out the kids' clothes.

One of the challenges was that 95% of their clothing was still in Spruce Grove. Ryder had left behind a "dress up" outfit for hockey in his closet in our house, so I packed that up to give to Fran. As for Radek, I was only able to find him a pair of jeans and a button-up shirt but I had no 'ginch' for him. That little detail broke my heart. How could they dress my little boy without any underwear? And how did I not have any of his underwear in my house?

Brent again was a calming presence for me as I went through the motions of what needed to be done. I sat down and wrote each of my boys a short letter of goodbye and placed my special messages in the pockets of each of their dress shirts. Once finished, Brent and I retreated to our bedroom, closed the door, lay on our bed holding on to each other, and again cried. We had not had a lot of alone time in the past few days, so it was comforting to be together as we searched for the strength to do what was necessary in these moments, helping each other through the insanity of what we were experiencing.

Too soon, the doorbell rang. It was Fran arriving to pick up the boys' clothing. I went downstairs and handed her the bag filled with their outfits. I started to cry as I shared the fact that I had no underwear for Radek. Fran's eyes were again soft as she squeezed my hand and said she would make sure Radek had a pair of undershorts on before he was cremated. That simple gesture on Fran's part was very soothing to me as a mom and a true blessing in the madness of that moment."

The Spruce Grove Vigil

Thursday, December 22, 2016

SYK to TRS: Please share your experience of the evening in Spruce Grove when the boys were honoured by the community where they had last played hockey.

TRS to SYK: It was incredible, Sandra. For the boys having only been in Spruce Grove a few short months, the ceremony was an amazing, touching tribute to my sons. Spruce Grove, like Whitecourt, is a wonderful community and the support we received from both communities helped us through those initial days of grief and shock. It seemed that everyone in that arena was feeling our pain. Amber Stoby, a talented musician from Whitecourt, sang a Dixie Chicks' rendition of the song (Godspeed) Sweet Dreams[6] which strongly resonated with me, as I reflected on my own little men and the love I was sending them each and every day on their heavenly journey. We changed the singular to plural.

Amber added a last verse:

God bless Mommy
And matchbox cars
God bless Brent
And thanks to the stars!

---

6   Godspeed (Sweet Dreams) Lyrics by Radney Foster. Songfacts.com

Her personalizing the song for our family was very touching for me.

Brent and I spoke briefly, thanking everyone for their love and support. My insides ached as I struggled to keep my composure as the reality of why we were celebrating again hit hard. The mayor of Spruce Grove spoke of his nephew being great friends with Ryder. After the speeches acknowledging the boys ended, we were accompanied into the rink where there was a display set up on the ice with flowers and pictures of Radek and Ryder. The score clock displayed the boys' numbers #3 and #8 along with the year 2016.

The young teammates from Radek's Sabretooth Pee Wee team and Ryder's Timberwolves AA Bantam team, as well as another Bantam AA team, were assembled on the ice in their uniforms, skates all laced up with their sticks held in the air, as the lights were turned down and the music played. Brent and I stood in the player's box with Ryder's coaches. The captain of each of the boys' teams skated up to the players' box, bringing me flowers and presenting me with the boys' white jerseys. We were all crying. Oh My God. It was so very sad. I kept asking myself, *Is this really happening?* I hugged all of the players, thanking each of them for their courage and their kindness. They were just kids going through an experience that was so unfair for young hockey players who should have been chasing the puck that night rather than trying to hold back tears because of the actions of one man who decided to kill their teammate. I ached for these boys as I sat with my family in the owner's box, watching the skills competition that followed, which provided the players an outlet for the intensely emotional evening that had just transpired.

As I sat there, I could not help but think of the last games I had watched my #3 and #8 play the previous Sunday, wearing the jerseys I now held in my hands. How could this be my life this 22nd day of December 2016, three days before Christmas? I was numb as the reality of the beautiful tribute to my hockey boys set in.

The Spruce Grove score clock, honouring #3 & #8 at the Spruce Grove Vigil Ceremony

Chapter 3

PLANNING A FUNERAL

RATHER THAN CELEBRATING THE CHRISTMAS SEASON WITH JOY AND LAUGH-ter and family time, the Stark family was planning a funeral. A few months after Tracy and I begin working together as therapist and client, we engaged in an email exchange.

SYK to TRS: What was going on inside you, Tracy, as the days unfolded during the Christmas season between the shooting and the funeral?

An email arrived shortly with the information I had requested.

TRS to SYK: It is hard to put into words, Sandra. I would say shock took over completely. I became a zombie. I truly could not figure out if it was a nightmare or a movie I was watching. It is next to impossible to think straight. I again kept blinking my eyes as if to clear my scattered mind almost like trying to find a different channel with a different show. This kind of thing didn't happen to people I knew, let alone me!! Us!! In my mind my boys were still alive. They would be home on the 29th. They were just in their dad's custody for his share of Christmas holidays. I was going to wake up and Radek was going to be coming through the front door with his big hello letting us know that he was home and Ryder would be dashing up the stairs to his room to call his buddies. I kept going with the thought, *They are just with their dad for the Christmas holidays. This was just a bad bad dream.*

Each morning I would wake up and go into one of their rooms and lie on one of their beds praying to God that this wasn't happening. Praying that my boys were not gone from me forever. The thought of my boys never sleeping in their beds, never walking in that front door, never talking to me or hugging me ever again, took my breath away. It is as though someone had punched me in the stomach and I couldn't catch my breath. My heart physically HURT. I had an ache I could not describe, but I know that any parent who has lost a child knows exactly what I am talking about.

Every day, following that Monday, my home was full of all my besties. Friends tidying what needs to be tidied. Friends prepping snacks for the day. Friends making sure the liquor cabinet was well stocked. Friends trying to get me to eat. People kept coming and coming and yet, even when under extreme duress, I greeted everyone who landed at our front door to express their deep sorrow with a hug. I never for a moment hid in a back room grieving alone with my overwhelming devastation. Those individuals, who braved the threshold of the Stark home, sustained me and their words and their hugs gave me strength to carry on.

When Corry and I had split up, as in many breakups, friends chose sides. People entered my home who had not spoken to me in years. Corry was their guy. I was genuinely touched by their empathy and their courage in coming to pay their respects. I was deeply moved by the men and women who chose to be there for me and my family. All of our guests, who had been Corry's friends as well, were shaking their heads in disbelief that their friend, Corry MacDougall, could commit such a hideous act. It was as though we all grew up that week of December and I will be eternally grateful for the love and consideration of all who showed me such kindness and empathy in the days, the weeks, months and now years following the death of my sons.

Good Friends, Good Stories, Good Whiskey and Good Wine

Each day following, when I was ready, my dear friend Carla, who had put her life on hold for me since she heard of the tragedy, was there preparing me a shot of whisky to dull my pain. We sat at the table and often just stared blankly at each other or out the window, crying and praying that all this was simply a horrible nightmare and that tomorrow all would be back to normal. Gradually the truth began to settle firmly into my bones and how my body ached.

Our table held eight and every day, all places were filled along with many more chairs being added to the circle of friends sitting with us. We told funny stories. We reminisced about the boys. We were there for each other as we had all been traumatized by what had happened to Ryder and Radek.

With help, I planned out the days to follow until the funeral on December

29, 2016. We listed everything that had to be done, from getting my kids' things out of Corry's house to planning the funeral. The thought of organizing such an event for my only two sons over the season they loved the most made me nauseous. I was not eating. I was not sleeping. I was zoned out or checked out much of the time.

Although Christmas was the following weekend after our boys died, no one left our table all week except to sleep. Then, they would return the following morning. I often thought of all the families at home without their loved ones who were now sitting at our table supporting us through the trauma and pain of losing the boys in such a senseless act. Not only was our Christmas season destroyed, but so was that of everyone in our circle of friends. How could anyone celebrate Christmas knowing two beautiful boys who loved Christmas so much were spending Christmas in Heaven not only this year, but in every year to follow?

The Hockey Bag

It was Christmas Eve when Brent and our friend Brett went to Corry's place to get the boys' belongings. When they returned home, I could tell they were both emotionally exhausted. Brent explained what they seen when they entered Corry's home. I continued asking questions, but they would not answer me, which made me angry. It wasn't long before I was to understand the reason they were avoiding my questions.

I needed to grab something out of the garage and there, in a laundry basket rather than in his hockey bag, was Radek's hockey equipment. I looked around. His hockey bag was nowhere to be found. I came inside, confused. Brent was sitting at the kitchen table. I asked him why Radek's equipment was in a laundry basket rather than in his hockey bag.

Brent shrugged and looked down.

I could feel myself heating up. I said to him, "Where is Radek's hockey bag, Brent?"

He looked at me and said, "I don't know, Tracy. His equipment was in the laundry basket when we got there."

I said, "I seen his bag at the bottom of the stairs when I was looking in the front window that morning."

Brent stopped and looked at me and there was an edge to his voice as he said,

"You know why Radek doesn't have a hockey bag for his equipment, Tracy? I'll tell you why."

He choked out the words. "Because there was blood all over it!!"

OMG. How much more could my heart handle? Whose blood? My baby boy's? Ryder's? Corry's?

SYK to TRS: Tracy. Please take a break. This is so very raw. I am concerned that the material is too traumatizing to deal with unless we are working together on decreasing the activation in your nervous system before you write any more. Please stop and take a break!

She ignored my response.

TRS to SYK: Christmas came and went. We travelled to my parents' place in Edson for Christmas. I was totally zoned out. When we returned home, the knocks on the door never stopped. People in our community continued to drop off food for the morning, noon, and evening meals. Some was still hot and ready to eat. Other people just dropped by to give us hugs and offer their condolences and prayers. My friends did not wait for anyone to answer their knock. They just walked in, grabbed me in a hug, their tears meshing with mine. That was what I needed more than anything. There was no protocol. Just friends dropping by, doing dishes, having a bite to eat, and bringing their love into our home. Some that walked into my house were friends I had not seen or spoken to in years. Other friends who arrived were totally broken, as they came through our door. Sometimes, it was me doing the comforting.

However, I can honestly say one's body stops making tears if you cry enough. At least, that is what happened to me. By the time the boys' funeral came, ten days after their deaths, I was completely out of tears. Although that day was the second hardest day of my entire life, my body just stopped. I could not cry another tear. I was totally done.

Our emailing continued.

No Time for Celebration

TRS to SYK: Most people do a celebration of life to honour those who pass. In conversation with Brent, he said to me, "This is no f*#king celebration, Tracy.

The boys should be here to live their lives. They should be here playing their games on their new PlayStations and laughing and joking in their excitement for Christmas. They should be outside playing street hockey! But no, they are not here, because Corry wanted to play God for a day!" He was adamant about his thoughts regarding a celebration. After hearing him share what was going on inside his head, I totally agreed. This was no time for a celebration.

We decided to call it a funeral service. The minister was wonderfully kind and caring. She came to our home to discuss what we wanted during our service. At first, she was very professional, keeping her emotions tucked deep inside the confines of her purse, which I am sure one in her position had to do when dealing with families of loved ones who had died. I asked if she would like to see the boys' bedrooms, and she said she would very much like that so she could get to know the boys a little.

I had spread their hockey blankets, on which were the images of their life-size hockey photos, on their individual beds. I shared stories about each of them. Their rooms told their own stories and pretty much spoke for themselves. Ryder's room had a few holes in the wall, a PlayStation and lots of hockey paraphernalia neatly placed. Radek's room, on the other hand, was cluttered with "stuff." LOL! There were teddy bears, knick-knacks, games and his PlayStation. Every corner in his room had something stuffed in it. That was who he was. Everything was important to him. Once, when he had gone to my parents' place, he had returned with an old trophy of my dad's, which he displayed with great care in his room. That was Radek.

The empathy and consideration Minister Ruth Lothotz shared with me that day was filled with compassion and is etched firmly in my memory during the most difficult ten days of my life.

A few days before the funeral, Corry's younger brother called, asking if it would be okay if the members of his family could attend the service for the boys. He estimated there would be approximately 20–25 family members wanting to attend the service.

Without hesitation, I said, "Of course." I told him that there would be a few rows at the front of the service opposite where Brent and I and the girls would be sitting that I would have reserved for Corry's family.

Chapter 4

THE FUNERAL

ON DECEMBER 29, 2016, WHITECOURT'S ALLAN AND JEAN MILLAR CENTRE was packed. Many hockey teams appeared amongst the mourners dressed in their team jerseys. The Stark and Ross families entered the facility to the emotional wailing sound of the bagpipes. Leading the procession were Alesha and Shelbey, cradling their brothers' urns in their arms. In a subsequent email exchange, Tracy and I discussed her experience of the day. As well, she shared the script of the proceedings.

> TRS to SYK: As Brent and I followed the girls down the aisle, I saw Corry's dad midst a number of Corry's family at the end of the aisle near the front. I stopped and hugged him, his wife, and Corry's brother before we passed by to our seats. Corry's dad hugged me back and then hugged my mom. My heart was breaking for Corry's family as well as my own. They looked as crushed as we all were. They loved Radek and Ryder and had not only lost the boys, but their own son/brother as well and that son was the whole reason we were all here, remembering two young boys with a funeral rather than cheering in the stands at a kick-ass goal or assist in the arena, a block away. I was sure the boys' paternal grandfather, who was very close to his grandsons, was going through hell, wondering as we did, why Corry did what he did. It was hard to fathom how the MacDougall family could possibly cope with such an unbelievable tragedy.
>
> A good friend of our family, Rodney Koscielny, the former head of the Whitecourt RCMP Detachment in Whitecourt, had said he would be honoured to be the Master of Ceremonies. He stood tall and in charge at the front of the room. He, of course, had had a lot of experience in dealing with pressure, the media, and his emotions—skills critical for guiding us all through this most difficult day.

Mourners at the service wiped tears from their eyes as the Mountie read the content of the individual letters I had written to each of my sons, his voice cracking with emotion.

"I hope Heaven is as beautiful as I imagine," I had written in my letter to Ryder. "I hope you hold your brother's hand tight. I miss you so much, my sweet boy, but I know I now have the most beautiful angels walking beside me. I can't wait to see you again. I love you to the moon and back Ryder. Love Mom."

The Mountie then read the words I had written in a second letter to my younger son, Radek. "I miss you so much, my boy, and I know you miss me too. I feel you with me. I know you have your big brother with you to protect you, and I've read there is no fighting in Heaven, so I know Ryder is being nice to you—a first for everything! Be there to protect Ryder too! You now are my angels and the most precious angels anyone could ask for. I can't wait to see you again. I love you to the moon and back. Love Mom."

The Master of Ceremonies spoke well of the boys and our family, and Brent and I were very touched by his kind and compassionate words. Miles Valiquette, a second RCMP officer, who had been Ryder's hockey coach the previous spring, spoke next. Prior to his current posting, he had been stationed in Whitecourt and had become a friend of our family. In doing his rounds in the community, he would often drive by our home and if the boys were outside, he would suddenly turn on the siren in his cop car and scare the heck out of them, laughing all the way. He ended his eulogy with, "Ryder was a kid I would have play for me day in and day out. I wish I had had him longer than one spring. Ryder and Radek, my little buddies, may you rest in peace and make sure you watch over us all!"

The Master of Ceremonies concluded the ceremony with the following statement: "It is my hope that Ryder and Radek will be remembered not for how they died, but rather, for how they lived. Let us remember two beautiful boys and from all the people here, you can see the impact they had on others, including many young kids just like them. That is what we should remember—the positive side of what those two boys brought to this world."

The service ended. It was over. The haunting, majestic sound of the bagpipes played over one thousand mourners out of the hall. Most everybody had in their hand, their pocket, or their purse an **R&R** decal to follow my dream of having my boys see the world by asking people to find a special place to attach their sticker.

In a subsequent email, Tracy shared more of her experience of December 29, 2016.

TRS to SYK: As the service ended, I just needed to get out of there. I was on the edge. I needed to be amongst my closest friends and family. I loved that so many had come to pay their respects, but I was barely holding myself together. I needed to retreat to my safe place as quickly as possible. We invited close friends and family back to our home.

I was so thankful for those dear friends responsible for catering such a wonderful meal in our home as it made the day a little easier as it was one less thing to think about. Everyone helped to ensure all who entered through our front door left well fed and "watered." I couldn't have handled sitting in a hall, eating bites from an egg salad sandwich or a turkey bun and hugging people for hours. I just needed to go HOME. I wanted to put on some comfy clothes and pour a damn shot of whisky into my glass and drink it down among those I sincerely loved and who loved me and my boys. Anything to ease the piercing pain in my heart.

The evening of the funeral, our home was filled with friends and relations sharing much love. However, as the last stragglers left our home, it was as if a heavy weight had been lifted from my shoulders. No more housefuls of people. No more planning. No more looking at old pictures for the video. No more talking when I just needed to be quiet midst the difficulty of saying goodbye to my boys. I so needed a break. A break from everything. I was exhausted physically, mentally, and emotionally. I needed the pressure of the last eleven days to be over.

The next morning Brent and I drove to Edmonton and boarded a plane for Cabo, Mexico, where we would revisit the last place we had holidayed together with our family. I needed the healing rays of the sun, the long walks on the beach and the calming rhythm of the ocean to ease the aching in my soul.

As Tracy's recollections had been written after she and I made the decision to work together on the book, sometimes the writing was very tough for Tracy. Often, we were able to do a therapy session after such writings to ease the activation in her nervous system. Retraumatization was my greatest concern in revisiting the trauma of what she had experienced. After emailing me her writings regarding the Christmas season of 2016, she sent me a text.

> TRS to SYK: It was very hard writing this, Sandra. I'm going to take a little break for a bit. This has hurt my heart so much. I hadn't really gone back to that week in a long time. However, I will be back. Promise.

Within a few days of her email, we had the opportunity to process what she had written. It was a good session, again following the trauma protocol, to remind her that such traumatic events were in the past, letting her body gently know… such events…. were over.

Chapter 5

AFTERMATH:
A NEW YEAR, 2017

Sandra Young Kolbuc, Counselling Therapist

THE AIR CONTINUED TO BE HEAVY WITH SADNESS IN WHITECOURT AS WE welcomed the New Year, 2017. Our community had been deeply touched by the death of Radek and Ryder. My heart, as a mother and grandmother, ached for Brent and Tracy and their families. Friends of the boys struggled. Children hearing their parents speak in whispers were curious yet frightened to hear of a dad actually shooting and killing his sons and then killing himself. Those engaged in the hockey world, as we were with our son coaching and our grandson playing, were a part of the grieving hockey family. However, at the time, I felt I did not know Tracy well enough to cross the threshold of her home as did so many kind and caring people.

I did not feel comfortable intruding in her life by offering my services as a therapist. That wasn't my way. In good time perhaps I would reach out, but not now. Right now, Tracy was still in shock and incredible grief and being surrounded by those closest to her was most important.

Anyone who heard about the murder of the boys was horrified at what had happened. We were all still distressed weeks after the murder/suicide as details continued to surface. There was no recourse. No retribution. No further investigation. No trial. It was over.

As well, there was much pain in the hearts of those who considered Corry a friend, many of whom continued to shake their heads in disbelief, shocked by his bizarre behaviours. He had been an integral part of our town. Upon hearing the gruesome story, however filtered by their parents, young boys who knew either

Ryder or Radek were unable to sleep, their anxiety boiling over from what had happened to their friends, their former teammates, their prior school buddies.

It was also disturbing for parents who did not even know Tracy and Brent or Corry or the boys. Female clients sharing custody with ex-husbands were terrified that if such could happen to Tracy Stark, did their tumultuous relationship with their 'exes' have the potential to mirror what was in the air? Could this be the fate of their own kids?

How did you tell a young boy that his friend's dad purposely shot and killed his friend? Young boys looked differently at their fathers when Dad would get angry at some of the typically weird behaviours of young boys with their immature brains. Little boys who should be playing fantasy good guys vs bad guys were confused. They asked questions that parents tried but struggled to answer. What did Radek and Ryder do that had made their dad mad? It was beyond the comprehension of the boys' teammates that one of their friends had been murdered by his own dad. Dad should be someone you trusted and who protected you! Dad should be someone on your team.

Dads and moms attempted to dial down the horror of what had happened to Ryder and Radek in ways that did not traumatize their own kids. But kids were curious. They asked many questions. To some, the dark of night brought fear. Moms and dads had children who suddenly wanted and needed someone to sleep with them. They needed someone to reassure them that they were safe. That it was okay to go to sleep.

In our AIM[7] counselling practice, my daughter Kristin, a registered counselling psychologist, and I worked with parents, assisting them in finding the language to help settle their children as they reassured their kids that something like this would never happen in their house. That Ryder and Radek's dad was "sick." Men cried out in rage that a man could actually do this to his sons. This was big city stuff! Not in our town! Women became hyper-vigilant, wondering if such could happen in the lives of those they knew—could it become a reality in their lives when things got extremely tense in their own homes? Was

---

7   AIM is the acronym for the family-based human development company, Accendo Incedo Magnus (AIM) International Inc., established in 1988 by David J. and Sandra Young Kolbuc and dedicated to the well-being of those within its circle of influence. It is now known as AIM Counselling Services (aimcounselling.ca) and operates under the auspices of their daughter, Kristin LeCoure, MA, R. Psych.

this event alcohol or drug-related? What had happened to cause this dad such despair, rage, or whatever had figured into his decision to kill his boys?

When working with parents, I became even more attentive of emphasizing the importance of parents 'regulating' themselves before disciplining their children. We discussed appropriate discipline strategies. We talked of logical consequences. I had heard many times over the years from too many men who said, "My dad never spared the rod with me and it didn't do me any harm. I turned out all right." Did you really, man? What about your anger bubbling barely beneath the surface, which your children witness, buddy? We educated mothers, dads, and children about managing anger appropriately. People were looking for answers and men were realizing how unsettling this event had been for their children and their wives, which, in most cases, was a good thing.

My counselling room became the safe place for a dad sitting in my blue chair to express his fear of repeating the violence he'd experienced at the hand or fist of his own father in his dad's handling of his own adolescent behaviour. We educated about intergenerational trauma that many parents experience by carrying the stresses of their own parents. I hoped we were squashing the old-school mentality of the unequivocal "might makes right" as I introduced self-regulation therapy[8] to my clients. There were discussions of how adult dysfunction was strongly connected with prior experiences of childhood trauma.

Asking for signs of the danger of which they should be aware, some moms shared behaviours they'd witnessed between their husbands and their boys and their girls that worried them. Still others brought in their children, who could not sleep as they lay in their beds at night, because of what they had heard in the low voices emanating from living rooms and around kitchen tables as well as at the Scott Safety Centre where, until the previous fall, the McDougall boys had played their hockey. Little "big ears" were taking it all in and then afraid to close their little eyes at night.

Friends of the boys who were broken apart by the loss of their friends and teammates also crossed the threshold of the AIM counselling room with parents worried about their own son or daughter's grief.

---

8   Self-regulation therapy (SRT) is a noncathartic mind/body approach aimed at diminishing excess activation in the nervous system. It has its basis in neurobiology and reflects our innate capacity to flexibly respond to novelty or threat. SRT assists a client in becoming more grounded and centred, enabling the nervous system to integrate overwhelming events and bring balance to the nervous system. (CFTRE.com)

We had been traumatized as a community and as individuals. Women did not know how Tracy would be able to go forward in her life after the darkness of the events that had devoured her sons and filled her with the trauma of finding her babies that devastating Monday morning. Some of her girlfriends needed advice on how to be there for her as they themselves worked through not only the anguish of Tracy's grief, but also the vicarious trauma of their own. Others were afraid of sharing any positive experiences of their lives regarding their own children with Tracy because she was no longer in an active mothering role. There was survival guilt, for they were still tucking in their children at night, kissing and holding their children tight while their friend could no longer physically do so. How could they be happy when their dear friend was so sad? It was excruciating. However, it was not until January 27, 2017, a little more than a month after the death of Ryder and Radek, that Tracy Stark would directly enter my life in a tragic and dramatic way.

Chapter 6

THE KEY

Sandra Young Kolbuc, Counselling Therapist

I HAD NOT MADE CONTACT WITH TRACY, ALTHOUGH I OFTEN THOUGHT OF the staggering sadness and traumatic reactions she would most likely be experiencing. Of course, in my work and in our small community, I heard rumours of how she was supposedly coping.

Then it was 1:45 p.m. on January 26, 2017. I turned the key in the lock of my AIM office after returning from a beautiful and serene kick sled on the ice of Rotary Park to see the clients listed in my afternoon schedule. Once inside my office, I reached for the iPhone on my desk to check for messages. There were three texts, all from my youngest daughter in Calgary, Alberta, five and a half hours away.

First: "Mom. Call me."

Second: "Mom. Call me. Important."

Third: "Mom. Call me. Emergency!"

My heart raced out of my chest as I quickly dialed her cell.

The calmness in Meisha's voice unnerved me as my daughter began to speak. "Mom," She paused. I was frantic. What was it? The names of my dear ones flipped through my mind.

She continued, "Mom," she repeated, speaking slowly. "Trevor collapsed at the gym and was rushed to the Foothills Hospital. He had a heart attack, Mom, and they don't think he is going to make it."

Visions of Trevor's wife, my niece, flew into my mind. "OMG Meisha! Where is Trish?" I countered.

"Warren and I are here with Trish at the hospital. We are going to go with her to see Trevor so she can say goodbye to him!"

"Oh my God, Meisha!" I couldn't see. I couldn't think.

"Mom. I think you should come." I breathed in deeply as I listened to the unfathomable exchange I was having with my third daughter, another counselling psychologist , who had obviously taken control of the situation at the hospital. I, on the other hand, was a mess! Trevor was a young man, barely past 40!

"Of course, I will come!" I replied. "I will be there as soon as I possibly can! Oh honey, I am wrapping my arms around you all. Breathe deeply. Thank God you and Warren are there with Trish! I will leave right away. Hug her tightly for me!" *Was this really happening?*

We hung up so Meisha could join Trish. I sat for a minute, taking in the reality of what my daughter had shared, my head spinning with what I needed to do to head immediately for Calgary.

The phone rang. It was my brother, Trish's dad, calling me from Victoria. We were both in shock of what was transpiring in that Foothills hospital room. He assured me he would be on a flight as soon as he could get to the airport. I did what I needed to do to close my office. My mind was frantic. I had to get a hold of myself.

I sat and took in three deep breaths, pressing my feet into the floor. I cancelled with my client in the waiting room and made two quick calls to my other clients rescheduling their appointments. I grabbed my briefcase, tossed it into the back of my SUV, and headed up Dahl Drive to my oldest daughter's home, wondering how to tell her what her younger sister had just shared.

I was still in disbelief as I exited my vehicle and walked briskly to her front door. From the look on my face, Kristin knew immediately that something was amiss. I shared the devastating news. Heartbroken, she called her husband to share my news and asked him to come home and be with their little ones. She packed quickly to accompany me to Calgary. I needed only to stop at my country home so I too could quickly pack a bag. We were on our way to Trish and her young boys, Maxym, aged six, and Maddox, aged three. I was sick at heart for Trish and those beautiful little boys who absolutely adored their father. OMG!

The weather was abominable. The blowing snow of a cold January careened over the highway as we headed south on Hwy 22, the Cowboy Trail. As we talked on route, Kristin reminded me of the Tracy Stark/Trish Hayter connection which had not entered my thoughts at this point.

Trevor Hayter had been Corry MacDougall's best friend. He had dated Tracy for two and a half years until he went to work overseas. After Trevor left town, his best friend Corry and his best girl, Tracy had started to hang out together just as friends. However, the sparks flew between the two and they started a relationship. That of course initially distanced Trevor and Corry. Within a short period of time Tracy and Corry were a newly married couple with a small son. Trevor, on the other hand, met and fell deeply in love with my niece, Trish. In 2009 Trish and Trevor had tied the knot in Las Vegas.

I said, "I remember Corry being at Trish and Trevor's wedding. He and Trevor must have reconnected."

Kristin replied, "They did. But you might also remember that Tracy was not at the wedding. She and Corry had split by then. Trish and Tracy had become close friends. However, Corry had made it next to impossible for Tracy to come to the wedding as it was her time with the boys and he would not change times with her. Then unbeknownst to anyone Corry drove from Whitecourt to Vegas and showed up unannounced two days before the wedding in time for Trevor's stag and expecting a seat at the wedding feast!

I replied "I remember Trish saying Trevor had been angry with Corry but as a man of few words he had simply said "That fu*kin' MacDougall!" All I could remember of Corry's presence in Vegas was that he was 'feeling no pain' at the Hayter wedding.

I began piecing together the intricacies of the relationships. Corry had moved out of our community in 2011. Trevor and Trish had lived in Whitecourt until the fall of 2016 when they had moved to Calgary. By this time, they were the parents of two beautiful little boys. My husband David and I had missed connecting with the Hayter family on our after-Christmas run to visit our Calgary families because Trish and Trevor had been in Whitecourt at the funeral of the MacDougall boys. OMG. The intertwined connections in a small town.

***

Kristin and I were exhausted from our blustery drive, but we relieved my two Calgary daughters, who then headed home to their families after being with

Trish since they had become aware of what was transpiring in that room in the Foothills Hospital that morning. Trish, of course, was still in total shock. Her phone never stopped being and ringing as she fielded calls, many from her and Trevor's friend group in Whitecourt. People wanted to know when they could come and be there for Trish, how they could lend support. Others to simply send her their love.

The next morning, we all accompanied Trish to the funeral home, where we got things in order for Trevor's celebration of life the following Saturday. Things were happening so fast. So many decisions to be made. How I ached for my dear niece and my grandnephews.

Trish and Tracy were a part of the same friend group who were still recovering from the shock and devastation of the death of Ryder and Radek and their friend, Corry, father of the boys. Tracy and Trish had dated the same man ... years apart. Tracy had lost her two boys, **R&R**. Trish had lost the father of her two boys, M&M. Both women had suffered extreme bereavement. It seemed uncanny that both were embroiled in such pain less than forty days apart.

Trisha's phone continued pinging and beeping the following morning. Once we completed what needed to be done at the Chapel of the Bells, we proceeded to one of her favourite restaurants. Sitting down at the round table, we ordered food and drink. I glanced over at Trish, sitting across from me. She was looking past me, her gaze extended over my left shoulder. For the first time since we had arrived in Calgary, I saw that suddenly her eyes had some light in them. I turned to see what had captured her.

Breathe!

There, striding down the aisle of the restaurant, was a force to behold. Heading our way was grace and grit personified oozing from every pore of the woman leading the charge. By her stride, I knew this woman knew where she was going and what she was doing as she led a posse of women toward us. The power in her step was undeniable. She was in charge of that room and nothing was stopping her. She said not a word and headed directly to my niece Trish, smothering her in her arms. All of us turned our tear-filled eyes toward the two women. Trisha melted into her. We stood stunned by the intimacy of the connection we were witnessing. Thirty-eight days prior, this woman had found her two precious young boys murdered in a horrific, devastating event. Now, Tracy Stark had cleared the way to hold and love and simply be there for her friend. The rest of the feminine entourage following Tracy moved in, bringing Trish into their loving circle. This heartfelt connection with her was breathing life into my newly widowed niece.

As they disengaged, the "Leader of the Pack" removed a silver chain supporting a metal key from around her neck and placed it over Trisha's head and around her neck.

Looking directly into Trisha's eyes, she recounted to my niece the history of the key. "This key was given to me the day my boys died by another strong woman, Trish." She paused. "By a kind and caring friend."

Trish grasped the key like a lifeline as Tracy, with her own tears flowing freely, spoke simply and directly to the heart of her friend. "As my friend told me, Trish, the key is to breathe." She placed her hand over Trish's. "This physical key is to remind you to breathe." She again tightly embraced my niece.

I watched the unfolding of such a beautiful gesture of love. There was profound caring, unselfishness, and connection in the quartet of women as they shared the deep sorrow of my niece. I felt privileged to witness such love. As the four moved back from Trish and joined us, I hugged them individually, thanking each of them for coming to be there for my niece, their dear friend. I approached Tracy last, wrapped my arms around her, and told her of the light I had seen in Trish's eyes as she saw her friends coming down the aisle of the restaurant.

"Sandra," she said, "when my boys died what sustained me through the inconceivable shock and the ghastly reality of what had happened, what got me through the days following their deaths was the unbelievable support of my friends. I just knew I had to come."

I was in supreme awe of the strength of this incredible woman. She, of all people, would know far better than me what my Trish needed at this time, and she had driven five and a half hours from Whitecourt to ensure that was exactly what my niece received.

Tracy, Angie, Stacy, and Kristina, some of Trisha's remarkable core of women, joined my daughters, my brother, and me in surrounding Trish and her M&M with our love and support that evening. I was particularly sensitive to how Tracy must be feeling as, for sure, this whole Trevor experience would be a profound "grief burst" for her. I watched her, the grieving mother of Radek and Ryder, being comforted by Trish's dad, my brother Ross. Her wound was still so very fresh from the loss of her beautiful sons, as Trevor's broken-hearted father-in-law shared his unbridled appreciation for her decision to spearhead the trip to support his daughter that day. The love in the room was palpable. Just being there together with each other, both crying and laughing, sometimes at the same time, took the edge off the pain overriding all else as the reality of loss permeated the walls of the Hayter home. We had all come together in remembering Trevor Hayter and to be there for his wife, and here, in our midst, we had a woman whose heart had been cracked wide open a little more than a month before. The camaraderie amongst us in the Hayter house combatted the cold, blustery January evening. We were bonded in trauma. We were connected in compassion and love.

Chapter 7

A CHANCE TO HEAL

IT HAD BEEN OVER A MONTH SINCE MY ENCOUNTER WITH TRACY AND FRIENDS in mourning the death of my nephew-in-law, Trevor, that fateful January night of 2017. After Trevor's service, Tracy had told me she would be making an appointment to come and see me. When I had not heard from her by the end of February, I sent her a text:

> SYK: Still haven't seen your name in my roster, kiddo. Where are you?

> TRS: Good morning Beautiful! Just giving you a chance to heal. I really do need to sit in your chair. It's been a rocky road of hurting for everyone.

> SYK: Grief certainly is a rocky road Tracy, isn't it? Please reserve a space in my online schedule.

I remembered Ryder's birthday was March 1. I read a message she had posted on Facebook and sent her another text that day

> SYK: Hello Little Mama. Just read your Facebook Post. Sending you much love today as you remember your Ryder with the words to the amazing song you shared. Did Michaela write it for you?

> TRS: Aw, thank you Sandra. Yes, she did! It was such a hard day. Hard to have kids in Heaven when I love birthdays so much. It was just so different this year as we celebrated Ryder's birthday. Here's the words to the song. You can get it on iTunes.

Love You to the Moon

by Michaela Clarke [9]

Hey it's me
You say you're doing okay
But between you and me
You know you don't have to be
Ya. It's good to see your face
I know it's been some time
But it don't have to be that way
Just close your eyes
And I'll be there for you
Anytime you need me to
I know I went away
Left you to stay
Some days you think you've gone crazy
Cause you can't figure out what this is all about
Questions with no answers
I wish I knew
Oh, I was taken too soon
But I know you're listening
You know I love you to the moon
Oh, you know I do
Days go by
And you still fake that smile
Ya. I see you cry
Wishing you could turn back time
But don't look up to the sky
Cause I'm right here by your side
I know I went away
Left you to stay
Some days you think you've gone crazy
Cause you can't figure out what this is all about

---

9   Michaela Clarke is a talented Nashville, musician, singer and songwriter. The song Love You To The Moon is available on iTunes. Michaela grew up in Whitecourt, Alberta.

Questions with no answers
I wish I knew
Oh, I was taken too soon
But I know you're listening
You know I love you to the moon
Time heals all wounds
But it feels like time's stopped
So, I'm holding onto you
With every inch I've got
And I promise you
I'll keep on loving you from Heaven to the moon
From Heaven to the moon
Hey it's me
I know you're gonna be okay.

SYK: What a beautiful gift for you and for Ryder!

TRS: I am really touched by it. It is as though my boy is talking directly to me.

SYK: And how wonderful to blare it out to him on his birthday. To make his favourite cake! To have a food fight in his honour! Whatever would make him laugh. When someone dies, the relationship does not end. It simply changes. The love lasts forever and ever. There is no amen. Ryder and Radek will always and forever be your sweet boys.

Each time you think of either or both of them, send your love to them across the sky. They are the gentle breezes of the new spring surrounding Ryder's birthday, the roar of the thunder and the flash of the lightning as we welcome the end of winter. They are your brilliant stars in the north sky at night after the long summer days. They are the golden leaves falling in the beauty of Canadian Thanksgiving around Radek's birthday. They are a part of you and you them, Little Mama, FOREVER and nothing can take that relationship away from you!

Cry when you need to cry. Tell their stories not of how they died but rather, as your friend said at their funeral, of how they lived. How Radek giggled! How Ryder burped! How they breathed in their life on earth in great gulps! How they loved their mom and how they did life with your family and their friends on and off the ice! There are so many connections between you and your boys that you will continue to experience.

TRS: I do get lots of signs too. It's amazing. They let us know they are always with us. I seen a great psychic as well, which has been helpful.

SYK: If you are open to it, please write about your psychic experiences and send them to me. You and I will need to deal with the trauma in your nervous system … very, very gently so you can gradually find a degree of peace, little by little. I know you want to ensure the boys will be remembered in a way that makes their having lived make that difference in this unpredictable world. I am off to Mexico soon, so let's meet before I head'er.

And then. It is there in the online schedule: Tracy Stark*March 07, 2017*11:00 a.m.

Chapter 8

MOURNING

Sandra Young Kolbuc, Counselling Therapist

IT WASN'T THAT I DOUBTED MY ABILITIES TO ASSIST TRACY WITH THE COM-
plicated grief and trauma she would bring to the AIM office. I was well-trained
in dealing with both. I knew I would find the grace and grit to work with the
"blonde bomb." I, as a therapist, was ready.

I had always believed that skill and knowledge were critical for a therapist
but in my mind, the "person of the therapist" was perhaps right up there as a
most critical component in healing. The relationship was paramount. Me and
Tracy? Well, we already had the strong beginnings of a relationship, and besides,
I wanted to provide that space for her to grieve and to heal right here, right now,
in her home community.

As I sat, anticipating our first counselling session, I flipped through a pam-
phlet entitled "Moments" written by Dr. Alan Wolfelt, author, educator, and grief
counsellor, which stated, "Mourning in our culture isn't always easy. Normal
thoughts and feelings connected to loss are typically seen as unnecessary and
even shameful. Instead of encouraging mourners to express themselves, our
culture's unstated rules would have them avoid their hurt and 'be strong.' But
grief is not a disease. Instead, it's a normal, healthy process of embracing the
mystery of the death of someone you loved. If mourners see themselves as active
participants in their healing, they will experience a renewed sense of meaning
and purpose."

I believed I could facilitate that.

I wanted Tracy to feel safe and secure in her grieving, to be recognized for her
strengths, and to know that all of what she was feeling was okay. I wanted to be

the therapist that this Little Mama deserved. I wanted the therapeutic relationship I knew we could forge.

The critical factor in my analysis of what was needed in Tracy's healing was based on my knowledge of how to work with trauma. In this area, I was highly trained. I knew, in the depths of my being, that we would do good work together. I breathed in as I regarded the clock's minute hand moving to the top of the eleventh hour. I settled myself, thinking about our upcoming session and the questions filtering through my brain.

How did she deal with the heart-wrenching pain? How did she manage the flashbacks? How did she live with her rage at Corry and the systems and the individuals she believed had failed her? The depth of her sadness must have reduced her at times to a curled-up ball of humanity, her rage at Corry's actions tightening her body like the drying rawhide on a drum frame. But at whom did she rage? Hmmmm. That must be why Brent continually referred to Corry as a coward. Never had I, or any of his very closest friends, ever expect this from Corry MacDougall.

I grabbed a file folder and wrote the name Tracy Ross Stark on the identifying tag. I got up, breathed in once again, and walked to the waiting room to greet my new client.

The Walk Down the Hallway

I saw the blonde sitting there alone, absorbed in her cell phone, waiting for her first appointment with me, her now-therapist. I was focused. I knew thoroughly from my work what had helped me in companioning others when they had lost loved ones. I had been happy to see her name in my online scheduling roster.

I was nervous about this first encounter in our new roles, but I knew the butterflies in my stomach would be fluttering to attention at my command and would spur me onward as I worked with the grief of loss—separating out the normal grief reaction from the trauma of the dramatic way the boys had perished and in Tracy's experience of that dreadful day. I was eager for the challenge presented me. The prospect of beginning to reset her nervous system and of normalizing her reactions to abnormal events? That was my game.

I engaged in this encounter with my client from the moment I observed her sitting in the chair in my waiting room. My visual depression inventory began.

Good colour in her cheeks ✓ Well put together. ✓Faint scent of perfume. ✓ She had heard my footsteps and raised her head, giving me a beautiful smile, totally unaware of my ongoing assessment. ✓ We hugged. I noticed she was in bare feet, toenails immaculately painted a pink hue.✓ She accompanied me down the hallway to the AIM office as we chatted aimlessly about trivial things, reconnecting. She laughed at some mundane statement I had made.✓ I directed her to my blue chair.

Her smile was wide and sincere as she took in this new experience, no doubt wondering what to expect from what would be such a very personal encounter with me as we assumed our new roles. She, the client, and I, the therapist, were about to be engaged in a most intimate encounter.

Intimacy—In*To*Me*See. The breakdown of that word in this manner was helpful for many of my clients. In*To*Me*See. That was what our connection was all about. What would she allow me to see? I faced her directly.

She was stylish in her physical demeanour. ✓ Hair coiffed. ✓ Makeup impeccable. ✓ Clean, ripped jeans and a stark white, sleeveless blouse. Rings on her fingers and rings on her toes! Ah ha! Good. ✓ ✓

She was sitting straight up in the chair. I noted the tension in her body. **XX**

I could see she was settling more comfortably into the chair. ✓ ✓

I waited, as she and I began to connect our "internal WIFI." We sat and did just that … connected.

Chapter 9

THE BLUE CHAIR—
FIRST SESSION

I SMILED AND TOLD TRACY HOW BRAVE SHE WAS TO COME AND SEE ME. HER fearless demeanour suddenly evaporated and as the tears began, she said, "I promised myself I wouldn't cry here!" She reached roughly for a tissue from the coffee table beside her chair and dabbed at her eyes.

Quietly I said, "Like many of my clients, Tracy." My statement, an attempt to make her feel more at ease.

She smiled a little smile.

I saw the activation rising in her body **XX** as the vulnerability of being here in my counselling room took hold.

Again, I smiled gently at her and asked, "What is going well, Tracy?"

She appeared startled by this question, as were many clients. "What?" they would say. "I'm not here because things are going well, Sandra. I am here because things are falling off the rails!"

I explained that I wanted to have her expand her awareness rather than simply focus on the presenting problem of what I knew was trauma, grief, and loss.

She looked at me quizzically and I responded to her gaze. "Whatever you focus on expands. If you focus on the sh*t, the pile just gets higher and deeper. Through everything you have experienced, I am wondering if you can think of anything that you might be able to identify as going well."

She looked at me again rather curiously, tilting her head as tears continued to leak from her eyes. **XX** Her shoulders drooped and the falling droplets drew her head down. **XX**

"Just feel the support of the chair, Tracy, and if it's okay, just notice your breath."

She took another tissue in her hand and wiped the tears as they caressed her cheeks and began to drip into the recesses of her neck.

I sat with her in her grief, silently allowing it to wash through her in this sacred space as I bore witness to her deep despair. I had no expectations of my client other than attempting to be fully present to her breath in this moment.

Two women sitting together quietly. The seasoned therapist respectfully acknowledging the tears of her client. The younger woman embarrassed by her flowing tears. Together we breathed in the mutual molecules in the air, feeling the comfort of the connection of our two nervous systems.

The younger woman looked up, eyes rimmed with red as she said, "Jesus. I can't stop crying! Look at me! I'm a mess!"

I attempted to lighten the heaviness of the air in the room as we began. "Correction Tracy. You're still a hot … mess."

She issued me a slight grin or … was it a grimace?

I wanted to allow her to be exactly where she was. No pressure to do anything other than be right here, right now.

I started. "You have every reason to cry wherever … whenever … forever … if you wish. The most dangerous tears are the ones you keep inside. Besides, you, my girl, are still a beautiful soul, even when you cry."

She looked up and breathed in deeply, managing a very weak smile and regaining some of her composure as she adjusted to this therapeutic encounter.

Again, I asked, "So … what is going well?"

She sighed. "Well, Sandra … I am here."

"Yes, you are! You are indeed! I am curious, Tracy. How did you get here?"

She looked confused. "I drove here in my Range Rover."

I chuckled slightly. "Sorry! What I mean is, what finally got you out the door coming to do some therapy with the old babe, aka me?"

Now she actually laughed and again, breathed in deeply. I began to see her settling into the chair. "It was actually Brent who suggested I had better come and see you. I have been really struggling lately, with anger mainly. Mad that my kids are gone. Mad at that son of a bi#ch who took them from me. Brent told me that you were good with his daughters when he and their mother split up. I also remembered all the times you would come to the boys' hockey games when your grandson, Gavin, played on teams with my boys. You were always nice to me. I figured you knew my boys and maybe you would be a good listener and be able to help me. And besides, I promised you I would come see you when we were together in Calgary!"

I said, "Well, please thank Brent for his endorsement and tell him there is another chair in here, just waiting for him."

She laughed. "I told him he should come too, but he says he's good."

"Men always say they're good, even when to us women, it is very obvious that they are not so good." We laughed together again.

"I have to admit, I felt a lot of anxiety coming today and almost cancelled," she said. "It is so hard for me to talk about what happened, and I knew I would be an emotional mess." She dabbed at her eyes. "I hate people seeing me like this. I try to keep my 'bad days' to myself or when I am alone with Brent. I know it's hard on him when I am so sad, but he is my safe person and sometimes I just can't keep myself from losing it."

The tears in her eyes welled up again and we waited until she gently blew her nose and took in a deep breath.

"Tracy, I am so glad you made it here. What are you noticing as you think about being brave enough to sit in my blue chair?"

She sighed. "I notice that I am very emotional all right, but ... it's not quite as bad as I thought it would be ... yet!"

I saw her shoulders coming away from her ears as she settled even more into the chair. "You spoke briefly of the bad days when you lose it. What happens differently on the good days?" I asked.

"Well, sometimes the whisky helps change a bad day to a better day!" she joked.

I nodded. "Yes. Your whisky is one way to check out from the depth of sorrow you are experiencing inside. Listen, my friend. After a traumatic event, some people may turn to drinking a little more booze or smoking a little pot or something worse or sitting in front of a screen for hours on end. Others may become totally focused on work or stay busy all the time or engage in another addiction. Anything to ease the stress of the pain and loss. There are a variety of ways people who have been traumatized check out, or as we say in my business, find ways to 'dissociate' from what is going on inside. The difficulty with such practices is that they may become habits that do not serve a person well in the long term. Alcohol is a way of getting away, but you may want to take a moratorium on alcohol for a while because you are not going to metabolize the experience of losing your boys by using drugs or booze or even some pre-scribed medications."

I took the opportunity to explore my concern with how I had heard she might be handling things and with great respect and gentleness, said, "I have heard whisky is your best friend these days, Trac."

Her face remained neutral.

I went on. "You know throughout our work together I won't pretend not to know what I have heard. We both know small towns. I want to be real with you in hopes you feel you can be real with me. So, I want to address our friend, 'whisky,' up front so you will understand the ramifications of using booze to check out if … if that is what you are doing. What you do with this information is, of course, up to you."

"Hmm." She nodded. "Thanks, Sandra. I appreciate your candidness already. You heard right. Whisky has been my coping mechanism since the moment I returned home from Spruce Grove after finding my boys. That is how I got through the days, the nights, the vigils, the funeral, the …"

I put up my right hand. "Hold on, Tracy. We will get to those events, I promise. Just not yet. We have some work to do to decrease the activation in your nervous system first so we have room to process what happened to Ryder and Radek and your experience of finding them. If I go with you immediately to revisit the tragedy, you will find a way to check out on me because you will be overwhelmed by revisiting the events surrounding the death of the boys."

I reached for my tall glass cup of clear water to continue the teaching portion of our session. "Tracy, it is as though you have a cup filled with every 'oh sh#t' moment that you have experienced since the time you were in utero with your own mom and you could neither fight or flee during such experiences. All that 'trauma' is in your cup."

I waited as she took this in. "My job," I said, "is to help you empty that cup. Post-traumatic stress doesn't just occur in soldiers returning from battle. It is caused by having too much activation in one's nervous system, which can result in an individual developing many dysfunctional behaviours to stop the pain. When you can't physically flee from or fight through an event, trauma gets frozen in your body. Such activation needs to be released."

I wanted her to understand that "talk therapy" alone was only a part of the healing process. The trauma of her boys' death was residing in her body and we would be using appropriate interventions to deal with that activation.

She was engaged in what I was saying.

I continued in my "professional" teaching voice. "My job is to assist you in decreasing the activation in your nervous system. Anxiety and depression result from the nervous system being too activated, and then, it is extremely difficult to learn new things—new ways of being. Right now, you are learning to live without the physical presence of your sons and yet continue in a beautiful relationship with them. I need you to know there is a path to living with the 'new normal' you are now experiencing."

Again, I saw her eyes clouding up.

My voice softened. "Tracy. Your boys are within your soul now. They are already giving you the courage to make it through each day."

"It's funny you say that, Sandra," she said haltingly. "I feel their presence all the time and they do give me that strength to carry on." Once more, she wiped her eyes. We were quiet together as Tracy focused on her breathing.

I cleared my throat as I continued gently. "What I meant was, you absorb what has happened because you cannot change it. You learn to live with this new relationship with the boys and cherish it."

I saw the sorrow in her eyes and asked, "As I said that, what did you notice?"

"I'm not sure what you mean, Sandra."

"Tracy. I want you to tune in with your body and just notice any sensations: tingling, shaking, feeling hot or cold. Those types of things."

She nodded. "Okay. But I can't say I feel anything different right now, Sandra, except I am feeling very sad."

I saw her processing what I had shared but I feared I had overwhelmed her with too much information. I asked her if what I had said made any sense.

"I think so," she said. "So, I gather we are not going to talk about what happened to my boys today?"

"That's right, my friend. Not today. My job, as your therapist, is to help you decrease that activation in your nervous system. So yes, the death of your boys is the most critical trauma we will work with, but before we discuss it, we need more room in your trauma cup to process what happened. If the cup is too full, you will simply check out on me. The feelings will be too intense to manage. We need to slow it down and decrease the trauma in that cup with smaller 't' trauma experiences rather than the big 'T' trauma, which occurred on the day of their deaths."

I took a sip of the water from my glass cup, giving her a visual of decreasing the level of trauma in her "cup."

She nodded. "Okay. I think I get it now."

I revisited my initial question. "So, I am again wondering ... what is going well?"

She looked at me and said, "Going well? Hmmmm. So many people are still so supportive of me and my family. We have a great group of friends who never leave us alone. They are still there to support us 24/7, which is okay, but difficult too because sometimes I just crave some alone time to be with my thoughts and my boys and ..." she paused, "my tears."

She breathed in, wiping the tears that were again beginning to spill over from her eyes as she continued. "Right now, there are too many people around and Brent doesn't like it when people come in and make my 'good days' sad. He is very protective of me. It is extremely difficult for him to see me upset, so sometimes I try to hide my feelings until I can't anymore. Even he and the girls don't talk to me about the boys, and that is very hard for me." Her voice broke.

I took my time and then said, "Just feel the support of the chair, Tracy and again, notice your breath if that is okay."

We paused our verbal interactions as she experimented with what I had asked her to do. We were beginning the process of emptying her trauma cup.

After a couple of minutes, I could see she was more settled and said, "I am glad you are here, Tracy, in this safe space where you can talk about the boys all you want and cry and scream and yell if you so desire."

She managed another weak smile as I continued, "Don't worry. We will talk lots about Radek and Ryder. In fact, I have an assignment for you already. Over the course of our work in the next while, I will be asking you to do some writing. Would you be willing to write your autobiography and biographies of each of your boys? How's that for some heavy-duty homework?"

"Well. Brent told me you were a teacher in one of your past lives, so I guess I should have expected this!" she said.

Laughing quietly, I moved my rolling chair forward and grasped her hands. Looking directly into her tear-stained eyes, I said, "And you, Little Mama, will be giving me the precious gift of getting to know your boys through you and your stories of them and of how you decide to honour their memory. I want to say hello to them. I want to know the essence of each of them. And I want to get to know you as well, Little Mama. Thus, the homework." I squeezed her hands before releasing them and rolled back my chair. "Your job right now is to allow whatever you are feeling to emerge and be okay with it. Right here. Right now. In this moment."

Again, I slowed down our interaction as I continued. "Feelings are neither right or wrong, Tracy Stark. They just are. And tears? Well, they are simply discharge. Letting go."

She nodded slowly, obviously attempting to take in what I had just shared.

"What do you notice when you think about the support and kindness of so many people, Tracy?"

"It feels good to have such caring in my shattered world, and right now, I am beginning to feel more relaxed," she responded. "Actually, I'm not feeling so revved up anymore." She looked surprised.

As we came toward the end of the session, Tracy reached into her purse and handed me a creased piece of paper.

I unfolded it and saw it was an email.

She explained. "People have been so very kind. Friends, acquaintances, hockey fans from the Wolverine Games, people I do not even know have sent messages. Whitecourt and Woodlands County citizens and those across Alberta, Canada, and the USA have sent me emails expressing their sorrow. People actually email me from all over the world with sympathy and love filling their messages. Sometimes, it is very overwhelming. People want **R&R** stickers to place in their businesses, on their car windows, on their hockey helmets. That email you are holding arrived shortly after the boys died. I did not know this woman who wrote it but when the boys passed, she said she was called to write this poem and send it to me." She paused. "I am so touched that she took the time to write this verse. It soothes me when I think about my little hockey players being in Heaven."

I began to read the poem silently.

She stopped me and asked quietly, "Will you read it aloud, Sandra? It is comforting to hear it read and think of my boys in THAT WAY."

"Of course I will," I said. I began to read the poem out loud.

Heaven's Team

by
Lisa M. Kovacs[10]

The boys entered Heaven hockey sticks were in their hand
And as they met their loved ones they grew to understand
The ice where they now skated was as clear as ice could be
And as they did the warm-up lap, they set their young souls free
The wind that caught their locks under helmets that fit just so
Made them feel as if they could fly if they'd only just let go
The team that they now played on was full of faces once thought gone
But they recognized their teammates and knew they weren't alone
The reason they were traded to the team up in the sky
Is the question with no answers for no reasons fit the why?
The world is left to wonder how someone chose to pay this cost
Even though the boys now play for a team that has never lost.
They joined the team of angels for a season that does not end
And now forever they will skate as teammates … brothers … friends.
They will be the best they can as they skate in Heaven's lands
Until the day they see once more … their mom waving from the stands.

Mom … waving … from … the … stands. Our eyes met and I teared up as the vibration of the words resonated in the soles of my feet. We sat in silence, locked into the beauty and kindness in the caring words from the heart of a mom reaching out to the broken heart of another mom. We took turns with the Kleenex, the box now almost empty. She straightened and I encouraged her to notice the support of the chair, once again inhaling and exhaling, as we shared this moment in time. Right here. Right now. The end of our first session was approaching.

"So, my friend," I said. "I am so glad you found your way here."

"Me too … I think," she said. "This isn't exactly what I expected but it was okay!"

She smiled as I continued. "You may feel a bit weird for a couple of days.

---

10   A stranger who reached out to Tracy with the touching poem "Heaven's Team." See Appendix for a subsequent email from Lisa Kovacs in December 2020.

We are closing down old brain pathways and building new ones in your brain, Tracy! This is how we begin to work with trauma and grief."

She stood up. "That must be why I am feeling so exhausted! Lots of jackhammering, rippin' up the old pathways and building those new ones!"

I laughed softly at her ability to come back at me in a joking manner. I too stood and shook her hand. "If you have a little time, maybe you could begin writing your autobiography."

"Hmm. That sounds scary," she said.

I laughed. "Well, you can work on it just a little at a time."

She did look exhausted.

I returned the beautiful poem to her and she tucked it in her purse. "I hope I will see you again soon, Tracy Stark," I said.

She looked me straight in the eye. "You will." And with that, she turned and left the office.

Therapeutic Debrief

I literally fell back into my chair and breathed in deeply, reviewing our session and wondering what had been going on for Corry to murder those he loved most in life. Where was his head? I sat. I breathed in as I thought of the young man I had known as a boy in his growing-up years and then as the hockey dad of Ryder and Radek. I selected a piece of music, stood up and moved to the melody emanating from my phone, letting go of the activation in my body. Gradually I sensed a calming and felt gratitude for the privilege of sharing the healing strategies I was so privileged to carry in my therapeutic kit bag. I wondered if Tracy would find her way back to work with me again.

Chapter 10

THE BLUE CHAIR— SECOND SESSION

THERE IT WAS AGAIN IN MY ONLINE ROSTER THE FOLLOWING WEEK: TRACY STARK Wednesday, March 14, 2017, 2:00 pm.

As I entered the waiting room to retrieve my client, the big, beautiful smile again greeted me. We walked together down the hall to the AIM counselling room. Again, she was wearing a sleeveless blouse and as she settled into the blue chair, I got a full view of her sleeves of tattoos.

"Wow!" I said. "Those tattoos are mighty impressive, Tracy. You are just a walking work of art!"

She smiled.

"Tell me about your sleeves … if that is okay," I said as I took a closer look.

She extended her arms.

"Oh my God, Tracy!" I rolled my chair forward to get a better view of the image on the lower part of her right arm. I had remembered the sleeves of tattoos from our night together in Calgary in January of that year. At that time, the lower right arm was … blank. I remembered because it was the only space on both arms that was actually without an image. This tattoo on the right lower arm was brand new.

"That tattoo is so amazing! When did you have that done?" I asked, pointing to an obviously recent picture of #3 and #8.

She was happy to share. "It is an interesting story, Sandra, and symbolic of the love people have been showing Brent and me." She began by holding her left hand over the image of the boys as she spoke. "I never wanted to finish this right lower arm. I had half a sleeve from my shoulder to my elbow—a cross with a king's crown on the upper arm that read 'King of Kings' for my boys, which I had done when they were very young. I liked the look of not finishing the lower part of that arm. Then, when they passed away, I knew, oh how I knew, that the lower part of my arm would be for them. I guess … I guess that's what I was saving it for." She gulped in a deep breath as she continued her story.

"Shortly after the boys died, my friend, Candice Zemp, called and said a friend of hers had something for me, and would they be able to come by the house to deliver it? I said, 'Of course.' However, after the boys died, receiving gifts from people gave me anxiety. I would become so emotional. There were gifts … just gifts and gifts and more beautiful, heartfelt gifts. So many people were just wanting to share their love in such deeply personal ways. Everyone was so kind and generous, but it hurt my heart so much because the whole reason we were receiving gifts was because my boys had died. That reason made my heart ache even more. My heart has had a stabbing, physical pain within it all the time I am awake."

I interjected. "What are you noticing as you tell me this, Tracy?"

She stopped and took a minute to determine what was going on in her body. "My heart feels very heavy and that pain is still ever evident," she responded and placed her hand over her heart. We processed the sensations in her body until I could see her settling in the chair.

She returned to the story of the gift giving and said, "The reality of what has happened hit me harder each time a gift arrived. Don't get me wrong. People were so wonderful to do such beautiful acts of kindness. I was just struggling with the 'why' of why we were the recipients of such love, of such gifts.

The knock at the door came and it was Candice and her friend, Steven Ayles, who I knew from Haze Tattoo. With me covered with 'works of art' as you call them, it was so fitting to have him come to my home. He was carrying a beautiful canvas when he arrived at my door. Ugggggggg. It was a drawing of my boys depicting them from when they were little to the year they passed away. Of course, I started bawling. It too was such an amazing 'piece of art.' A gift from a guy I barely knew.

The Canvas

"Steve shared the history of the canvas with Brent and me, saying he was getting a tattoo done at The Calgary Tattoo Company and there was an artist there named AJ Smith, who also did airbrush paintings. Steve told AJ about Radek and Ryder and asked if AJ could capture their images on a canvas and that is exactly what he did!

"I reached out to AJ right after receiving the painting. I thanked him for doing such an incredible job telling him I felt blessed to receive such a beautiful piece. He was very sincere and sent his condolences to our family. That was when I knew he would be the one I wanted to finish my arm, to etch my boys onto my body. I booked an appointment and worked with him on my vision. He made it come true, drawing my boys walking the stairs to Heaven's Gate."

She referred to the tattoo on her arm and continued, "Each of the boys is wearing the hockey jersey from the last team he had suited up with—Ryder #3 and Radek #8. Radek is positioned ahead of Ryder as he reached the heaven's gate first. Ryder followed. AJ added two doves surrounding the boys and I had him add the boys' **R&R** black, red, and white heart."

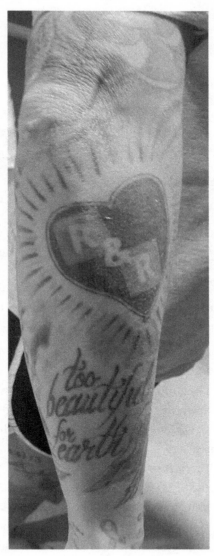

Tracy's tattoo of the R&R heart and "Too Beautiful for Earth"

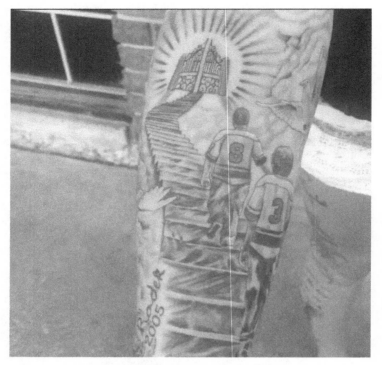

Tracy's tattoo of the boys walking the staircase to Heaven

"Another beautiful story, Tracy! What do you notice as you think about Candace and Steven and AJ?" I asked.

"I think it is such a beautiful tribute to my boys," she replied and remembering, she breathed that in, feeling the support of the chair and noticing her breath.

We were in self-regulation mode again, decreasing the activation in her nervous system wherein the trauma lies. We were dipping into the story of losing her boys with baby steps.

"So?" I asked my leading question. "What is going well, Tracy?"

"I'm ready for that one today, Sandra." She laughed. "I knew you would ask me that! After our session ended last week, I went out to my SUV and honest to God, I felt I could breathe again. It is hard to describe. I got in my truck and cried all the way home ... but not in a bad way, though. It was just the first time that I really had gotten in touch with how my body was experiencing what had happened and how I felt, other than simply being pissed off all the time. I realized we didn't talk a lot about the boys directly, but it was calming to work with you. Yes, I would talk to my friends and Brent, but they were living the same nightmare with me, so it is different with you. The fact that I can breathe again—that's big!"

I nodded. I could visually see her calming.

She closed her eyes as I sat quietly. I observed the woman sitting in my chair as she imagined taking the deepest possible breath. She began to appear even more grounded. More centred. We had already begun to do good work in releasing the trauma in her body.

Chapter 11

RADEK'S POCKET

WHEN THE BOYS DIED, TRACY'S FOLLOWING ON FACEBOOK EXPANDED EXPO-
nentially from places near and far. I, Sandra, as a follower, on her Facebook, was
privy to a message she shared three months after the deaths of the boys. She
prefaced the post with a text exchange with Radek that had occurred in early
December of 2016.

Tracy's Facebook Post: March 17, 2017

Since my boys passed away, I looked everywhere for this "Christmas gift" that
Radek had said he had bought me. I couldn't find it anywhere. I even called the
school to see if it was maybe left behind … Nothing. This morning I go into
Radek's room looking for a hat to wear. I come across his hockey jacket and of
course every pocket is filled with stuff from Canadian Tire money, his money
clip, and on the inside pocket is even a Day-Timer. LOL … and surprise, surprise … what I'm thinking is my Christmas gift. Two beautiful necklaces. One
for him and one definitely for me! It just kills me. I want them back!

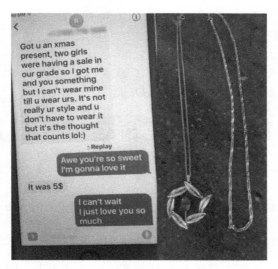

Radek's gift to his momma – Facebook Post

I sent her a private message:

> SYK to TRS: What a wonderful exchange and post on what you discovered in Radek's pocket, Tracy! A beautiful testament to your connection with your Radek. I always say, people never really die unless we quit talking about them. Keep telling the beautiful stories of Radek and Ryder, Little MAMA. These stories are always and forever yours.

Chapter 12

LIFE GOES ON THE WAY IT DOES

Sandra Young Kolbuc, Counselling Therapist

TRACY HAD TO CANCEL TWO SESSIONS, BUT BY THE END OF APRIL SHE WAS back again. She and Brent had been away on another adventure. He was diligent in ensuring his sweetheart was always on the move, so afraid of her going into a downward spiral. It was good to see her again. She shared stories of her latest travels. I administered a symptom checklist. Her results showed that since the kids had passed, she continued to have intrusive imagery and flashbacks, nightmares and night terror, frequent crying, depression, feelings of impending doom and the need for alcohol to relax. I assured her that these were normal responses to abnormal events and that they would settle down as we continued to work together, releasing more of the trauma in her system.

"What is going well, Tracy?" I asked.

She took a moment. "Well," she began, "we have bought a house in the country and are moving there in the summer. The thought of staying in our house with all the memories of the boys is too much. I still expect to see them playing hockey in the street or on the driveway when I am coming home. Then every time I pass by their rooms, I get this anxious, gut-wrenching feeling in my stomach. So, Brent and I talked and decided to buy a house in the country. We are doing some renovations, adding a gym, and doing a few other things to make it ours. I am so looking forward to the serenity of living in the country."

We processed what moving to the country felt like in her body and then she continued. "All that is good, but however much as we try not to be, Brent and I are in a funk. I am having trouble getting motivated to do anything. I am just so angry with the lack of an intervention by Child Services after reporting what the kids had shared regarding Corry's treatment of them and the unwillingness of that department to help me remove the boys from his home. And … the flashbacks of finding the boys are ever-present. I can't seem to stop that tape running in my head."

In her imagination, I ask her to put filter paper on the death scene of Ryder, moving it forward and away in hopes of dimming the imagery that continued to pass through her brain. We talked about possible ways of taking action with Child Services in following up on what had happened. I asked her about favourite memories of the boys—from taking Ryder to Los Angeles for summer hockey to all the holiday times that she and Brent had shared with the boys which were filled with fun. We revisited those times as she talked more about the boys.

I attempted to differentiate between grief and depression, reminding Tracy that it was important to continue to learn new things to keep the depression from taking over and to allow herself to actively grieve the boys, which was so important in her healing.

She recounted precious memories. We talked and talked about the boys. This was a safe place to do so and I felt privileged to get to know Radek and Ryder as she shared her stories about each of them. She was frustrated with not only Child Services, but also with the justice system that she felt had let her down, her frustration leaking from her pores as she spoke of court orders not being monitored to ensure such orders were followed. She began to formulate the changes she would like to see to prevent another mom from experiencing the horror of what had happened to her. In an effort to assist her in emptying that trauma cup, we titrated her distressing experiences.

She began to feel a degree of peace and tranquility as we worked together, and I expected she would see me again soon. But I did not hear from her for a while and in July, I sent her a text, just checking in.

It's OK To Have Fun!

SYK: 2017-07-08: I've been missing your sitting in my chair, Tracy Stark!

TRS: i miss you too, Sandra. i do want to reach out to you again … we finally got moved into our new home so i feel like i can breathe again!

We set up an appointment. It concerned me when it was so long between sessions, but I had to trust that she would come when she was ready. Two weeks later, on the day of her appointment, another text came beeping in.

> TRS: 2017-07-26 Good Morning Beautiful. Soooooo, i am sorry i have to do this … but i totally forgot we're leaving for Calgary this afternoon for a tattoo appointment. Brent just reminded me this morning.

> SYK: You have an awesome time in Calgary. Be in the moment. Please sprinkle your love over Trish and the boys if you see them! I heard a rumour that you girls were going to see Lady Gaga sometime soon. May you rock with her as well. Did you know she is finding her voice and sharing her thoughts regarding the impact of trauma based on her own experiences? Hope you have fun! Love to both you and Trish.

> TRS: Yes! i can't wait to see Trish. The 6-month marker is a tough one. We will take her out and share some memories and laughs. And yes! Lady GAGA here we come! It's going to be a blast.

> SYK: And … please stop using that small lower case "i" when you refer to yourself! You deserve a capital 'I' big time Tracy Stark.

> TRE: OK! Honest Sandra. It is just because I am writing on my Ipad and it is easier to just use the small 'i' character! LOL!

> SYK: OK. I get you. You are forgiven! But I mean it! Take the time to write that big "I" and remember, it is okay to have fun.

> TRE: Thanks. I will. I know that it is okay to have fun. I know that is what my boys would want me to do! By the way … Just want you to know I have just about finished my homework! I am sending my autobiography up until Corry and I got together via email. I will work on that next section when I get back from Calgary.

> SYK: OMG! A star client!

Chapter 13

THE HOCKEY CARD
OF LITTLE MAMA

Whitecourt Wolverines
Tracy Stark—First Draft Pick
History & Stats

By Tracy Stark, Mother

I WAS BORN TRACY LYNN ROSS ON JANUARY 12, 1979, IN MELFORT, Saskatchewan, Canada. I was older than my twin brother Trevor by seven minutes, which in retrospect was perhaps foreshadowing that I would be continually looking out for him throughout our lives. I was the independent twin. My brother Darin was eighteen months older than Trevor and me, and it was a crazy busy time for my mom, with three little ones under the age of three toddling through her kitchen. Until 1984, my family lived on a farm outside Hudson Bay, Saskatchewan. My dad's parents lived right next door, and me and my brothers spent a lot of time with our grandparents. Even at a very young age, each of us would pack a favourite cereal box under our arm and, in our pjs, toddle over to our grandparents' place next door to eat our chosen breakfast under the watchful eyes of our grandparents. Mom would call over and Gramma would say, "Yes. They're here!"

As kids, we were surrounded by aunts and uncles and cousins, all of whom lived in or around the small community. It was a safe place to grow up amongst people who looked out for each other. I considered my life to be perfect! I had no problem keeping up with the boys and at a very young age was riding mini dirt bikes in the summer and driving mini snowmobiles or snapping on cross-country skis in the winter. I loved the outdoors and was well up to challenging and usually beating any boy in a race on one of the machines. Life was good.

In December 1984, when I was five years old, I moved with my mom and brothers to Edson, Alberta, to join our dad, who, for months, had been living and working there, hauling logs as the forestry industry in Alberta paid much better than farming in Saskatchewan.

Upon our arrival, me and Trevor were enrolled in kindergarten, where it was determined that the twins should be split up. We were put into separate classes. This was the first time we had ever been apart. I had no problem with this, but Trevor was absolutely devastated. I was the more free-spirited twin, always looking for new adventures and open to new friendships, so I had an easier time than my twin.

I had fun growing up in Edson with many friends with whom I basically hung out from grade one until I graduated high school. Thirty-five years later, my gaggle of girls still kept in touch and were right there on my doorstep with arms open wide when Radek and Ryder died, crying compassionate tears and offering heartfelt hugs to me, their long-time friend.

My parents assumed traditional roles when I was growing up. Dad would be gone before we kids woke up and was home just in time for supper or sometimes even later, when he would stay at the shop and have a few beers or whiskies with his buddies. He had gotten into that pattern after being away from our family for many months. This was the norm for many men back in the day. Men worked hard and felt they deserved a drink or three with their buddies after work. For my mom, who was basically a stay-at-home mom, with three kids in tow and no time for herself, that didn't seem fair to me.

On occasion, I sensed my mom's frustration, but that was the way it was. Mom took care of the kids and the household responsibilities, which was typical of many women in that era. Mom's role as a stay-at-home mom in small town Alberta hadn't been swayed by the women's movement of the sixties. However, the home was her domain. She would wake us kids up, get us ready for school, make sure we had completed our homework, and then hand each of us a brown-paper bag lunch with our name handwritten on the front as we headed out the door to the school bus. Mom did this until we graduated. After the school day ended, she continued feeding, watering, and bathing kids before going to bed herself. She was very dedicated to her role as a mom and assumed the role of the main parent in the household.

In my mind, my parents were very strict. I had a curfew until I finished high school, even though Trevor and I had turned eighteen in January of our graduation year. The phrase "As long as you are living under my roof, you will obey our rules" was heard many times as we kids sat at the Ross kitchen table.

To me, being the only girl in the family was not at all fair! I was definitely more protected and had stricter rules than my two brothers. I remembered hearing the expression, "When you have two boys, you worry about two boys. When you have a girl? You worry about every boy in town!" My mom was the gatekeeper. I could not spend the night at friends' houses unless my mom talked to their parents and made sure me and my friends weren't slipping out to any parties. I maintain I had an earlier curfew than every kid in my class and I was not allowed to date until I was sixteen.

As a teenager, I considered my mother much too strict. However, she instilled in me some of the values that influenced me in the raising of my own boys. My children were going to be well taken care of. With my boys, I even did the brown-paper bag lunch thing, just a little upscale with lunch kits instead of brown-paper bags! I looked after my own boys with the same dedication I had learned from my mom.

In junior high school, I was an honour roll student and got along well with my teachers. I had many friends and athletically, I absolutely loved the sport of basketball. One day I signed up for a free-throw competition at my school and won it! I was elated as I had qualified for provincial competition. However, travel for sport was not in the family budget. I was unable to attend further competition. I was crushed.

That was the end of sports for me. However, I vowed that when I had kids, I would find the ways and means to allow my children to play any sport in which they showed interest. I kept that promise to myself and to my boys.

The basketball experience was one of the reasons I felt so passionate about eventually establishing the **R&R** Memorial Foundation. I wanted to provide opportunities for other kids whose parents had difficulty finding the funds for their kids to be fully involved in athletics.

As I grew into my teens, me and my mom, in typical daughter and mother fashion, were often at odds. Mom was more traditional in her thinking and I was wanting to try out my growing teenage wings! I was continually grounded for things I considered minor infractions, such as talking back to my mother or coming home late, even when I thought I had great reasons for both behaviours! Mom would definitely ground and reprimand me for finding my voice and defending my ideas with great passion. She called such behaviours being "sassy." To me, it seemed like Mom was doing everything to keep me within the confines of the home until I was forty!

In retrospect, it was obvious that Mom was wanting to give me good values and keep me safe. However, I was growing up and experimenting in finding my voice about things important to me. Dad was rarely home, as he was always working. Me and my brothers always found something to do. Dad role modelled putting food on the table and a roof over our heads. My parents did the best they knew, following the path of many parents of their generation. Dad made the money and looked after the outside work. Mom looked after the kids and the home.

Twin Trevor was my built-in best friend. We hung out with the same crowd until high school, when I became more popular with the high school crowd. I was no longer the awkward girl with the geeky braces. Thanks to my parents, I now had a beautiful, metal-free smile! The Grade 12 boys liked that smile. I liked the attention. My parents, on the other hand, did not!

As my parents became more protective of me, I got sneakier, which in turn got me grounded for what seemed to be my whole sixteenth year. I was aching for greater independence. Mom was so much harder on me than she was the boys, maybe because she felt it was a tougher world out there for girls. However, having two brothers, that's what made me tough! And maybe that is what I needed to survive the life that, unbeknownst to me, lay ahead.

Quest for Independence

Once I graduated from high school, I could not wait to move out on my own. I moved into an apartment with my friend, Michelle. I savoured every minute of being an adult. I loved paying my own bills, buying my own groceries, making my own decisions, and living my life in the way I wanted to live it. Michele ended up getting a job offer in Whitecourt, an hour away. She moved and soon met the man she would eventually marry. I couldn't afford our apartment by myself, so I moved in with my boyfriend at the time. My parents were not at all fond of this idea but they had no choice. I was now an adult! I had been dating the guy for three years, but I soon discovered that dating someone was a heck of a lot different than living with someone. It seemed that soon our place was becoming a party shack. His friends were there all the time and truthfully, I got tired of it.

I knew there was something more for me in life. I was ready to venture out of my home community, so I packed up my things and my mom and I moved me initially to Red Deer, Alberta. I believed I would have no trouble finding a job. However, it wasn't quite that easy and when Michelle, my former roommate, called telling me of a chance for a job in Whitecourt, I was on it. I packed up and headed north again. I got the job and soon found myself loving the energy of my new community. It was the turn of the twenty-first century and Whitecourt, situated in the middle of the oil and gas industry, was booming. Lots of young people with lots of money were having lots of fun. And now, I was one of that crowd!

What Happens in Vegas ...

Shortly after moving to Whitecourt, my friend Michelle became engaged. She asked me to be the maid of honour in her wedding in Las Vegas, four and a half months away! Michelle had begun opening my eyes to life. I had never travelled much with my family, other than going back to Saskatchewan each summer. Michelle had taken me to Mexico the year before and I had loved the experience of going on a trip. I was over the moon with excitement at the possibility of flying to Vegas and being party to "What happens in Vegas stays in Vegas!"

There was only one small problem. Well, it was not really that small. There was no way I had the money to go to Vegas. I could barely afford to pay my rent and eat, let alone go on a trip. So being the adult I was, I found another job that paid better and allowed tipping. I applied and was accepted as a waitress at Boston Pizza. I was up for a challenge, thinking, *This should be very interesting. I've never been a server. I was new to town and although many of my friends would disagree, I was very shy.* However, I fell in love with my job and made many more amazing girlfriends and yes! I made it to Vegas and came back filled with a lust for even more adventures. I was loving my new home and the independence I felt. I had this "living the dream" thing down pat. Then, I met a handsome young man named Trevor Hayter. He was a little older than me and we hit it off. Soon we were dating and he asked me to move in with him. I did and ... so did my twin brother Trevor!

Trevor Hayter was a good guy. He was very quiet but we had a lot of fun times with a great group of friends. We were together for two and a half years. We played a lot of slow pitch in the summers and enjoyed an equal amount of time sledding in the winters. Then Trevor went overseas to Yemen to work. When he left, I started spending time hanging out with his best friend, Corry MacDougall.

Best Friends Divided

I definitely enjoyed Corry's friendship. We would simply drive around in his truck and listen to music. At first, it was nothing more than a friendship, but the more time we spent together, the more we started to think we were a pretty good match. He was a hard worker. He was caring. He loved kids. He was a good person. He could give me a good life. That friendship soon developed into a more serious relationship.

* * *

Shortly after Tracy wrote this, she and I sat in the AIM counselling office discussing what she had written. I asked haltingly, "So, my friend. You got together with your boyfriend's best friend when your boyfriend was out of the country?"

She nodded.

"How did that go?" I asked.

She laughed softly at my remark. "Well. Not great at first. Trevor and Corry had been pretty tight. Trevor was angry at Corry and at me, so we didn't speak for a long time, but things had been changing between me and Trevor. I think we were basically done when he went overseas. I wasn't ready to stay home each night pining away for a guy thousands of miles across the ocean and we both weren't ready to move to the next step in our relationship. Then, Corry literally swept me off my feet. Besides," she smiled. "I had to move on so Trevor Hayter could fall in love and marry the true love of his life, your beautiful niece, Trish."

I shook my head. "Just a minute, Tracy. Let me get this straight. You and Trevor break up and then you meet Trish once she gets together with Trevor and you two become great friends?"

"Exactly right!" she said as she smiled brightly. "Well, I had to share all my 'tips' about Trevor with her, Sandra! You know how women stick together!"

I shook my head and smiled. The joys and intricacies of young women living in a small town and supporting each other in their love lives!

Chapter 14

LIVING THE LIFE WITH CORRY MACDOUGALL

WITHIN A COUPLE OF WEEKS, TRACY WAS SITTING IN MY OFFICE WITH THE next section of her autobiography.

"Tracy?" I asked as we sat together while she prepared to share more of what she had written. "What attracted you to Corry?"

She sighed and replied, "He was very outgoing. He was funny and a great country dancer. He asked me to come with him to a slow pitch tournament and dance where he told me, 'If you come to the dance Tracy, I will spin you around like a buckle bunny!'" We were having fun!

She stopped. "Here … I have my homework. I'll read you what I have written about my life with Corry." She reached for the file she had brought to our session, opened it, and began.

In the Beginning …

I was dancing on air at the beginning of our relationship. My parents loved Corry! He was charming and attentive. We were having a great time together. I was definitely falling in love. We moved in together. Two months later, I discovered I was pregnant. I hesitated to tell Corry as I was so afraid he would be upset. However, when I did share the news, he was literally ecstatic!

I was scared. I was not sure I was ready to have a baby and be a mom. Our relationship was so new! I was only twenty-four but Corry's enthusiasm for being a family spurred me on. Besides, I had always wanted to someday be a mom and now a beautiful child was growing in my belly.

I quit my job at Boston Pizza a few months before Ryder was born and became the bookkeeper of Corry's company. I completed the necessary safety courses and created a safety program for the company. Soon, my part-time job became full-time.

However, as my pregnancy progressed, Corry started changing, or maybe I was just getting to know him better. He began to go to the bar more and more with his friends. In the beginning of our relationship, we had some of his buddies, as well as my brother Trevor, living at our place. They would bring the bar crowd back to our home when the bar closed. I found myself again in a party house! Corry didn't see a problem with this, which caused problems between us. In retrospect, when I became pregnant, it was as though he now had me. I was his property. I was blind to this for a while, but gradually I saw our relationship changing. It was as though he wanted total control of me and my life. However, I was still okay. We were still having great fun and he was so excited at the prospect of being a dad.

Our first son, Ryder Patryk MacDougall, was born on March 1, 2003. After having Ryder, I told my mom that brother Trevor had to move back home. I couldn't look after my twin anymore. I had a baby now and little Ryder was my focus. Things between Corry and me became the "new normal" of being neophyte parents. Corry proved to be a very hands-on new dad. The bar crowd was no longer welcome at the house.

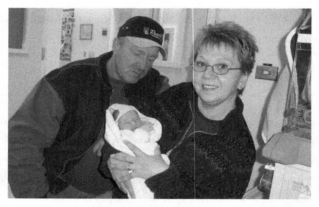

Ryder Patryk, first grandchild for Larry and Donna Ross

Corry and I became engaged on Valentine's Day 2004. Ryder would be one year old the following month. Our wedding was scheduled to be in Cancun, Mexico. It would be an amazing party as many of our friends would be joining us. It was interesting, though, how Corry's need for control seemed to increase even more once we became engaged. For a time, I was quite oblivious to this behaviour. I was in love with my life. I was in love with being a mom. Corry was an attentive dad and good with his new baby, Ryder Patryk. Even though we were not yet married, we were a family already! I was in love and happy being a wife and doing the things my mother had done to look after the home and us kids when I was a child. I was truly living the dream! New man. New baby. New house. New vehicle. New job. Corry made good money in his business. I did not want for any material things. Life was good and … we were getting married!

Game On! Marriage 2004

We pushed up the wedding in Cancun, Mexico to October 2004, and there was a great party atmosphere. However, a couple of interactions startled me and I suddenly realized that Corry would not stick up for me over his friends. I did not want to fail in this relationship, but once married, sign after sign pulled me away from the connection I had hoped would happen with Corry. I was totally in love with my new husband until his need for control began to penetrate all aspects of our life. It was his way or no way.

One evening, in mid-December of that year, when Ryder was almost two years old, I kissed our little boy good night, tucked him into bed, closed his door, and entered the living room where Corry was sitting. It was not long before Corry and I were in a heated argument. I have no recollection of what it was about but, he got up and looked directly at me before he grabbed our decorated Christmas tree, opened the patio door where we had not yet built a deck, and threw the tree as far as he could onto the frozen ground outside.

Little Ryder heard the commotion and came flying out of his room. He saw what was happening and started yelling over and over. "What did you do to my Christmas tree? What did you do to my Christmas tree!"

I scooped him up and told him not to worry. Mama would fix his tree. I put him back to bed, went downstairs into the darkness of the cold winter night and recovered the tree from the frozen ground. I hauled it back up the stairs and spent the next few hours making it perfect again for our little boy. Corry was sulking in our bedroom. He never apologized. I got over it … or did I? Life went on. I became pregnant with Radek.

Foreshadowing

Corry continued to go out with his friends. One evening, he just didn't come home. When I called his phone, looking for him, he told me he was not coming home and was going to sleep on his buddy's couch. I was incensed that he would do this. That was not how I pictured my life with my new husband. He was a married man. His wife was pregnant. He had a little son at home.

With Ryder asleep in his bed, I locked all the doors to the house, jumped into my vehicle, and literally raced to his friend's house. I woke up my drunk husband, got him into my vehicle, and brought him home. I was livid, screaming at him, worried about having left Ryder alone at home. In my mind, what married man, father of almost two kids, didn't come home at night and was drunk and sleeping on someone else's couch? I pulled into the garage and left Corry in the passenger seat of my vehicle. I dashed into the house to check on my little boy. Thank God he was still asleep. He looked so tiny, nestled in his bed and I realized I should have left Corry sleeping on that bloody couch rather than racing to get him and bring him home, putting our son at risk by doing so. My imagination went wild as I thought of things that could have happened when I was gone. I cuddled up next to Ryder in his little car bed and went to sleep. Later, I heard Corry noisily finding his way into our bedroom down the hall.

The next morning, I left Corry in bed and carried Ryder into the garage as I was about to head into town. As I went to put my boy into his car seat, I noticed two shotguns out of their cases, sitting on top of some boxes beside my Jeep. Now Corry had always had guns. I think his dad had given them to him when he was young. He had never hunted when I was with him and the guns were stored in a closet. Out of sight. Out of mind. When I saw them just sitting there in the garage, I was totally shocked. I continued strapping Ryder into his car seat, telling him Mommy would be right back. I proceeded to march back into the house, upstairs to our bedroom. My heels clicked angrily on the stairs. I confronted Corry, who was still lying in bed, saying, "Why the hell are those shotguns out in the open in the garage, Corry?"

He turned toward the wall, ignoring me.

I didn't stop. "Where did they come from and why are they there anyway?" I asked.

He just shrugged his shoulders.

I asked, "Were you thinking of killing yourself … or Ryder and me?" He said no to both questions, but I was furious.

I grabbed my phone and called his dad, telling him to come and get the guns off our property or I was going to call the police.

His dad came immediately and removed the guns.

Knowing what I know now, was this simply foreshadowing of what I was about to live through a little more than a decade later?

* * *

Tracy closed the file from which she had just read.

"Wow." I paused. "Good job Tracy," I said. "What was it like writing about that time in your life?"

Tracy responded. "It was okay. Actually, I didn't mind doing the writing. It was as though it gave me some peace of mind as I thought about how things had been with me and Corry. We had had some good times too, but as I wrote, I began to remember some of the things I had pushed way down in my memory, things that eventually pushed me away from my marriage."

Bit by bit, Tracy continued her story in emails, texts, and our sessions together.

Building an Empire

SYK to TRS: So, Tracy, tell me about how things were after you had Radek.

TRS to SYK: Our little buddy, Radek, arrived on the scene in October of 2005. It had been a stressful pregnancy, but I was excited to have a second child. However, with a full-time job in our company, I was struggling to manage everything. I was a mom, a homemaker, a bookkeeper, a safety coordinator, an inventory person, and a hot shot driver taking equipment to leases when needed. As Radek grew into toddlerhood, I talked with Corry about putting the boys in a day home for two days a week. I would devote those two days to the office and the rest of the days, I could do my most important job—that of being a mom. I felt I was missing out on quality time with our kids as I was in and out of the office all day long, tending to whatever needed to be done in the company, catering to Corry's every whim. Surprisingly, Corry agreed to this and that made a big difference in our home. I loved being a mom. I loved working for our company. Corry and I were working as a team. Together we were building an empire!

Corry as a Partner

However, the more successful we became as a company, the worse Corry became as a husband and father. He started going out with his buddies more and more. He spent every second weekend during the winter in the mountains riding snowmobiles. He figured he was entitled to do whatever he wanted, whenever he wanted because he gave "the wife," aka me, and his boys, a good life. For this, I was grateful. I was not the wife to cause issues. Besides, our home ran better with him away. Life was still okay.

It was not until Corry started to throw things in my face that our relationship began to deteriorate even more. With my company wage of $2,500 a month, I paid all the household bills, made my Jeep payment, bought all the groceries and anything for the home, or anything the kids or I needed. The money didn't stretch too far. However, Corry figured he was giving me the golden life and wanted to make sure I knew it. He had bought me a "sparkling" new Jeep, which I loved, but he was always making comments like, "So Tracy. What did you do to earn your Jeep today?"

Ummm. How about I paid for it with the wage I received for busting my ass in and out of the office?

I could no longer take having to explain myself to my own husband, convincing him why I deserved the things I had. He was someone who drove a brand-new, jacked-up pickup truck, a brand-new dirt bike, a brand-new quad, and a brand-new boat. I had always strived for independence growing up and here I was, married to someone who continually attempted to have me justify my existence. What did I do to earn my new Jeep? He had picked the wrong lady to pose that question to, too many times, for the seeds of discontent were beginning to fester within me. I had grown up struggling with someone attempting to control me and here I was again …

I continued to battle with Corry's need for control. Although we partied with friends, we never drank together at home, which was probably a good thing. The business continued to grow and many of his evenings were spent away from home having "business meetings," aka "drinks" with friends he called his "business associates" in one of the many lounges in Whitecourt. Terrible as it sounds, I continued to be happier having him away from home. Life was simpler when he wasn't trying to run my life and those of the boys.

Corry as a Parent

Corry was good with his first-born son. However, as Ryder entered the toddler stage, Corry started to become a "hard ass" with our little boy. On one such occasion, at my parents' place, we ordered in pizza and it arrived with little containers of sour cream. Corry opened the sour cream and began putting it on Ryder's pizza. Ryder protested, saying he didn't like "that stuff." Corry insisted and would not allow Ryder to have any pizza unless it was laden with sour cream. When Ryder pushed his sour-cream-covered pizza slice away, Corry physically forced him to eat it! Corry always had to be in charge.

Radek had an easier time with his dad, probably because he was a more compliant child. Even as a little boy, Ryder always thought we all favoured Radek. I would say to him. "Ryder, we love you as much as Radek but sometimes, son, you gotta make better choices." He was far more determined than his younger brother.

However, Corry "first-born" MacDougall seemed to put more pressure on his own first son. He was not a patient man with either of our sons but was beyond strict with Ryder when he acted out or became upset. He made Ryder bend over his bed with his pants down, his bare little ass waiting for a lickin', until his father was ready to spank him. It was almost as though he wanted Ryder to be waiting in fear of what was to come. This was brutal and infuriated me. He put the boys in time-outs for the stupidest things like not eating that damn sour cream on pizza. They continued to tell him they didn't like it. Corry did not care if they liked it or not. If he thought you should eat it, you had better eat it! He had a continual need to show them that he had the power. He was the man. He was in charge. But, the strange thing was, there were times when he could also be so much fun and that was confusing for me and the boys.

Corry introduced the boys to a lot of outdoor activities, which was great. He was always teaching them to do what he called "boy" things but when it came to the nurturing side of things or reading them stories or tucking them in? Well, that was not his idea of a dad's responsibility and he did not believe it was at all necessary. He always said I was making them into "puppies." Too soft. Too tender.

Chapter 15

TROUBLE IN PARADISE

SYK to TRS: So how were things between you and Corry during this time?

TRS to SYK: Like I said, Corry could be lots of fun. However, there were many instances when Corry would treat me with total disrespect. For example, I was scheduled to get together with a group of girlfriends for supper at Boston Pizza before heading to Girls' Poker Night at your niece Trish's place, actually. I was so excited to be going out with my girlfriends. I needed a break away from the demands and responsibilities of parenting and my job in the company.

Corry had been out sledding all day with his friends. I had told him I had plans that evening and asked him to please be home by supper time. I cooked up a shepherd's pie and was holding off feeding the kids, waiting and wondering if I would even make it out for supper with my friends. Of course, Corry wasn't home in time for me to leave for dinner nor had he called to alert me to his being delayed or of his unavailability. Rather than waiting for him to feed the kids, I finally dished them up just as I saw Corry walking up the path to the house. I quickly grabbed my coat, kissed Ryder and Radek goodbye, jumped into my Jeep, and pulled out of the garage. I rolled down the side window of my vehicle and sarcastically said how much I appreciated his consideration of being on time! He suddenly ran at me, dark eyes flashing in my face. He reached in my driver's side window, grabbed my Jeep keys out of the ignition, and threw them into the deep snow in the bushes before he turned and carried on into the house.

That being my only set of keys, I followed him angrily into the house. and asked, "WTF is wrong with you?" I was steaming mad. I threw my phone at him.

He winged it back at me.

I grabbed a flashlight and went to look for my keys.

In retrospect, I wonder what this was like for my little guys witnessing this and similar interactions, of which there were far too many.

When I arrived home that evening, I walked into the kitchen to see the casserole of shepherd's pie I had made for supper splattered all over the wall and broken pieces of the dish and chunks of the remaining casserole hardening on the floor. Corry was obviously sending me a message and again showing our boys his power. I proceeded to clean up the mess so that my children would not be walking through it when they got up in the morning.

My relationship with Corry was becoming hot and cold like the relationship I had witnessed between his parents. Things were either really good or really bad between us. Corry too was often either really up or really down. He had told me that when he was a kid and his dad was away at work, his mom had gathered up the kids and left his father. I have often wondered if my leaving Corry contained remnants of the pain of his parents' split many years before. Corry had been caught in the middle of that relationship and it continued into his adulthood. When we were first married, I would take Ryder to Corry's family reunions alone because the tension between his parents was too difficult for Corry to handle. We even had to do the kids' birthday parties separately with each of Corry's parents. If Corry was talking to his mom, then he wasn't talking to his dad. If he was talking to his dad, he wasn't talking to his mom. It was stressful for Corry and ... for me.

Corry rarely talked about his upbringing or what he'd experienced as the oldest kid in the family. He said when he was fourteen years old, his mom had a boyfriend he didn't like, so he moved away from his mom's place to come back to live with his dad. He spent a lot of time alone or with friends when he was a teenager as his dad worked the rigs and was away much of the time. Corry got used to having a lot of freedom.

On Ryder's third birthday, we were having a party at our house and we had invited Corry's mom, her husband, and Corry's sisters, along with many of our friends and their kids to celebrate our little boy. There was an unspoken agreement in Corry's family that we wouldn't do events with both Corry's parents attending. However, Corry's dad, who lived in a trailer at the bottom of our acreage, must have seen people arriving at our place. The party was underway when his dad burst through the front door and saw his ex-wife there. An intense verbal confrontation erupted between Corry's parents. Corry was mortified. All this was taking place in front of our friends and family, including the beautiful little grandson whose day we were celebrating.

Corry ended the party immediately, asking everyone to leave, including his father, sending him out the same way he had come in. Poor little Ryder's birthday party was ruined. My husband was totally humiliated and angry as hell, but I understood his frustration. I didn't see the whites of his eyes for three days.

I tried to figure out our own relationship. Maybe his relationship with me was coloured because of tension in his own parents' marriage when he was a kid. Maybe he thought all women eventually left. Maybe he was just used to having a lot of freedom in his life. Maybe. It was never something we talked about openly. Although, when I did ask him what it was like when his parents split up, his answer was short and defiant: "It never bothered me!" He was like Teflon, bouncing off any sadness, never admitting he had ever been hurt by what went on between his parents in his growing-up years. Just made him tougher, I guess ...

After Corry and I split, I still maintained a good relationship with his mother. I was in touch with her on a regular basis for a number of years. Corry's dad loved his grandsons and saw them regularly. He and I had a good relationship. I wanted my sons to know their grandparents. I still attended MacDougall family get-togethers with the boys when I was on my own until Corry told me I was to leave his family alone.

In December 2015, Corry's mom passed away after a battle with cancer. In December 2016, Corry's dad and his wife and his brother all attended the boys' funeral where, as I mentioned previously, I had a chance to give them all a hug. I have not been in touch with them since. I knew his dad would be suffering with what Corry did as he truly loved his grandkids. I was so glad Corry's mom did not live to witness the death of her grandsons at the hand of her own son.

Tracy continued to be on the move. In the hot Arizona sun, she continued to write, answering the questions I sent her

Working Together

SYK to TRS: How was your working relationship with Corry, Tracy?

TRS to SYK: Corry was very focused on making our company a great success. He worked hard in the business and then wanted to play doubly hard with his friends. I had no problems with this until we became parents of two little boys. As the business became more successful financially, he hired additional workers and was home more during the day. This had its downside for me. He was always attempting to control my every move. I would be in the middle of doing something with the boys and he would interrupt continually to have me work on some aspect of the business immediately, as if my engagement with the boys wasn't at all important.

He would say, "Why aren't you working more, Tracy?"

I would reply, "I am working, Corry. It's called parenting!"

He regularly wanted to exercise his domination over me. He needed to be the boss of me, of the boys, and of "his" business. I often felt like just another of his employees. I had never liked being told what to do. Telling me what to do was his forte. I had wanted to be independent since I was thirteen years of age, and now my husband wanted to control me just like my mom had tried to do those many years before. However, this time I again used the "I am an adult" card as his efforts did not go over well with this Little Mama, who he sometimes forgot was a mother of two precious children as well as "his" employee!

Sometimes, I simply wanted to play on the floor with our little guys. I wanted to snuggle them, joke with them, chase them, hug them. He didn't see such endeavours as having any value. I was to do the "pink" jobs, plus the parenting, plus the business responsibilities he had laid upon me. He did the "blue" jobs," or at least what he determined as "blue jobs," and insisted he was teaching the boys how to be men!

Questioning the Premises

I had learned growing up that the role of "the wife" was threefold:
1. You do for your family.
2. You have a full meal of meat and potatoes on the table for supper.
3. You do as you are told.

As time went on, I began to question each of these premises, but it was obvious these "rules" were in alignment with my husband's beliefs as well. I worked hard in our company, in our home, and in my parenting. I was a good mom and as Ryder became older, I had trouble with Corry's strictness in disciplining our boy. I was also beginning to realize this relationship between Corry and me that had initially felt so right was not what I had envisioned for myself as a wife. I was no longer willing to be controlled by anyone.

SYK to TRS: How was your relationship in general during this time, Tracy?

TRS to SYK: It was rocky. Corry's partying was so important to him. He needed his male friends, his male bonding, far more than he needed or wanted me. He did ignorant things to impress his buddies when he was with them. For instance, he would answer his phone when I called looking for him and put it on speaker on the table in front of his group of friends and have them listen to our conversation. It was simply another way to belittle me. I would hear the laughter from his friends as he attempted to humiliate me in front of them. His way to be a "big shot," I guess. He would call me names—names that later would come out of his mouth when he was angry at one of the boys. Was this the way to make MEN out of my boys, by calling them retards, idiots or stupid, to name a few of his choice labels. As well, I was continually portrayed to his friends as … the bitch. Maybe I was, but living with the likes of Corry and his temper, his need for control, and his disciplining of Ryder and Radek was difficult for me to ignore. He was now a dad with two beautiful little boys and I expected more of him. It was time for him to grow up and be a positive role model for our sons.

Many times, he would not come home at night. He had again slept on someone else's couch and arrived at his leisure, hung over the following day. I was still adamant that our home was not to be a party place. He needed to carry on his partying with his friends away from home, so I guess that was exactly what he was doing.

In some ways, I was glad Corry would go out because, as I said, things were so much easier for me and the kids when he was away from our home. He was mean to Ryder when Ryder was simply being a little boy. He was that strong disciplinarian. Sometimes … I wondered what it had been like for Corry in his family when he had been Ryder or Radek's age.

After another of Corry's failures to return at night, I gathered up my boys and headed to my parents' place an hour away. As I sat with my parents the following afternoon, Corry arrived, walked in through the front door, grabbed Ryder, and walked back out the door without saying a word to anyone. What was he going to do to my son?

I called the RCMP detachment. The officer on duty asked if Corry was the biological father.

I replied, "Yes."

"Sorry, ma'am," he said. "We can't touch him if he is the biological father."

I was both shocked and devastated. I felt totally powerless. I returned home with Radek to find Corry stretched out on the couch recovering from his previous evening of "fun" with his friends. Ryder was playing with his toys on the rug in front of him. Corry's brief response to me was simply: "Our sons should be in our home!"

Then, in June 2007, Corry went on a guys' trip to Phoenix, Arizona, with his buddies. When our financial statement from the bank arrived, there were several thousands of dollars in withdrawals from a place he obviously frequented.

I questioned him about the charges and he said he had no idea what the withdrawals were about. I phoned the number on the invoice. They faxed me the withdrawal slip on which were Corry's thumbprint and photo identification. The payments were to a strip club.

I was p*ssed as hell and said to him, "Don't make me feel like an idiot, Corry. Just tell me the truth!"

He continued to lie.

That sealed the deal.

I was biding my time until I could leave my marriage.

Game Over! Separation 2007

On July 15, 2007, Corry was in the garage putting together a new table and set of chairs. By this time, I had everything in place to leave him. I had spoken with a lawyer and filed for separation. I had my old job back at Boston Pizza, starting at the end of August, and an apartment waiting for me as well.

When Corry came into the kitchen, I said I wanted to talk with him. He sat down and I told him I was leaving him. He looked up in surprise.

I said simply: "Corry. You are not happy. I am not happy. There is no point in continuing this relationship. I have seen a lawyer and I have filed for a separation. You can bicker all you want about child support, but I have the figures all here in this file on the table. I am taking the kids and we can work out a shared custody agreement."

It was obvious that he was in total shock. He stood up. His eyes got even darker than they had many times before when he was angry. His eyes were black as coal on a good day. He told me he needed to get away for a little while and said he was just going to take the boys down to the river for a bit.

I could tell he was upset even though he never said anything. In retrospect, I realize how dumb I was to allow him to take the kids with him, but never did I imagine that he could ever be capable of seriously hurting them. He loved them! I knew that. I felt badly for him, but I had never been afraid of him. There had been times when we would fight that his dark eyes would again get even blacker as he screamed at me to punch him. Every time, I would refuse to engage. I knew if I ever started hitting him, I would never stop. I was not going to create that dynamic in our home. Furthermore, I was never going to do anything to jeopardize my custody of my kids if we were ever to end up in court. Foolishly, I trusted in the court process.

When Corry returned from the river with the boys, he asked calmly what my plans were. I told him I had rented a place and had gotten my old job back at Boston Pizza.

He said, "You can leave, but you're not taking the boys."

I replied, "I am taking the boys, Corry. They belong with me. I have been their main parent since they were born. We will work out a shared custody plan." I was firm and had done my homework. That week I had damn well "earned" my f'ing Jeep and the recipient of my good work was one Tracy MacDougall, an entitled company shareholder.

I moved downstairs. It was brutal on both of us, but we lived together for two more weeks until my new place was vacant. We tried to have meals together as a family but those two weeks were tough. We decided Corry would have the kids one week. I would have them the next. We would rotate custody. I sensed he was hurting but he never admitted it and went about his business as though nothing had happened. He helped my mom and me load up the truck.

My mom asked how he was doing.

His reply was simply, "Not so good, Donna."

That was it. Corry and I were done.

I had grown up poor and was ready to leave with nothing. Fortunately, my dad sat me down and reminded me that I would not have a husband to "take care of me" and to walk away without support for my two boys and myself was not a good idea. Corry paid out the matrimonial monies owed within the next few months. By his co-operation, it really was my hope that Corry and I could eventually get back some of the friendship that had brought us together in the first place.

I honestly felt sorry for Corry, but I was certain this was the best decision for me and my boys. I did not want my sons growing up in a home where they witnessed rage and behaviours that I knew were wrong. What was I teaching them by putting up with their dad's behaviours and his treatment of me? What were they learning from watching Dad treat me as though I was not fit to lick his boots? What were my boys learning from watching us fight?

As I walked through the kitchen one last time, I turned the corner and looked at the stain on the wall left from the shepherd's pie he had hurled in his frustration a few months before. I breathed in and reassured myself that I was making a good decision.

Corry told me point blank that I did not deserve his last name so I immediately changed my name back to Ross.

I remembered my father's words: "You are a hard worker and you will make it, my girl!" Those words are one of the greatest gifts my dad has ever given me. I left in August 2007. Tracy Ross and her sons were going to be okay.

Always together

Chapter 16

HELLO BEFORE GOODBYE

SYK: Good Morning Mama Wolverine! Great work again describing your relationship with Corry. Now, will you please write those biographies of Radek and Ryder so, as I write, I can make a connection with them. I want to get to know your boys better. I want to say hello to each of your precious sons as I learn their stories. I want to say hello … before I say goodbye.

I received her emails within a few hours of my request. It was obvious how well she knew her sons.

SYK: Thanks, Little Mama. I will create each of them a hockey card. Number 1 in your heart. Numbers 3 & 8 respectively on their latest hockey cards!

TRS: Thanks Sandra. I have included below a little blurb on the first appearance of the **R&R** symbol, which now represents them. When a good friend heard what had happened to my boys, she designed the **R&R** symbol and posted it to Facebook the day they died. As people heard of the tragic and untimely demise of my boys, many people, both known and unknown to me and Brent, changed their social media to display the red, white, and black heart logo **R&R** to show their support for us and our families and in remembrance of Ryder and Radek. The symbol went viral and, to this day, continues to hold reverence for all who know its significance. It felt good to write about my boys. Hope you enjoy getting to know my sons even beyond the **R&R** symbol and having watched them on the ice.

So, who were these boys who have touched the hearts of so many? Who were Radek Stryker and Ryder Patryk? Who were these young men who would become the forever **R&R**?

THE HOCKEY CARD OF RYDER PATRYK #3

by

His Mama

Ryder Patryk was born in the wee hours on the morning of March 1, 2003, weighing a whopping 4 lb 8 oz. After some initial birth trauma, Ryder became the perfect baby. He cried only when he was hungry or cold. He slept through the night at two months of age! He walked for the first time the day before he turned one. When he was born, it was basically like having an adorable accessory. I took him everywhere. I was so happy in my new role as a mom! I was the first one of my circle of friends to have a baby and he was the first grandchild on both sides. You could say my boy was very well loved. Ryder made being a mother seem easy.

Just after Ryder turned one year old, we moved into a shop on our land while we built our new home. My little boy adjusted so easily. He loved working in the shop with his dad. He loved to help out in any way he could. He soon knew what tools were what and he had amazing motor skills. My parents would always say, "That boy is going to do great things with his hands." At the time, I figured he would probably fall into mechanics like his dad, but now I know it was a kick-ass slap shot at which he would be amazing.

When Ryder was two and a half years old, he became a big brother. He loved his new baby, Radek. He always wanted to hold him and help with anything that Radek needed. He introduced Radek to anyone we would meet!

Ryder: "Hi, this is my little brother, Radek."

Living on an acreage, Ryder had the opportunity to learn how to ride his very first motorcycle (with training wheels, of course). He loved speed! When he turned three, his Grandpa MacDougall bought him his very first ATV (All Terrain Vehicle). How that made the grown men proud to see this little wee boy rippin' furiously around the yard. How his grandpa loved his first grandson! Ryder loved being outside. He loved going fast on anything! It wasn't a coincidence that his initials were RPM (Revolutions Per Minute)

Much of the rest of Ryder's story is contained in the following section entitled The Split—Game Over, as when Corry and I separated, Ryder tended to become Corry's target. Perhaps it was because he was the older of the boys as Corry had been in his family growing up. Perhaps it was because he was more like Corry in his temperament. The split seemed to affect Ryder far more than Radek, who simply went with the flow. One of the things I knew was that Ryder surrounded himself with people he loved and trusted. His friends were everything to him. If you were in his bubble, it was the best place to be! As my friend Carla said, "He made you feel amazing if you were in his bubble."

Some people didn't connect with Ryder, and it was because he wouldn't let you in for a reason, whatever that might be. He got that from his mama. I taught him, "Not everyone deserves to be in your bubble, Ryder"

"Hi, Mom, it's me, Ryder! Remember I am #1 in your heart!"

THE HOCKEY CARD OF RADEK STRYKER # #8

By

His Mama

Radek Stryker was born mid-afternoon on October 8th, 2005, weighing in at 4 lbs 13oz. He was my perfect Thanksgiving baby. I was so thankful to have another healthy boy. I had had a scare a few weeks prior to having Radek. I had a condition known as inter-uterine growth restriction with Ryder. My doctors figured I had it with Radek too. I had an ultrasound at thirty-six weeks and they measured Radek to be just over three pounds. Then, they did an amniocentesis and discovered that Radek's lungs were very underdeveloped, which could be a marker for Down's syndrome. At first, I was devastated. My doctor offered me a steroid that could boost his lungs, so that he would at least make it through the delivery. I was prepared to do anything to save my baby, and if he were a Down's syndrome child? He would be the cutest most-loved Down's syndrome child ever! I opted for the steroid. However, I was not sure what the doctors were talking about because even though Radek was born four weeks early, he weighed almost five pounds, not three, and he was absolutely perfect.

Radek definitely was not as easy a baby as Ryder had been. Initially, he had colic, which as any parent who has tried to settle a colicky baby knows, was very trying and exhausting. He was constantly in my arms as I tried everything to calm him. However, at the three-month mark, as many parents with a fussy baby also discover, he settled down. We got through it. Radek became the happiest, chubbiest baby ever. He loved being with people. He loved to be held as long as he could see his mama. He loved it when people talked directly to him. Once Radek learned to talk, he never shut up again! He would actually chatter from the moment his eyes opened until they closed at bedtime. As he got older, we sometimes put him in a brief "quiet" time out just to have silence in our home for a few minutes.

My younger boy had a heart bigger than anyone I knew. He hated to see people upset. If I were sad, he would hold my hand or just hug me. He would say, "Mom. Don't be sad." If he was in trouble, it literally broke his heart. He would write me notes saying how sorry he was and he would present me with punishment choices for himself when he'd mess up. Sometimes he would just hand me all his electronics at the same time and say, "Here Mom. I don't deserve these." And truly mean it! It was really hard to be mad at him. He would pick wildflowers on the trail home from school and leave them on my bathroom sink with a note saying 'I love you Mom".

Everyone loved Radek. He was a sweet, sweet boy. Teachers loved to teach him. Coaches loved to coach him, for although he was far from the best player on his team, he had the heart of a champion! His friends ... ohhhhh his friends! Just to think of his friends breaks my heart because he loved his friends with everything he had, and they loved him just as much. To lose such a special friend at such a young age, particularly in the way Radek died, was so hard for all his friends, his teammates, and his schoolmates. Even the weekend of his death, he was at the canteen at the rink, wanting to buy treats for his teammates. It has been very hard to see Radek's best buddies grieving my boy. When asked to share words that would describe Radek, his buddy, Kent, wrote the following verse:

Radek
Loving * Caring * Believing
Sporty * Funny
Best Friend Ever

Radek & Kent

Kent spoke clearly about his friend, his voice deep and strong. "Radek said he was going to make it to the NHL and play for the Chicago Black Hawks. In hockey, he was a sniper and a playmaker. He didn't seem to like his dad much. He told me once that his dad said he [Radek] didn't belong here on this earth. Radek was smart but would say dumb things to make people laugh. I miss him so much!"

Radek had a great imagination. He loved to make videos. He was always in the basement making hockey videos. When we went on a holiday, he would be videoing shots so he could follow up with a movie of it. He loved YouTube. Basically, he just loved having fun and being a kid. He loved playing with Lego. He loved board games, riding his bike, and going to the skate park. He loved to help in any way he could, unless it was a lot of physical work. Then it was "No Thanks!" LOL! He loved sleepovers with his friends. He loved pancakes. He loved to bake. He was a kid you wanted to be around. Once, after having come home from his weekend with his dad, Radek entered the living room and asked if he could pour Brent and me a drink. He loved being the bartender. I told him no, as we weren't going to have a drink that day. He looked at me, shrugged his shoulders and said, "Come on! Where's the Stark spirit?" He just made us laugh! Needless to say, we had a drink!

When things were a little quiet in our home, he always upped the ante! Being around Radek made you happy. I would always say the world needed more people like my boy, Radek. He also had a great imagination. However, my poor boy also lived in fear. He was scared of everything. He was scared to make anyone mad. He was scared of the dark. He was scared there was a monster under his bed. He slept with me any chance he got right up to our last weekend together. He wanted to sleep in my bed that last Saturday night and I had said no. I wanted him to feel the comfort of his brand-new room in our brand-new home in Spruce Grove. I told him he had to sleep in his own room. As you can imagine, that has been one of the biggest regrets of my life.

"Hey, Mom, it's me, Radek! Remember I am #1 in your heart!"

Chapter 17

THE SPLIT—GAME OVER

SYK: GOOD MORNING STARKSHINE! Today is a Good Day to Have a Good Day! When you have a chance, can you write about life after you left Corry?

TRS: Good Morning to you too Beautiful! I will do so later this week.

The email arrived.

TRS to SYK: When Ryder was four and Radek was one, I left Corry. It was August 2007. Things had become rough between us. Corry was a very angry man. When we would fight, he would scream and call me his favourite derogatory names: *Retard, Idiot, Bitch, Useless.* Those were the nicer ones. Parents often do not believe that little kids pick up on what is going on in their parents' relationships, but I know they definitely do. As incidents of Corry's raging increased, our fighting became more frequent. I did not want my boys being raised in a home where this was acceptable. Corry had told me that as a young boy he had grown up in a home where this was the norm and he really didn't see anything wrong with it. After all, he had turned out all right. Yeah, right.

We had a problem. It seemed he was bent on controlling me and our sons, and I was not going to be controlled nor could I handle his ways of disciplining the boys. When he was angry, he really was that "hard-ass" dad. He needed to be a domineering force with the boys and that worried me. What kept me in the relationship for as long as I stayed was because I worried about how things would go if I had to share custody with him and was not able to intervene on their behalf if he was angry with either of them on his time.

This was my first foray into the court system where we had to each hire

lawyers and make custody arrangements and decide on child support payments, all of which had to be documented in a court order. We began by sharing
custody of the boys 50-50.

Parenting with Corry, after we separated, went somewhat smooth, aside
from the fact that Ryder had a really tough time with our separating. This was
not because we didn't live with Dad anymore. Rather, it was because our custody
agreement became a week with Dad and a week with Mom. I had been the major
caregiver of the boys their whole lives to this point and now they had to live one
full week without me? This was excruciating for me and for Ryder. Corry would
throw my little boy over his shoulder and carry him out of my house with Ryder
screaming for me. Of course, Corry blamed me, saying I had brainwashed Ryder
to act like that. It was the most heartbreaking experience ever. Ryder and Radek
were just two little boys wanting to be with their mommy.

It wasn't that they didn't love Corry and all the great adventures they had
when they were with him. For the most part, after we separated, the boys very
much enjoyed spending time with their dad. They just had trouble being away
from me, as I did from them. They did a lot of camping and motor sports—
boating, ATVing, dirt biking, and sledding (snowmobiling) with their dad. The
boys loved the fun opportunities he shared with them. I had always heard it
said that children did best when both biological parents were in their lives and I
knew that Corry, regardless of the way he disciplined and sometimes interacted
with them, loved the boys and loved being a dad. I was not going to interfere
with that male bond.

Even when they were small, I heard little of what went on at Corry's place
from Corry or the boys, except for Ryder's reaction when he had to return to
Dad's place. I guess that was the kicker. The boys didn't want me getting angry
at their dad even when they were small. As they got a bit older, they learned to
share little of what was happening while in Dad's care if they thought anything
might upset me. They definitely did not want to see us fight. So little and yet
so astute.

They still needed their mom to do the things I had always done—cuddle
them, wipe their tears, tuck them in at night, read to them, and allow them to just
be little boys rather than little men. That wasn't Corry's way of parenting.

However, after a time, the boys got used to the new schedule. They were
okay being with their dad more and living with Dad's rules, which, in my mind,

were beyond strict. He could be so intimidating. Corry was the boss man and things were always going to be his way. End of story. However, there was nothing I could do. Corry was their other biological parent and he had legal rights.

One of the things that bugged me most was that Corry would not let the kids just be little kids. They weren't allowed to have stuffed animals as those were baby toys. They could not speak highly of their mommy. Corry made sure the boys knew I had torn apart our family by leaving. I was painted as a horrible person by breaking up our family. He never let the boys forget that.

They were being raised to be MEN. "Stop crying or I'll give you something to cry about!" or "Don't be such a girl!" or "Quit being a baby!" I can see now how, in his desire to make men out of the boys, he abused them verbally, mentally, and physically. He obviously instilled fear in them. I see so clearly now things I missed or simply tried to ignore when they were younger. Bloody hindsight? So often 20-20.

Baby

When Ryder was very young, he had a favourite teddy bear named Baby. He dragged that bear everywhere he went. He even rubbed Baby's nose off from snuggling it so much. Baby was Ryder's security blanket. No matter where he was, whether my house or Corry's house, Baby was the only constant he had, other than our dog, Keaton, who went back and forth with the boys as well.

One day Ryder came home after a week with his dad and I noticed he didn't have Baby. I asked, "Where is Baby, Ryder?" He just looked down and shrugged his shoulders.

I kept asking, "Where's Baby, Ryder?"

He said he must have lost him. This made no sense as they were inseparable.

I called Corry asking where Baby was or where Ryder could have left him as I needed to find him. Corry said he must have left the bear at the rink. I immediately bundled the kids up, got into my vehicle, and headed to the arena to look in the Lost and Found. No Baby. We searched through all the dressing rooms, in the washrooms, and in the stands. No Baby.

My mom wrote a letter to the Town of Whitecourt asking if they had found a stuffed bear and stating how important that bear was to a little boy named Ryder. NOTHING … BABY was GONE! To some, this may sound silly, but losing

Baby destroyed Ryder. He was completely lost. Bedtimes with Ryder became extra hard. For two Christmases, Ryder had me write his letter to Santa Claus saying, "If you find Baby, can you bring him home please? He's light-brown with a green bow tie. I miss him so much." It wasn't until a few years later when Ryder and I were chatting that the issue of Baby came up.

Ryder said, "Yeah, Dad made me throw him in the garbage because he said I was too old for baby toys." Ryder had kept this a secret for years, probably because he knew I would lose it on his dad and then he would get in trouble for telling me. Ryder was good at keeping everything bottled up inside and ensuring he did nothing to make Dad mad.

Ryder and his "Baby" & friends

Ryder's Struggles

After Corry and I split, Ryder's whole demeanour changed. He was an angry little boy. He continually lashed out at Radek and at me. He just wasn't the same kid. He seemed filled with rage or would just shut down and not talk. In kindergarten, his teacher requested that he speak to the family-school liaison worker as his anger was spilling over into the classroom where he was showing signs of aggression. The liaison worker was a beautiful, sweet young woman with pretty blonde hair and the kindest eyes. It took Ryder a while to warm up to her, but when he did, he absolutely adored her.

After months of seeing Ryder on a regular basis, the young woman called me in for a meeting. She was leaving her position and said that Ryder had come a long way and that she didn't think that he would need to see the new worker who would be replacing her. Ryder had trouble with her leaving. He had always been excited to have his time with her where he could just be himself and relax into his regular counselling sessions. For a time, he was one sad little fella after his 'break up' with his counsellor.

Seeing a Shrink

Then, when Ryder was seven, I received a phone call after one of his hockey practices from a mom with a child on his team. She was very forthright and said that she was worried for Ryder's safety. After practice, she said that Corry had grabbed Ryder and started yelling and belittling him in front of the whole team.

I talked to this hockey mom for quite a while. She was going through a divorce herself and her kids were struggling with the split. She recommended a therapist in Edmonton. I got the therapist's information and called her. She agreed to start seeing Ryder. When I ran this idea by Corry, he said it was me just being dramatic and refused to take Ryder to see a "shrink" on his time. However, I took Ryder to see the therapist when he was with me. She worked with Ryder for almost a year and made good progress with him as well. He started to come around. He was not as angry and started talking more about his feelings. The therapist ended her sessions with Ryder, saying she believed he was doing well. She said I did not have to make that four-hour round trip to Edmonton anymore and suggested using a local counsellor if I ever felt Ryder still needed to talk to someone.

Ryder again took this hard. I believe he thought that every time he got close to someone, the relationship ended. Sometimes those seven days he was with his dad were hard on both of us. No denying it. He loved his dad very much, but being with me, he could be more himself, a little boy. He could get angry at me, do stupid things, make poor decisions and, though I might get mad at him, he knew I would still think he was one of the two greatest kids on the face of this earth. He trusted me enough to know that no matter what he did, I would always love him.

Little Mama & her boys

One day I picked up the boys from school after a week with their dad. Ryder had a butterfly stitch on his forehead.

I asked, "OMG Ryder. What happened?"

He replied, "Nothing!"

I said, "Well, obviously something happened! You have a gash on your head!"

He screamed, "NOTHING HAPPENED!"

That is when Radek jumped into the conversation. "Dad threw a plastic toy at Ryder's head yesterday, and it wouldn't stop bleeding, so we had to go to the hospital."

Ryder yelled at Radek to shut up.

I called Corry and started yelling at him that I was taking the kids away. I drove to the hospital and got the record of the hospital visit. Corry continued to contend it was an accident.

I definitely wanted to take the kids away from Corry at that point, but when I talked to a couple of people familiar with separation and divorce issues, I became afraid I might not win such a fight and my boys would be the ones hurting if I took Corry to court. I calmed down and life continued.

Chapter 18

RECRUITING A WINNER

SYK to TRS: So, Tracy, how did you meet Brent?

TRS to SYK: I was on my own for a while, dating occasionally, but nothing serious. I was happy to have no one directing my life. I missed my boys like crazy when I did not have access to them for a full week, but I was doing okay. I worked lots, taking all the shifts I could when it was Corry's week to have the boys, so that I could spend every waking hour with them when they were in my care.

When they were with me, and me alone, I was able to be the mother I wanted to be. I had a place of my own and having my boys with me every second week without interference from their dad made everything so much better. They were just little boys and I got to be their mommy, parenting the way I wanted to parent. I played on the floor with them. I snuggled them. I read to them. We enjoyed our pizza without sour cream!

My life went on as a single parent, sharing custody of my children with my ex-husband. It was like living two different lives actually, sharing custody. One week on and one week off. Corry and I seemed to be working together okay. I enjoyed my work at Boston Pizza, meeting many interesting people. Then, in 2008, I met a definite "person of interest"; a very compelling man who would change my world. A man who would become an all-star player on my team.

Brent Stark captures Tracy's Heart

Hockey is the Game

Who was this man who became Tracy Ross's teammate and a crowd favourite in her game of life? Who was this man who had moved to Whitecourt, Alberta, as a young boy and had such a strong passion for hockey like no other? The boy, turned man, was an individual committed to his community and to Canada's game. He became an entrepreneur and businessman in the Whitecourt community. His name was Brent Stark, owner of the future Whitecourt Wolverines Junior A hockey team. It was to him that Tracy would lose her heart and begin to wear the Wolverine team jersey.

Initially, Brent became involved in a spring hockey team called the Whitecourt Wolverines, which had been started through the efforts of another hockey enthusiast. In 2007, Brent Stark and his partner put their heads and wallets together and turned that spring hockey team into a Junior B club, fulfilling Brent's lifelong dream of being more involved in the Canadian hockey scene. After a few years, Brent bought and ran the Junior B team solo and eventually purchased the St. Alberta Steel Junior A club, moving the team to Whitecourt. Whitecourt finally had a Junior A franchise! Before long, Brent initiated an upgrade for the Whitecourt arena and became more involved in the Whitecourt Minor Hockey Association. Hockey had a new look in Whitecourt and the hockey program itself was filled with young aspiring hockey players, all wearing the red, white, and black.

Now Whitecourt, Alberta, Canada, is surrounded by beautiful lakes, rushing rivers, and boreal forests. The forests are filled with big game—bear, deer, moose, elk, wolves, and cougars. It is here in the boreal forest where "the wolverine is considered a rare and wondrous sighting." The wolverine is a powerful animal resembling a cross between a small bear and a wolf. Its Latin scientific name *Gulo gulo* means glutton, referring to the animal's willingness to eat anything. It is the size of a dog, from 65-107 cm long, excluding the tail. It likes the cold weather and has large paws that act like snowshoes. Within those paws are claws that get longer when the wolverine wants to climb, dig, or attack. They are generally antisocial and somewhat shy but they do not scare easily. Wolverines will take on animals much bigger than themselves and they do not back down.[11]

Brent Stark wanted a name for his team that would exemplify ferocity, strength, and tenacity. So, was it any wonder that Brent opted to resurrect the name of that initial spring hockey team for his Junior A franchise located here in the wilds of Alberta? Thus, the Whitecourt Wolverine name was revitalized. In fact, so enamoured was Brent with the wolverine that in 2008 he "styled" one as tenacious as any of his Whitecourt Wolverines when he met and began dating Tracy Ross.

Gossip Fodder in the Dressing Room

"So, Tracy," I asked in one of our sessions. "How was your life once you and Brent got together?"

Tracy waited for a minute before she replied. "My relationship with Brent was amazing and continues to be to this day. I had never felt so loved in my

11 CBC.ca CBC Kids -4 things you might not know about wolverines

entire life. However, once Brent and I were a couple, Corry's attitude toward me changed even more. Everything became a fight. He obviously did not want me to be happy with another man."

She paused as she took a sip of water and continued. "When I got together with Brent, many people were extremely unkind. They called me a trophy wife. A dumb blonde. A gold digger. I put that down to small-town gossip and a degree of jealousy for the life I was finding with Brent. Corry particularly did not want me to be happy without him in my life. I knew Corry continued to paint me to others in a very poor light. He was singing that 'She Done Me Wrong' song. However, I was truly very happy! Brent was happy. My boys appeared happy as did Brent's girls." She laughed. "Most of the time!"

"What about after you heard you were being called a gold digger?" I asked.

She replied, "The gold digger stamp? Hmm. At first, I took total offence to this label as I knew I was the furthest thing from it. Initially, it hurt. I would always explain myself until I realized that people would always have their own opinions. I could not change what they thought of me or said about me or to me. Then Brent asked me what was worse my being called a gold digger or people saying he couldn't get a girl like me without having money? That was when I immediately stopped caring about the insults and what others were thinking or saying. It was extra challenging in a small town, but it was truly what you said Oprah would say, 'What others think of you is … none of your business!' What was my business was what I thought and I began to seriously respect my own opinion of myself as a mom and a woman and Brent and me? We were very happy together. Perhaps people were simply envious of our good fortune of finding each other in this crazy world and having such a caring relationship."

Tracy and I processed what she had shared. Then she said, "I love Brent very much. Sometimes I worry about him because I know he too has been deeply impacted by the loss of the boys, but, like most men, he continually says, 'I'm okay'. Sandra, he is my everything! I couldn't handle losing him too!"

I saw the tears beginning to form in the corner of her eyes and interjected. "Just feel the support of the chair, Tracy, as you think about the wonderful relationship you have found with Brent and how he continues to want to take good care of his very favourite Wolverine!"

She breathed in and responded, "I can already feel my toes tingling."

The release of activation went on. We continued to establish resources in her body as we did the therapeutic work. She began to settle more fully into the chair as she continued her story.

"When I left Corry, aside from splitting the assessed value of our new home and his paying me child support, I was willing to walk away from everything else. We had assets: quads, snowmobiles, dirt bikes, a brand-new Mastercraft boat, a brand-new motorhome, eight acres with a brand-new home and shop, plus all the company assets. In our separation, Corry retained all of these items plus the house. With the monies I was granted in the separation agreement, I purchased a new mobile home for myself and the kids, made monthly payments on my brand-new Jeep, and purchased all the necessary furniture to set up our new home.

"I left everything in the house except a furniture set and the bed from the spare room so the boys would feel 'at home' when they were with their dad. Needless to say, according to the laws of the land, I was entitled to so much more. Corry should have thanked his lucky stars, but nope … he never got over it. Like many men, he figured that since I had walked away from our family, I should leave with nothing.

"In 2013, I came home from a city trip with my girlfriends and when we arrived at my house, there was a man sitting in a vehicle in my driveway. Once I parked, he got out of his vehicle and walked up to me and asked if I was Tracy MacDougall. In my naivety, I said yes. He handed me an envelope and told me I had been served. I opened up the envelope to find I was being sued by the Royal Bank of Canada for $310,000. Apparently, Corry had defaulted on a company loan and my name was still on the loan from when we were a couple. I had to hire a lawyer and fight this and ended up with my name being dropped from the charges. Thank God. I was already tired of going to court and yet the worst of my court experiences had not yet even begun."

Chapter 19

THE MAMA WOLVERINE

The Whitecourt Wolverine

SO JUST HOW DID TRACY ROSS FIT THE WOLVERINE PROFILE WHEN BRENT made his "rare and wondrous" sighting? She was not particularly fond of cold weather. She was far from antisocial, as evidenced by her enthusiasm in bringing people into the Wolverine family in her community. She was unwilling to eat certain foods, contrary to her namesake of *Gulo gulo*. However, she did have large claws, always painted a bright hue. She was powerful. She did not scare easily. She did not back down, and she willingly took on predators much larger than herself. In those regards, she was truly a representation of the WOLVERINE. Even more telling was the fact that after the death of her boys, she was still alive, her strength in breathing in deeply every day, putting one foot in front of the other and willing to fight to the death to make sure the lives of her boys made and continue to make a difference in the world.

These stellar qualities have given Tracy Stark the strength to share her story in the hope that neither another mother nor another child will ever know what she and her boys have known. That another woman will not become a "childless mother" because of a calculated killing spree by an angry father. That, in finding her voice, both men and women will join her in her quest to lobby for laws that will provide greater safety and security for all children caught in the craziness of relationship breakdown and domestic violence. That the telling of the *R&R* story will provide an impetus to review and create superior policies and procedures in guiding Child Services and the Justice System in their dealing with issues of custody and access. That the *R&R* story will give other women the courage to find their own voices, speak truth to power and leave unhealthy relationships where women and children are brutalized by verbal, mental, physical or emotional abuse. That men will see the importance of teaching their boys respect for women by how they treat the mothers of their boys. That men and women will work together to change the reality of domestic violence. Yes! Men will stand up to those of their gender abusing women physically, emotionally, mentally, verbally and financially. And, that those in positions of power will increase their awareness of the brokenness of systems that leave gaps in the area of child protection, custody and access, and criminal investigations, and bring forward new laws.

With those qualities of tenacity, resilience, and strength, Tracy Ross is truly a representation of a WOLVERINE. These qualities have given her the courage to share her story and that of her two youngsters on their journey to become known as FOREVER WOLVERINES eternally represented by the *R&R* logo.

Chapter 20

MERGING THE FRANCHISE

TRACY SAT IN THE BLUE CHAIR IN THE AIM OFFICE AS SHE CONTINUED HER account of her relationship with Brent. "We dated for three years before we took the next step to move in together with our children. Corry was not at all happy and caused me grief whenever he could. I would so often wish he would have fallen deeply in love with someone and found some happiness of his own. I knew he was afraid the boys would love Brent more than they did him.

"Of course, like most children from split families, so often what the kids wanted was for their 'bio' parents to be back together, but that was definitely not going to happen! Brent and I had moved on from our former lives and were focused on making a good life together for ourselves and the children we brought into this 'merger.'"

"So," I asked, pen in hand, "how was it with Brent's girls?"

She breathed in before she spoke. "I knew blending our kids would have its challenges. Brent and I took our time with our kids getting to know each other. We did not want to push them into too much too soon. When Brent and I became serious, Shelbey, Brent's younger daughter, who was eight at the time, was instantly attracted to her dad's new girlfriend. She loved the attention and the girl time, even if it was simply going for a ride in her dad's Corvette to grab an ice cream cone. She always wanted to be with us and we loved having her around.

"Alesha, on the other hand, was not around my kids much. She was ten years older than Radek, eight years older than Ryder, and five years older than Shelbey. When I met Brent in 2008, Alesha, at thirteen years of age, was a young teen engaged in the challenges of growing up through those teen years. Her parents had split, which was difficult for her. She was mad at the world and understandably so. She was close to her dad and I was an intruder, as were my boys. However, I got along great with Alesha when she was willing to give me her time."

Tracy became reflective as she shared more of her relationship with Alesha. "It was definitely tougher to bond with Alesha as she was going through her own issues. I totally understood and gave her the space she needed, I think, but I also jumped at the chance to be around her when she was open to it. Once Brent and I moved our families into the same home, things got even better. The kids liked each other and everyone respected each other's space."

I nodded before I asked for another clarification. "I understand Alesha went away for high school. How did that come about?"

Tracy continued, "Alesha is super smart and Brent wanted to give her every avenue to have a successful life and prepare to go into post-secondary education if she chose to do so. A private boarding school was Brent's choice for Alesha for high school. At first, she was not fond of the idea, but in 2011 she entered Grade 10 at Brentwood College School in Victoria, BC. Brent and I visited her twice a month on the two weekends Corry had the boys. She came back to Whitecourt for Grade 11, but returned to Brentwood for Grade 12, and graduated in 2013. We did many of our family vacations according to the Whitecourt school holiday schedule, which did not align with Alesha's school calendar when she is in BC, so unfortunately, she was not often able to come with us. Those vacations were good bonding times, definitely fun times, and great picture times. It is sad that often Alesha could not join us.

"Like many teenage girls, Alesha did not like having her picture taken! Ever! We had few vacation time family pictures, so I would book a sitting for a family picture and she wanted nothing to do with it. Brent would say, 'She hates pictures! She's just like me!' Fair enough. So much for family pictures. Since the boys died, that has been a real regret.

"I loved having our blended family of six sitting at our family table. However, it was short-lived as Alesha again left home to attend university right after high school. Even in the later years, with our trip to California for Ryder's hockey tournament in 2016, Alesha was at university and unable to join us. However, Brent and I were lucky enough to get a picture with her at her high school graduation!"

Alesha's high school graduation

Chapter 21

THE LEGEND OF THE
FOREVER WOLVERINES

The Initiation into Hockey

THE STREETS OF WHITECOURT ARE RELATIVELY QUIET IN THE DARKNESS OF the early week day mornings. There are the occasional shift workers heading to and from the local mills and pick up trucks filled with 'oil patch' workers getting ready to travel on the icy gravel roads into the wilds to maintain Alberta's oil and gas reserves. A few early morning workout fanatics drop in to the local fitness facilities. The line ups begin to form at the local Tim Hortons, McDonalds and A&W.

And there.....there..... inside the Scott Safety Arena.... Moms and Dads are already up and at 'er in the dressing rooms, tying skates, putting on helmets, blowing noses and grabbing the remnants of their child's 'in car' breakfast from the bench beside their little hockey star player. Some enthusiastic coach has "The Hockey Song" by Canada's own Stompin' Tom Connors resonating from his phone welcoming his team. It is CANADA and HOCKEY! HOCKEY! HOCKEY! Is on the early morning menu as youngsters begin the Wolverines Chant as soon as they hit the ice!

"WOLVERINES! WOLVERINES! WOLVERINES!

SYK to TRS: Tell me about the "FOREVER WOLVERINES" initiation into hockey, Tracy.

Shortly, I received the following reply:

TRS To SYK: Corry literally threw the boys into hockey once they each turned five years of age. Ryder began his hockey career in the fall of 2008 and Radek the fall of 2010. At first, like many little guys, Ryder hated hockey! Every day he had to go on the ice was a struggle. He just cried and cried. He'd come to the boards surrounding the ice, where I was sitting, and would bang on the glass screaming for me to come and get him off the ice. It was the saddest thing ever!

My mom had worked the early shift at the Edson Arena. She believed it was not at all fair to a young child to have to get up early and brought to practices in the wee hours of the morning, chewing on a piece of toast as he/she walked half asleep to the dressing rooms where those committed parents would be helping put on equipment and tie the skates of the young kids still half asleep.

I so wanted for Ryder to love the sport, but when he was so unhappy, I wondered if maybe we were making the wrong choice. However, about half-way into his first season as a Timbits Tiny Mite, he finally warmed up to being a hockey player. What I learned very quickly, and what my mom didn't realize, was that 90% of those kids she watched during those early mornings would soon be fanatic about hockey too, and once they were on the ice, they were different people than the bleary-eyed kids she saw entering the arena at 6 a.m. or those other little kids struggling in their initiation into the game on the ice as my Ryder did at first. Hockey soon was in the Canadian veins of those little hockey players and they wanted to play 24 hours a day! At least, that was definitely the story of my boys and their friends.

Corry and I had enrolled Radek into CanSkate, a learn-to-skate program, before he even started hockey and when he entered hockey, he loved it right away. He didn't have the natural abilities of his older brother, so sometimes he would flounder. However, he wasn't giving up! LOL. He wanted to be just like Ryder!

I absolutely loved being a hockey mom and was always excited watching my sons play. I rode the buses and put many miles on my vehicles, hauling the boys and their friends to games in some treacherous winter driving conditions. Anything to get to the game! When we were extra lucky, we were sometimes able to travel in style on the Whitecourt Wolverine Junior A bus. It paid to have connections! LOL!

What was especially fun for me was to see that once my mom saw how much her grandsons loved the game, she too became a fan and turned into a loudly cheering gramma! Now that my nephew plays, Gramma rarely misses a game. I sometimes wonder if my life had been different if I had been able to continue in competitive sports, as I absolutely loved watching my boys compete as a mom waving from the stands!

When the boys entered the world of hockey, Corry became a very involved dad. He always wanted the kids to be who he'd never been. Like many dads, he pushed the boys to follow his unachieved dreams. It was him wanting them to do things he always wanted to do but never did. Maybe I was a bit like that too. I wanted to give them every opportunity to try activities they were excited to experience. Corry however was very strict with the boys as they learned new skills. In my mind, he pushed them far too hard. Corry expected so much from them. For someone who had never really played the game, he should never have had such high expectations, but his easing up never happened. Again, he was in charge and his boys were going to follow his rules and fulfil his dreams. He seemed to be reliving his life through the boys. Interestingly enough, the boys came to absolutely love the game.

As time went on, like so many little Canadians, in both winter and summer, the boys ate, slept, and played some form of hockey with their friends in our drive-way, at the arena, on the outdoor rinks, and on the roadway, moving the goalposts very quickly when a car approached and just as quickly returning them to play after the vehicle had passed by. They were always firing pucks and leaving their marks against the garage door, knocking over the barbecue, breaking windows, or denting the fridge doors in the garage with an errant shot. There was always a hockey stick nearby that they would grab to take a quick shot or two with a rolled-up sock or tennis ball. They engaged in a fight for the "puck" with anyone willing to challenge their prowess. For Ryder, it was also a way for him to release some of the tension, frustration, and emotions that lay inside my first-born.

I stopped caring about the insults or what people thought about me and Brent. We were happy and our house was filled with fun and laughter and a heck of a lot of hockey!

As well, my sons played golf, soccer, and baseball. They rode dirt bikes and snowmobiles. They were also involved in boating sports from the time they were small. Corry introduced them to many great opportunities. I, too, was committed to finding ways to support them both financially and physically, getting them to the practices and games in any sport they wanted to attempt. As they matured, hockey was highest on their list.

All went well with Brent and me in the merging of our families. Well … sort of, anyway. Corry and I still maintained a week-on and week-off schedule with the boys. Brent stayed out of my business with Corry. However, as with many blended families, there were challenges in sharing the custody of my most precious "free agents," or rather, "shared agents."

The Shared Agents

I ended up quitting my job at Boston Pizza when Brent and I moved in together. Corry figured that since I didn't need to work anymore, he should cut my child support in half.

I said, "No way, Corry. I am still their mother and I have financial responsibilities to support them." He said he would just change his income to say he made the minimum, and he could do that because he owned the company. However, I was privy to all the information on his company as I had done the books when we were together, so I reminded him that he probably wouldn't want to bring that "can of worms" into court! He eventually dropped the child support issue. However, he continued to fight me on every other possible issue regarding the boys. So much of our shared custody of the boys had to be settled in the courts. It cost me so much money as Corry opposed everything. He breached orders. I would have to take him to court to have his hand slapped and that was all it was. A slap! No one was going to control Corry MacDougall and … no one tried.

Chapter 22

CORRY MAKES A MOVE

IN THE EARLY SPRING OF 2011, OUT OF THE BLUE, CORRY CALLED TRACY TO say he was moving to Kelowna to seek work opportunities and he needed her to keep the kids until he figured out what his plans were. Ryder was eight and Radek was six when the parenting schedule then changed. Tracy now had full custody of the boys. Corry did not see the boys until their summer holidays for his court-ordered access. Then, he started coming to get them every second weekend. Tracy went to her lawyer to have the custody order changed. Corry was incensed. He, of course, was angry because he did not think his child support should double even though he no longer had the boys for his week. Tracy and Corry talked and came to an agreement. The child support could stay the same if Corry paid for the boys' sports. He was good with that or at least said he was.

SYK to TRS: So how did things go once you had primary custody, Tracy?

Ryder! Ryder! Ryder!

TRS to SYK: By the time Ryder was nine, he was already in full-blown puberty. He was too young for this! This was a trying time for our household. He was so damn moody. He snapped at anyone who talked to him, mainly Radek, of course. We tried to give Ryder some space as his body was changing dramatically and yet … he was still a little boy. He started to get sneaky—stealing and lying. I got on this right away and took him to the police station after he stole my credit card and charged up $6000.00 for Clash of Clans. Needless to say, that kid had the best Clan ever.

I spoke with an RCMP officer whose son played on the same team as Ryder, to determine how best to handle his behaviour. The officer did not want to scare

Ryder. Rather, he wanted the police to be people who Ryder would go to if he ever needed help, not officers he detested because he got "sh#t" from them for stealing his mom's credit card. However, like most moms would be, I was concerned. Then, when I found out he had bullied another of his teammates by throwing all his hockey buddy's gear into the urinal in the dressing room, I was livid, incensed that he would do something like that!

But something was wrong. I know that those who have been bullied often became bullies, and I was beginning to fear that the experiences Ryder had in his dad's household and Dad's displays of anger during these tender growing-up years of living in two totally different households were coming home to bite him. I needed Ryder to understand that there were consequences for his actions, but not through beatings or extreme disciplinary measures. He needed those logical consequences I had read about in dealing with disciplining kids.

I tried to talk to Corry about this, but Corry told me I didn't know what I was talking about. He said his disciplinary measures when the boys were at his house were none of my business! I wondered where he was getting his ideas on parenting two active little boys and if our boys were suffering because of his need for such rigid control. My boys, like many kids living in two homes, were hesitant to ever share the slightest negative experience they might have been having at Dad's place because they knew I would be on it and it would not be pretty!

With Corry gone to Kelowna and subsequently only having the boys every second weekend once he returned to Alberta, Ryder started to come more and more out of his bubble.

SYK to TRS: What do you mean he came out of his bubble?

TRS to SYK: Ryder loosened up. He had always been so afraid of upsetting his dad and being away from that pressure seemed to allow him to be more of the boy I knew he really was. He definitely needed routine and parents who loved and supported him. Ryder never talked badly about his dad. He loved Corry but it was evident from his behaviour that he was constantly on edge, fearing that his dad would be mad at him or call him down. When his dad's rage came out, it was brutal and devastated him. Now he was starting to laugh again. He cracked jokes. He had a ton of friends around him, as did the easygoing Radek. Our home was continually filled with the boys' friends! Ryder was a leader and both boys and girls were attracted to him and his personality. He loved to be outside playing and riding his bike. He grew to love hockey more and more. I finally got my Ryder back and in Radek? Well, the sweetness just continued.

However, I began to sense a change in Corry. I didn't know what it was, but I had a bad feeling about the changes that seemed to be taking place. I had heard rumours about an "intense" lifestyle that may have contributed to the changes. He had left Whitecourt with a lot of money and built a huge house in Kelowna overlooking Lake Okanagan. Both my kids, as well as Corry, told me that he had a suite in his basement built so I could have somewhere to stay if I wanted to come visit when he had the kids. What? Who was this guy? Why, all of a sudden, did he even think that I would ever stay in his house? This seemed bizarre to me. He even offered to take Brent and me boating with the kids when we were in Kelowna. His change in behaviour was hard to figure out. At one point, when we were getting along, he even suggested in one of his texts that if things did not work out with Brent, that I should come back to him. Well, that was definitely not going to happen.

Once Corry got his business organized in Kelowna, he bought another house just up the street from me in Whitecourt as he still had business deal-ings here. I was thinking this was the best opportunity for our kids, having both parents close and in their lives. Corry picked up the kids on the third Saturday of the month and kept them for nine days, taking them to school and hockey on his time with them. However, his dad and brother were living in his house so he rented a motel room for himself and the boys for those nine days and did his parenting from there.

He had work around Whitecourt, so he was busy when they were in school. His time with them worked out well. He took them to school, grabbing them lunches from a convenience store on the way, and then they would eat out at night or bring in take out. It seemed to work fine for the boys and for Corry. We agreed on a two-week rotation between us in the summer time, a week at Christmas with Dad, and access again during Dad's scheduled spring break. I believed my boys needed their dad's attention. I had heard heartbreaking stories from friends about the challenges of raising young boys without their fathers having a role in their lives. As mentioned previously, I had also heard that kids did best when both biological parents were engaged in their kids' lives. I believed that! But never did I imagine the havoc Corry would continue to cause.

In the summer of 2011, when the boys were with Corry for his summer holiday access, Brent and I were having a bite to eat in Kelowna before we had to return our rental car and fly home. We had been in Kelowna for the wedding of good friends. Brent looked past me to the doorway of this little restaurant where we were eating and said, "Your kids are here."

I was like, "What? There is no way!" I turned and sure enough, my boys were standing at the front door waving at us as they were enjoying a couple of ice cream cones on a hot summer's day. I got up and went to them, giving them each a big hug, and I asked, incredulously, "What are you boys doing here?"

They said, "Eating ice cream! DUH Mom!"

The weird thing was that they were not surprised to see me. How did they know I would be in that particular restaurant? I wondered how this "chance" meeting came to be? Just coincidence? Sometime later, I became aware that Corry had hired a private investigator to follow me, and in thinking about this … was I already under surveillance that summer?

Chapter 23

HARASSMENT/
COURT ORDERS/DIVORCE

TRS to SYK: In March of 2012, we were to leave with another family on a holiday to San Diego. Corry refused to sign the necessary documents so that I could take the boys out of the country. The dad of the other family we were to be travelling with made a call to Corry, pleading with him to give his permission to allow the kids to go as he had kids and we were all looking forward to the trip. Corry finally relented, but so often with Corry everything was a hassle. I went to my lawyer and got a permanent order to allow me to travel with my kids without Corry's permission. His harassment was continual and began to get even worse.

Later in the summer, a van was parked down the street in front of the home of some friends for a few days. There was always a man sitting in the driver's seat. Thinking the driver was a creep and having two little children of his own, our neighbour confronted this character. The man said he was a private investigator. I learned that when a private investigator was called out, he had to disclose what he was doing. He told our friend that he had been hired to watch me.

When my neighbour shared this information with me, I was totally freaked out as Brent was hunting in Alaska. I invited another friend and her kids over to stay with me. I called the RCMP and they came over and the guy in the van said he was a private investigator hired to watch me as well as a home at another location where my friend, who was now staying with me, lived. Needless to say, this man reported back to Corry with no inappropriate findings. SHOCKER! After Corry's suicide, it was released in the media that Corry had refused to pay this man as he felt the investigator had not done his job properly. Not sure what "dirt" he was hoping to find.

Corry and I had been apart since 2007. Since that time, my ex-husband had continued to refuse to sign the divorce papers. Brent and I had dated for three years before we made the move to blend our family and live together. In November 2012, after Brent and I had lived together with our kids for over a year, a judge finally granted me a desk divorce.

One of Corry's first orders of business, after he returned permanently to Alberta, was to request a bilateral assessment to attempt to prove me an unfit mother so he could gain full custody of the kids. The cost of the bilateral assessment was $15,000. Corry wanted me to pay half. I told him I would pay half but that in the event the results came back in my favour, he would have to pay me back my portion of the assessment. He agreed.

A bilateral assessment allows a psychologist to question each parent individually, to question the kids without the parents, and then to question the kids with Mom and then with Dad, all in her office. Then a home study was conducted where the psychologist visited each of our homes when the kids were in individual custody time with each of us. As well, the psychologist requested from Corry and from me the names of three or four friends who would speak on our behalf. I hadn't realized that Corry's friends would have the opportunity to share their perceptions of me as well.

In relaying this experience during a counselling session, Tracy said, "I could not believe some of the totally untrue statements that were made by Corry's friends about my parenting. They were cruel and vicious. I found it hard to think that anyone could share such lies about me. Again, I recognized that I had to let these statements go. I knew they were untrue, as did Brent, and that was all that mattered. It was interesting to note that the psychologist also was able to discredit the accuracy of these statements made by the people Corry had chosen to support his case. Without a doubt, the psychologist's findings clearly stated that I was to continue to have primary custody of the boys and that Corry had just wasted her time. Fighting to recoup my portion of the cost of the assessment proved to be simply another costly challenge in dealing with Corry.

"Corry had also been ordered to pay me back my portion of the cost of the bilateral assessment in yet another court order. However, there was no follow-up by the court. Corry had also stopped paying child support and was three months in arrears. In March 2013, another order was written. Nothing happened. Since the courts could not make him pay me, I finally registered with Maintenance Enforcement.

"On November 19, 2013, I again needed to contact my lawyer to get an emergency order to locate my children. They had been with Corry for his weekend and he had failed to return them home as per our court order. Corry was not answering my calls. His family was not answering my calls. The order was faxed from the court to my lawyer in Hinton, Alberta. My lawyer emailed me a copy, which I took to the Whitecourt RCMP Detachment and they said they couldn't read it. It was not clear. There was nothing they could do. Holy Mother of God! Corry was still trying to control me and the courts appeared to be helping him do just that! I felt helpless when the court order itself was not respected nor enforced.

"Thankfully, I found my children without the intervention of the RCMP. During my attempts to locate them, Ryder secretly returned my call and whispered where they were. I was furious, frustrated, and concerned that Corry would continually defy all court orders with no retribution. It was clear that Corry thought he was above the law and why wouldn't he? In my experience, never once was a court order enforced.

"Finally, on February 26, 2015, our 'Matter(s)' made it into Special Chambers, where all our history was to be reviewed by a judge. This meeting had been set three years prior! Three bloody years! I retained a new lawyer, who I hoped would fight harder for my kids. This sitting was again at my cost. All court orders I'd had to initiate were at my cost and my scheduling. As you can gather from what I have written, I had my fair share of experience with the courts, and what I have shared here is far from all of the court orders needed to correct Corry's behaviours that were way out of line. He had a blatant disregard for such court orders. I wanted to get paid what I was owed from Corry. The money was not forthcoming so I needed to register with Maintenance Enforcement. I wanted my kids returned to my home when they were missing. Corry breached his order and I was frantically trying to locate my boys. I got an emergency order in place, but the RCMP said it was not clear?? There was no accountability whatsoever for Corry."

SYK to TRS: So, what did you learn from all your court order experiences, Tracy?

TRS to SYK: I learned that as long as someone was the biological parent, they had "rights" to their children and there was nothing anyone could do about it. This lack of accountability for defying court orders began that path down the road that led to the eventual death of my only two children. Why at no time did a judge say, "Hold on. Wait a minute. This poor mother. These poor kids. Something has to be done to stop this harassment." Who was accountable when the justice system, in place to protect, failed to protect???

After sharing my experience, I heard from so many other women who had had similar encounters regarding court orders. Women who were concerned that their children might be experiencing abuse or, after hearing of my experience, terrified that something similar to what had happened to Radek and Ryder could happen to their child or children.

I believe these injustices will keep happening to families over and over and over again, unless something is changed. Laws must change! Those in positions of power must look seriously at how the "systems" are not serving vulnerable women and children. Funny how the courts—lawyers and judges—could take $50,000 of my money in bits and pieces without blinking an eye and do F*#K all for me. What about those women who do not have the resources to fight as seriously as I had to, with little result? The emotional stress involved with each of these breaches was so difficult to handle. Those without the financial resources would very likely be double stressed or reluctant to follow up regarding situations such as I found myself on many occasions as the mother of two boys dealing with a self-centred, narcissistic, and vindictive father. Corry was simply laughing in my face and my boys paid the ultimate price! A bit of a rant, eh Sandra?'

SYK to TRS: Understandably, but maybe better between us right now rather than on Facebook, Little Mama.

Chapter 24

LITTLE SNIPPETS FROM DAD'S HOUSE

WHEN CORRY LEFT KELOWNA, HE RETURNED TO WHITECOURT FOR A WHILE and then the boys began to see him every second weekend. Then he moved to Blackfalds before he finally moved to Spruce Grove in 2014. The boys continued to see him every second weekend. He still attempted to have a strong say in what was happening when Tracy had the kids in her care. In Tracy's words, "As well, he attempted to undermine me and maintain control with them at every possible opportunity."

The Girlie Boy

TRS TO SYK: Then, things started to drastically change between Corry and the boys. Radek, who was eight at the time, decided he wanted to take a year off hockey as he was excited to try dance class. From what the boys said, Corry constantly belittled Radek for this decision, calling him a girlie boy and telling him he would only be picking up his "son" Ryder from now on. Radek, never wanting to disappoint his dad, ended up quitting dance. I felt so sad for him, but what could I do? Then, when I got the boys back after a weekend with Corry, Radek would only eat vegetables. When I asked him why, he said he was on a diet. Dad had told him he was getting too fat and needed to be on a diet. I was furious!

Radek then spilled a few more "beans." He said Dad would ask him and Ryder if they loved their mother and if they responded yes, he told them to f*#k off and go to their rooms. He told the boys they should hate their mother and Brent for how they treated him. He would scream at them that Brent could be their new dad and he, their real dad, would be forgotten.

He demanded that the boys text him every day. If they did not, Radek reported that they were punished when they returned to his house. The boys both shared that he constantly yelled and screamed at them. Any time Corry was mad at me, they said Dad took it out on them by flipping tables, yelling, or breaking things in the house.

Hearing this from Radek was brutal. The boys and I decided we would have a deal. I told them they could tell me anything and we would talk about it, and I would keep it as their secret. I was so afraid that if I confronted him on anything, Corry would take it out on the boys. I gave them the option of leaving their dad's place and coming to stay with me, but they said no. They always seemed to feel they "owed" it to their dad to go back to his house. They both maintained they loved their dad. They just didn't want to go with "mean" Dad.

Ryder Says No!

March 1st was Ryder's birthday. The latest court order had stated Corry must email me if he were coming to get the boys, as sometimes, he would say he was coming and then not show up, which was upsetting to the boys and infuriating to me! As well, his noncompliance did not allow us to make definitive plans with the boys. This birthday weekend, no email from Corry arrived. Ryder and Radek pleaded with me not to let them go to Dad's after Ryder's hockey game if Dad showed up. They said Dad hadn't been nice to them the last few times they had gone with him.

I took Ryder to hockey that morning and left Radek safe at home with Brent. Corry was still trying to control our family. As he had not emailed me, it was now my choice as to whether or not the boys could go with him if he happened to show. The boys strongly indicated that they did not want to go.

After Ryder's game, I noticed Corry in the arena talking to a couple of people. My heart started to pound. I had not seen hm until that moment. I ran down to Ryder's dressing room and when I told him his dad was in the arena, a look of complete fear crossed his face. I said we would slip out the side door and get into my vehicle. Obviously, Corry saw us. Ryder started walking as fast as he could to get into my vehicle with Corry following after him, yelling his name. Ryder just kept walking. I stopped and turned around and told Corry that the boys did not want to go with him. He told me to let Ryder make that decision. I knew Corry figured he could intimidate Ryder and talk him into going with him.

Corry quickly jumped in his truck and pulled up behind me, blocking me in my stall. As other hockey parents were watching all this happen, I felt safe that no one would let Corry do something stupid. Corry exited his truck, walked up to Ryder's door and opened it. He asked Ryder if he wanted to go with him. Ryder said no. I could tell my boy was stressed to the max. I was so proud of him for standing up to his dad but at the same time was scared as hell for my son.

Corry then began yelling at Ryder and me. I told him to get away from my vehicle. There were people around, so he must have thought better of making a scene. He got into his truck and left the parking lot. I turned to Ryder and asked if he was okay. He nodded, although I could see this had not been easy for him to do. Corry clearly then drove straight to the police station.

When I got home, I received a phone call from the Whitecourt RCMP saying Corry was at their offices and would I please bring my kids to the station immediately. I told the officer I would come, but I was not bringing my children. I located my court order and drove to the RCMP detachment, holding it in my hand. I met with the officer who had called, shared my story, and showed him the document. The police officer told me he was sorry for wasting my time and to have a good day. I did not see Corry at the station. The officer said he was in the back with another of the constables. I was out the door first, my heart still racing at having to do this again and again when Corry breached court orders. It was getting far more than simply annoying.

But that was always just the way it was with Corry. Everything was a fight. I took the brunt of Corry's anger that day, but I am sure Ryder got in trouble for not wanting to go with his dad, although how would I know? For the most part, generally the boys were tight-lipped about what happened when they were under Dad's thumb.

Children of Divorce

SYK to TRS: Thanks for sharing, Tracy. Sometimes it is so hard for kids from split families because they are often in the middle, not wanting either their mom or their dad to be mad at them or to see either parent sad. It is as though each parent has one of their arms and the child is pulled back and forth, not knowing which way to lean. Some kids attempt to be peacemakers while others become angry kids because of being caught in the middle of two "warring" parents. It is far harder on kids than parents realize.

TRS to SYK: I know it was hard on my kids, although they often just seemed to shake it off. I think I got both kinds of kids. Radek was the peacemaker, for sure. The boys were so afraid to do anything to upset Corry. Ryder would simply remain silent. Radek would constantly be trying to cheer up his dad by being so loving toward him. Sometimes, it seemed like Radek was almost parenting his dad emotionally even though he, himself, was just the little kid! I would be so angry at Corry for some of his treatment of the boys, and I wasn't good at keeping my anger at him hidden from them either. But never did I think he would intentionally harm his own flesh and blood! Never!

I was always unafraid of standing up to him on issues which concerned me. Not that he listened. When I had to bring the issues into the courtroom to reach a settlement, I would do so. It was not fun. It was not cheap and Corry was not happy. He still did not want me to be happy without him in my life and he was still trying to manipulate both me and our boys.

Chapter 25

EVERY ROSE HAS ITS THORN

THE LIVES OF TRACY AND BRENT AND THEIR FAMILY CONTINUED TO EVOLVE. It was time to make their union official. Brent decided to 'pop the question' in a unique and fun-filled manner. Tracy describes the night of September 28, 2013:

"Our friends, Robin and Barb Lang and Brent and I had tickets to see Bret Michaels play at the Wild Horse Pass Casino in Chandler, Arizona. Knowing that Bret was my all-time favourite musician, Brent bought VIP backstage tickets to meet Bret before the concert. Our tickets were in the third row from the stage and as the concert was going on Brent had told Robin he wanted to propose to me at the concert. Unbeknownst to me, Robin located Bret Michaels' manager and told him he would make a large donation to The Bret Michaels Life Rocks Foundation if Brent could go up on stage to propose to me. That was exactly what happened! Brent asked to borrow Barb's ring as the engagement ring he had selected for me was back in our house in Scottsdale.

"I was singing along to the music, clueless of what was going on beside me, when all of a sudden, Brent was called up on stage. What? I was listening as Bret Michaels was singing 'Every Rose Has Its Thorn.' The next thing I knew, two guys were grabbing my hands and lifting me up on the stage as well. I wrapped my arms around the musician as I was closer to Heaven being on stage with my beloved performer than I had ever been! He peeled me off him and turned me around to where I saw Brent down on one knee. Brent looked up at me and asked me to marry him. I was totally shocked! However, there was no pause as I responded with a resounding YES!

"After the concert, we again met up with Bret Michaels and he gave me his concert-worn shirt, wet from sweat. I didn't even care! I put it on and wore it for the remainder of the night! It was truly one of the very best nights of my life. After that incredible evening, it is hard to imagine that the beauty of the rose could ever be tainted by the pain of the thorn that would penetrate my heart and that of my future husband, Brent Stark, on a cold winter day a little more than three years later."

Brent and Tracy Get Hitched

TRS to SYK: Brent and I set our wedding date for September 13, 2014, at the Whitecourt Golf and Country Club. It was a dream come true for me. I was totally excited. The night before the wedding, all my ladies in the wedding party stayed with me in our home while my beautiful little guys, Radek and Ryder, stayed with friends. Brent and his attendants bunked at the home of one of the groomsmen. In the morning, I brought in a beauty crew to perform magic on each of my women in the natural light of my fantastic dressing room. Girls just having fun! The house was rockin'. My boys got ready with the groomsmen. They were so happy to be one of the guys.

At 4 p.m., my ladies and I were in the clubhouse, waiting for our signal to start our walk down the aisle. The troop of men led the way to the front of the tent to the song "Best Day of My Life" by American Authors. Brent, my soon-to-be husband, stopped at the bar where a shot of Gibson's whisky was waiting for him before he took the longest walk of his life! It was his first time at the altar. Poor guy. He had to have a shot of "courage," I guess! Must have been scary. My beautiful team of women began the walk to the tent, where three hundred guests waited, excited to watch Brent and me get hitched.

At the entrance of the tent stood my two handsome boys looking so amazing in their tuxedoes with their hair combed just perfectly. I felt my tears already forming as I regarded my sons waiting for me. The song "How Long Will I Love You?" by Ellie Goulding started playing. Alesha and Shelbey, Brent's lovely daughters, led the entourage of beautiful ladies to join the groomsmen at the front of the venue. My sweet Radek and Ryder walked in front of me down the aisle and then stood beside me. I was so proud to have them accompanying me on such an important day! I felt so loved as they looked at me. That picture of them is truly etched forever in my memory.

Brent and I then said our vows. We kissed to seal the deal. We signed what needed to be signed and walked out as Mr. & Mrs. Brent Stark. I was so very happy to have found the man, who aside from my boys, was truly the love of my life. Outside, we had golf carts waiting to take our wedding party to the shores of the Athabasca River for pictures. I remember my boys seeming to be so happy, so very happy, to be a part of something so special. Ryder stood on his tiptoes in most of the pictures so he would look taller. He always wanted to be bigger than he was! And Radek? Well, he was just grinning from ear to ear in typical Radek fashion.

After the formalities of the dinner and speeches, my boys wanted to leave to hang out with other kids who had also attended the wedding. I tried to convince them to stay as I wanted them to see the surprise behind the curtain that would be unveiled later in the evening, but like typical boys, they had had enough wedding and just wanted to go and play with their friends. I kissed each of them goodbye and commended them for being such great members of the wedding party. I could tell they too were very pleased with themselves.

In setting up for the wedding, we had hung a huge white curtain across the front of the stage to conceal what lay behind. At midnight, the MC called Brent and me to the dance floor. The song "Every Rose has Its Thorn" began to play. All our friends stood and watched our first dance, wanting of course to see if Brent still had the moves. As the song picked up, the curtain dropped and … it was BRET MICHAELS and his band playing our chosen song LIVE! Oh My God! It was suddenly insane. Everyone was on their feet, cheering loudly. When our song finished, everyone rushed to the stage. The Stark wedding had now turned into a Bret Michaels concert! Brent and I went up on the stage and danced with the band. We pulled up Alesha and Shelbey as well and we all danced! The party went on for hours and at the end of the night, Bret Michaels was signing autographs and taking pictures with our guests in the Whitecourt Golf and Country Club. What a magical night! What an incredible way to formally start our life together as husband and wife. I was in a dream which I did not want to end! I was now formally Tracy Stark and I had two lovely stepdaughters, Alesha and Shelbey. My new husband officially became the stepdad of my precious boys.

The Wedding Photo — Gloriously beautiful.

SYK to TRS: Wow! Sounds like a wonderful party. So, what happened after you became Tracy Stark?

TRS to SYK: After Brent and I become man and wife, my light was shining so brightly. I felt such confidence in myself. I was pleased to be married to Brent and become Tracy Stark. I was walking tall. Maybe some people thought I thought I was too good for them. Maybe some people thought I was shoving my life in Corry's face! Corry's face was the farthest thing from my mind. That wasn't it at all. I was just so very happy, not because I thought I had it "going on," but because I loved being a mom, and I loved being loved by the man I had found in Brent. I also loved sharing our life together with my boys and Brent's girls. Radek and Ryder had been the star players on my team since they were born. Brent and his girls were now full members of our team! I loved the way he interacted with my boys, the way he treated them with such respect. He never spoke badly of their dad, although he could have. There was continual laughter at our table as he joked with the boys and actually, Brent's relationship with Corry was much better than mine.

On one occasion, Corry actually called my phone and asked to speak to Brent. He proceeded to warn Brent right in front of me about who I "really" was.

Corry plainly did not want me to move on. Brent tolerated Corry as he was the father of my children, and sometimes he made excuses for Corry's behaviour to make the kids feel at ease, which drove me nuts, but I saw and understood what he was doing. I think Corry hated the fact I was with Brent because Brent was giving me and the boys the life he couldn't or should I say, chose not to give us when we were together. Brent and I were truly livin' the dream! And Corry? He could not stand that.

Chapter 26

THE NANNY

SYK to TRS: Good Morning, Warrior Goddess. If it is okay, let's talk about the nanny.

TRS to SYK: Warrior Goddess? I like that! The nanny. Hmm. Corry became obsessed with the fact that I had hired a nanny. Sometimes people would say mean things about me. I would hear them and think, *You do not know me at all and certainly do not know or see what is happening in our home.*

People would comment and say a nanny was raising my kids, which was totally untrue! I initially hired a wonderful woman named Natasha to help out when I took over running the Goal-line Grill at the rink, where adults and kids could score a bite to eat or a drink of some kind, while watching the games on one of the two ice surfaces below. It was a fun place to be, but for me, it was also a full-time job. I took over managing the rink restaurant as well as taking the opportunity to run my own lounge, something I had always wanted to do. With my boys in hockey, I was at the rink six days a week anyway, so I figured, why not? It was also a place where I could bring my kids while I worked.

The boys loved that their mom "owned" the rink lounge. LOL! Hanging out at the rink? What young hockey player wouldn't love that! The boys even loved to help out with little tasks. It was a win-win situation.

I had a nanny so I could spend more time directly interacting with my boys, not less! Natasha helped with household tasks when the kids were in school and I worked. When I was not at home, I wanted my boys in their own space with their own things. I wanted them in our home rather than in a day home. Even when Ryder was a little older, I did not believe it was okay to leave the boys home by themselves when they were on my time. Natasha, my nanny, was not there to replace me. She was there to help me manage the household and help with the boys when I was away or at work. I still made breakfast for my kids, got them ready for school, cooked supper for my family, helped the boys with their homework and most importantly, tucked them in at night.

Sometimes, Brent and I would plan a short holiday around Corry's weekend and Natasha would be there when the boys were dropped off. She would look after them for a day or two until we got home. I'll admit I loved the jet-set lifestyle, as Brent mesmerized me with his sense of adventure and his many kindnesses to me and to my boys. I was with a man who loved me in the way I needed to be loved. He was a man who loved being with me and did not ask me each day if I was earning my keep or as Corry would say, "Earning my Jeep." I was with a man who could afford to take me on beautiful adventures. I was in love with my life, my boys, and my man. My boys knew how much I loved them and when we could do so, they too enjoyed many incredible moments with us as a family, both at home and away. I always felt that the more good people who loved my boys and were around them, the better. One of those good people was Natasha, our nanny.

The one who had the greatest issue with the nanny was the one, who after returning from Kelowna, only saw his kids five days a month. While everyone talked about my having a nanny, Corry, on more than one occasion after moving to Spruce Grove, paid the kids $20 each to watch each other while he went to the Oilers hockey game with friends. He left my boys at his home alone, with no one nearby to call if something happened. To Corry, perhaps they seemed old enough, but to me they were still my little guys in a new community without supports, and I was furious that Corry would do this. I let him know in no uncertain terms that it was unacceptable. As usual, he just shrugged and walked away.

Chapter 27

SWITCHING TEAM COLOURS

SYK to TRS: Good Morning Mama Wolverine! Remember…Today is a Good Day to have a Good Day! How did the boys end up living with their dad in Spruce Grove?

TRS to SYK: I knew Corry had always been on the boys to come and live with him although I never trusted his intentions. I always felt he just wanted to keep the kids to get out of paying child support. Ryder only wanted to start living with Corry after he played spring hockey in Spruce Grove in 2016. His spring hockey experience had been truly a self-esteem booster for my older son. It was as if the new team and his new group of friends buoyed him up! He had performed well in the hockey camps and it was so good for his confidence to make new friends and do so well. I knew too that for Ryder to make it to the level of hockey he wanted to play, he needed to begin to play in a larger centre and be playing a higher level of hockey. Maybe this could work with Corry. Maybe he could be the dad the boys needed him to be.

I was not able to just up and leave Whitecourt, although that proved to be untrue later that fall. Ryder was so insistent that living in Spruce Grove with Dad was what he wanted and needed to do. Corry had lived in a few places after returning to Alberta and had finally settled on Spruce Grove. To Ryder, this would be perfect. With his dad encouraging Ryder to come and live with him, my older son became even more determined to convince me that this would be a good choice. He, in typical Ryder style, was relentless. He was not about to be denied! So, it was actually my kids who made my decision. I couldn't rob Ryder of the experience of living with his dad and playing a mor4 intense level of hockey where he felt so comfortable. After much thought and discussion, I agreed to allow this to happen for the 2016-17 school term. Ryder was ecstatic.

Little brother Radek was not about to be left behind. He had always wanted to "try" living with Dad since he was about eight. He insisted that he was going too and would pipe up. "Mom, you and Brent have had your turn with me, so it would only be fair to give Dad a chance." I knew this was Corry pushing the idea. Maybe it was always his plan to convince the boys to come live with him. I knew that both boys were always wanting the approval of their dad. Radek would do anything to appease his dad, and he would do that until the day he died. My little peacemaker assured me, "It will be good living with Dad as he has been so nice to us on our last few visits." My greatest fear was that they would be so happy living with Dad that they would not want to return to live with me. However, I knew deep down that Corry would fail as a parent once the kids started living full-time with him as he had never been a full-time father—EVER! At times he was a good dad but it seemed like he was always going from one extreme to another.

The Unwritten Contract

Corry and I talked and I agreed to allow them one school year and within that year, Brent and I would figure out what we needed to do to move closer to the city. Brent's daughter, Shelbey, was in Grade 12 and still had a year of school left in Whitecourt. Brent and I both wanted to be closer to Edmonton, so with Ryder's hockey, we were thinking we would push it a little earlier than we had anticipated. There were big decisions to be made, but we were putting together a plan if hockey in Spruce Grove proved to be a good fit for Ryder and for Radek.

Corry and I agreed on the new living arrangements. Like most separated and divorced women, I wanted my boys to have a healthy relationship with their biological dad. In retrospect, I now wonder if Corry had been grooming them to come live with him by being, as Radek said, so nice? Did I too get caught in that honeymoon phase of the abuse cycle as he agreed to my terms? I began to believe that maybe living with their dad might be a good thing. This was his chance.

Corry and I went for breakfast with the kids to let them know how things were going to work. The boys would live with Dad for the 2016-17 school year.

We would not go to court to change the custody agreement. It would be strictly a verbal agreement between us. We would simply shift our rotation. Corry would have the boys during the week and I would have them every second weekend. As well, I would come to their games as often as I could. I would still be the custodial parent. He was so agreeable.

I signed the school papers, giving the boys permission to reside in Spruce Grove for that one school year, but I was to be made aware of anything involving the boys that went on at the school or at hockey. I wanted to be "in the know" on everything. After all, I was their mom. I was very clear about this with Corry. He agreed.

Needless to say, his word was not worth sh#t. Such information was never forthcoming from Corry. In fact, he just got weirder and weirder and more secretive and more controlling as time went on. My limited information came from Radek, my sweet little boy, who finally needed to tell his mom when things started going sideways.

After we had this conversation with the boys at breakfast, Corry had the nerve to ask me, in front of the boys, if he could borrow $60,000 of the money he "gave" me when we had split up. He said he had a business opportunity and he needed $60,000. I was ticked off. I told him he didn't "give" me anything. I was entitled to the money, as I had earned it as much as he had when I worked in the company and no, I didn't have $60,000 to "give" him. I asked him how he was going to afford to support two boys for the year if he had no money? Of course, as usual, he didn't answer except to say he would no longer be paying me child support now that the boys would be with him. It just killed Corry to pay me anything, even though he had paid only $833 a month for the two boys since the time I had left him. That did not even cover the amount of money it cost to take care of them each month. But whatever. Something was going on with him, but I didn't dwell on it. I was having enough trouble emotionally with just letting the boys go!

Missing My Boys

In late August, my hockey guys were off to live with their dad. I could not believe how much I missed them. In fact, I became somewhat depressed when they moved to Spruce Grove, missing them far more than I ever thought I would.

And, I had always worried about them at Corry's house as he had moments of being such a tyrant with them, and sometimes, I knew they would need the softness of their mom when they returned to my home. I had always taken good care of them. I had always tucked them in at night. It was difficult for me when they were not under my roof or close by if they ever needed me.

Strangely enough, those first two and a half months of Ryder living in Spruce Grove gave me the best Ryder I had ever seen when he was with me on our weekends or at his or Radek's games. He seemed genuinely happy with his new environment. He was handsome and witty and instantly became one of the "cool" kids in his school and on his hockey team. He started coming out of his shell. The girls loved him. The boys idolized him. He was beginning to develop confidence in himself with his peers. He was in a new school and on a new team. He made jokes, played really horrible music really loud, and laughed his butt off. Even Radek cracked up and said how funny Ryder was.

Ryder wanted to be around me on those "every second weekends" or when we came in to watch his and Radek's games. Everywhere I went, he would come too. Whenever we were together, he would wrap his arms around me. I knew he missed me, and I knew he loved me. I watched as I witnessed him becoming his own person. Absence truly was making his "heart grow even fonder" of his mom and his life. He was on top of the world and he was only thirteen. And Radek? He was just Radek, loving life and following his brother around, loving his new friends, but missing his mom and calling her every single morning … on the sly, so Dad wouldn't get mad.

SYK to TRS: So, when did things start to concern you, Tracy?

TRS to SYK: In November 2016, I started noticing changes in the boys. Ryder was becoming very gaunt, losing weight, and looking exhausted. Radek was quieter and seemed very sad when he had to return to Dad's household. The boys told me that Dad had been so nice when they first moved in with him, but now he was mean to them. When I asked what he was doing, they gave no details except that they could never ever have any candy or junk food. I didn't clue in to the extent of what this snippet of information actually meant. I should have asked more questions! The end of November I received a call from a parent of one of Ryder's classmates, who informed me that Ryder had been suspended from school for writing rude notes about teachers and students. His son had also been implicated in the incident. The man on the line actually wanted Ryder to take full responsibility for what had been done as his son wanted to try out for the school basketball team and this incident was holding him back from the tryout. I said I would speak to Ryder.

WTF? Why did I not know of the suspension? That had been part of the deal with Corry. He was to share any and all information regarding each of the boys. He shared nothing of this incident or any other. I called Corry and asked to speak to Ryder. He told me Ryder would call me after he finished his chores, and when he did, Ryder confirmed that he had been suspended from school. He admitted his part in the action that had led to the suspension, but said the other boy was not blameless. I called the father who had initially called me and informed him that Ryder would not be taking the full responsibility for what had happened. His son too would have to pay the price and I would be speaking further to my son to learn more about this incident. Other dad … was not pleased.

Chapter 28

BREAKING THE
CONTRACT

SYK to TRS: Did you have any involvement with the school, Tracy?

TRS to SYK: I did not feel I had a relationship with Greystone Centennial School where the boys attended. I had signed the papers allowing the boys to attend, but it soon became apparent that Corry had not included me in the paperwork as the primary custodial parent. The front office staff appeared to have no knowledge of me. On one occasion, I was picking the boys up to take them out for lunch and not knowing the school policy for kids leaving the school grounds, I went to the office to tell them I would like to sign my boys, Ryder and Radek MacDougall, out for lunch and would return them for afternoon classes. The lady working the front desk looked up their names and asked me who I was. I said, "I am their mother." She was reading something and said, "I see you don't have custody of the boys," or something to that effect. I looked at her with confusion and snapped back, "Actually I am the primary parent of my boys and they are just here for one year to play hockey and try out life with their dad." She looked surprised as I continued, "I will have them back after lunch." I turned, grabbed the boys and walked away.

This encounter unsettled me. It was never my intention to be rude, but what the hell? What had Corry told the school? I would have to follow up. When Ryder was suspended from school, I had not been contacted. I was beginning to wonder if Corry had altered/or even submitted the papers I had signed. I was beginning to wonder what Corry had shared with the school regarding the custodial parent of Ryder and Radek, aka me! I checked into this and found that I was listed as a guardian, but not a contact. Corry had the name of his latest girlfriend and his sister as the emergency contacts for the boys. I was not even mentioned. I was beginning to wonder what else was happening on his watch.

SYK to TRS: When the boys shared with you about Dad being physically abusive with them, what did you do?

TRS to SYK: Honestly, Sandra, I never heard a word out of their mouths about any kind of mistreatment from Dad other than when they shared the junk food thing. I picked them up from school on December 2 to take them to Whitecourt for my weekend. They were tight- lipped regarding what was going on in Dad's house until that very day on the drive home. That is when the sh#t hit the fan.

Misconducts

I was waiting at the school. Radek was out before Ryder and once he was in my vehicle, he immediately began opening up, telling me what had been happening. He was talking a mile a minute, wanting to tell me everything before Ryder got in the car.

"Mom," he began, "last week Dad took Ryder to Value Village and made him buy a dress and wear it to hockey. He shaved Ryder's head to the skin and wouldn't even let him wear a hat!" I just looked at him. I was in total shock! What? This was unbelievable! I was incensed that Corry would be so insensitive to our son! Once Ryder got in the vehicle, I asked him if this was true. He hesitated and then confirmed what Radek had shared regarding the dress the previous week. The boys were finally spilling their guts.

Radek said, "Dad was so nice before we moved in and for the first little while and now, he is so mean sometimes!"

On our one-and-a-half-hour drive home to Whitecourt, the boys shared what was going on at Dad's for the first time. The boys said:

1. Dad slashes Ryder across the arms with his hockey stick when he is slow coming out of the dressing room after hockey.
2. Dad beats us with the belt.
3. Dad constantly calls us names: Retard, Idiot, Pussy.
4. Dad throws things at us or at things in the house, breaking pictures, etc. when he is mad at you.
5. Dad bought us new cell phones which were going to have new

Spruce Grove numbers and we will not be able to have any communication with friends or family in Whitecourt.

6. Dad gets mad at Radek when he texts you. Radek deletes all messages between him and you so Dad will not find out. He never calls you from home because he doesn't want Dad to know he is talking to you because Dad gets mad.

Radek finished with, "That is why I call you every morning on the way to school, Mom, so Dad won't know I've been talkin' to you!"

Sharing this information was particularly difficult for Radek as he was conflicted, saying, "I feel like I am backstabbing Dad by telling you all these bad things he's doing 'cause sometimes he is so funny!"

I was more than upset! When we got home, I fired Ryder's hockey coach an email.

Chapter 29

FACING OFF WITH THE HOCKEY COACH

On Dec 2, 2016, at 5:48 PM, Tracy Ross
████████████████ wrote:

Hey there

Sorry to bother you on a Friday evening , but I had picked Ryder up from school and he proceeded to tell me that his father made him wear a dress to practice ?! Is this true ?

Tracy Stark

On Dec 2, 2016, at 11:01 PM, ████████
████████████ wrote:

Hi Tracy,

Sorry for the delay. Yes, when I showed up to practice on Thursday, that is what he was wearing. I told

Ryder that he could change into something else, but at that point, he seemed to be okay with finishing dryland in what he was wearing. I didn't want to make a scene out of the situation if Ryder felt okay about it, so I supervised the rest of dryland and Ryder left shortly after.

I'm not sure if Ryder or his father told you, but I asked Ryder to take a break from the team until he had served his school suspension. I also had him write me an explanation of what he did wrong and how he would handle the situation next time. Ryder did so and I am confident that Ryder learned a lesson from the decision that he made.

If you have any questions, feel free to email me back or give me a call at ████████

From: Tracy Ross
Sent: March 29, 2019 11:30 AM

Subject: Fwd: Ryder

Tracy Stark

Begin forwarded message:

> From: Tracy Ross
> Date: December 3, 2016 at 8:46:11 AM MST
> To:
> Subject: Re: Ryder

You know as a parent you're hoping your son is lying when he tells you he had to wear a dress to hockey .... wow

Well thanks for clearing that up and I'm glad you had Ryder write you an explanation!
I would never condone my child to do what he did but Corry's punishment is child abuse in my eyes ...

Please keep me in the loop if anything happens in the future!

Thank you

Tracy Stark

On Dec 3, 2016, at 11:34 AM,

> I definitely understand that sentiment. We are in the process of doing our individual interviews with each player, so I'll get a chance to talk to Ryder next week to make sure that he knows he has whatever support he needs from the coaching staff. I started coaching because I wanted to help the kids become better players and better people, so I will do my best to contribute to that, and I will let you know if anything comes up.

> Talk to you soon,

From: Tracy Ross ▮▮▮▮▮▮▮▮▮▮▮▮
Date: August 30, 2017 at 7:12:56 PM MST
To ▮▮▮▮▮▮▮▮▮▮▮▮
Subject: Re: Ryder

Hey ▮▮▮▮
Just going through my emails from last December
You mentioned you asked Ryder to write you about what he did wrong and
what choices he would make in the future regarding his suspension.
Could you email that to me

Also you said when I emailed you on December 2nd, about My son wearing a
dress to hockey .....
You were doing individual assessments the following week
And you would be talking to Ryder personally about the event that had
happened.... could you email me that too please

Thanks

Tracy Stark

From: ▮▮▮▮▮▮▮▮▮▮▮▮
Date: August 31, 2017 at 10:16:59 AM MST
To: Tracy Ross ▮▮▮▮▮▮▮▮
Subject: Fwd: Apology Letter

Hi Tracy,

Hope things are going well for you. This is the email that Ryder sent me in order
to get back to playing with the team.

I will have to do a little bit of digging to see where I put the log of our
conversation. I should be able to check when I get home tonight, but I wanted
to send this before I forgot.

I'll reply again as soon as I take a look at home, but if I can help with anything
else, just let me know.

All the best,

▮▮▮▮▮▮

Emails between Ryder's hockey coach & Tracy

From: Ryder Patryk
Subject: Apology Letter
Date: November 30, 2016 at 6:10:00 PM MST
To:

Dear Coach

I am writing this letter to say that i'm sorry that I got
suspended and couldn't play last weekend. We won both
games but I should've been there to help the team. I was
fooling around with my friends writing inappropriate notes in
class. I learnt that i shouldn't have to be inappropriate to be
funny and i shouldn't make fun of people. I'm glad to be back
to school and on the team. I had to prove that i am willing to do
anything to play hockey. I learnt my lesson and definitely won't
do anything like that again. I feel that i deserve to be on the
team because even though I wasn't behaving at school I am a
good leader in the dressing room and try my best to motivate
and help the boys have a good game. Usually i am good at
school but last week i was messing around at school and I will
make sure I go to school get my work done and that's it. I don't
want you to think i am a bad kid because i don't think i am, and
i think i proved that.

From: Ryder

Letter from Ryder to hockey coach

TRS to SYK: Not one word was ever spoken to me about Ryder arriving at practice wearing a dress until Radek told me what had happened. I received no communication from a coach, a manager, any concerned parent watching the dryland training, or anyone dropping off or picking up their kid. There were no words from any parent whose son had shared what he had seen at hockey that night—a thirteen-year-old teammate arriving at practice wearing a dress with his head shaved to the skin? I find it heartbreaking that Ryder's coaches were more concerned about getting an apology letter from my son regarding his suspension than they were about him arriving at practice in the state he was in. No alarms went off in their heads when he showed up and attempted to practice in a dress?

Shortly after the boys died, one of Ryder's friends texted me saying how sorry he was about what had happened to Radek and Ryder, indicating he felt responsible because he never said anything when Ryder had texted him shortly before they were killed. At that time, Ryder was serving a suspension from hockey because of his suspension from school.

Text Between Ryder and Friend * Nov 2016

> Ryder: My dad … …
> Me: What did he do. We won 4-1 btw
> Ryder: Good job. He's just being a f*#king d#ck. he came home started yelling at me and I started yelling … then he punched me in the head
> Me: Actually. Like bruh that's abuse you need to tell someone
> Ryder: I told my mom
> Me: What did she say … … … … … … … … …

That was all the script Ryder's friend shared. I reassured the boy that he was not responsible for Ryder's death but ached when I thought of the pain this young man had been experiencing since the boys died.

The boy also shared a video that he had taken in the dressing room of Ryder just being Ryder—making everyone laugh. He was a leader, comfortable in his surroundings and in that video, my boy definitely owned the room.

Ryder in a dress (as shared on his team's Instagram account)

NO ONE CALLED YOU MAMA?
NO ONE AT ALL
NO ONE CALLED YOU MAMA?
REALLY BAD CALL!

Chapter 30

MANEUVERS REQUIRING SEVERE PENALTIES

Alberta Child Services

TRS to SYK: I reached out to Alberta Child Services the weekend the boys shared the information about Dad's abusive behaviour with an email detailing what the boys had told me. I thought, given such information, someone would lead an investigation and help me to remove the boys from Corry's home and give them to me. I did not want to break any rules and knew if I tried to remove them myself, there would be hell to pay, if not for me, for my boys. I thought Child Services would immediately order a home study and make Corry get the help he needed to regain his rights as a parent. I guessed too that it would help my case to have the boys taken away from Corry and safe in my home until he sought help. Here is a copy of the letter I sent and the reply I received in return.

From: Tracy Stark
Sent: Sunday, December 04, 2016
To: Human Services Edmonton Region
Subject: Urgent Review

To Whom It May Concern:

I'm writing out of sheer concern for my children's safety. I have attached my most recent Court Order. First off, I would like to add that I, Tracy Ross Stark, am the primary parent of my two children, Ryder Patryk MacDougall and Radek Stryker MacDougall, age thirteen and eleven.

This past September my children begged to try living one school year with their father, Corry Gene MacDougall in Spruce Grove, Alberta. Both my kids are very active in sports, mainly hockey. Spruce Grove offers a better hockey league as well as numerous sports that our home town of Whitecourt, Alberta does not offer.

I agreed to let them try. I took on Corry's schedule of every second weekend where I pick them up Friday after school and return them Sunday at 5:00 pm. The past few times I've had the kids, they have shown signs of fear towards Corry. My older son is begging me to move closer to them, so they can live with me again. My younger son cries every time I have them, saying how much he misses home. I took this as typical kids missing their mother and the only life they have ever known as Corry hasn't had them much over the years of their lives.

Ten days ago, my son Ryder got suspended from school for writing a horrible letter about some people in his school. I heard this from my younger son Radek. When I texted Corry to ask him what had happened, he proceeded to tell me to "Fuck Off". Sorry about the language but you have to understand the person I have to deal with.

I asked that Ryder call me and Corry said he would have Ryder call me after he had done his chores. Ryder did call and we spoke about what had happened. I told him I would talk to him more when I seen him on the weekend.

So, this past Friday I picked up the boys from school. Radek got in my vehicle first and proceeded to tell me what had happened over the past few weeks:

Corry took my son Ryder to Value Village to buy a dress. He made Ryder put this dress on and go to his hockey practice and dryland training in it. The sheer humiliation he put my son through is NEVER acceptable. The coach had suggested to him that he remove the dress and Ryder hadn said he was okay. I confirmed this with Ryder's coach over email and it was in fact true.

Corry had also sat Ryder down and shaved off all his hair so he was bald, just to add to his humiliation. Then, when Ryder asked to wear a hat, Corry said "No. You can walk around like that!" My son has bad psoriasis on his scalp as well so I am sure the humiliation factor was heightened just a bit more.

Corry also punched Ryder in the head when he got home from school after being suspended. When I asked Ryder if this was the first time this had happened, he said "No. He does it all the time."

As of now, both my kids have phones that I pay for. Radek told me that Corry has ordered them new phones and new numbers and they would not be allowed in contact with anyone from Whitecourt.

THIS IS MENTAL AND PHYSICAL CHILD ABUSE ON EVERY LEVEL!

That is not all of it. He whips them with the belt when they misbehave or "lie" to him.

He slashed Ryder across the arm with a hockey stick because he took too long getting undressed from hockey.

He asked Ryder what he would rather be called an asshole or a retard? The name-calling is a constant in Corry's household. He constantly refers to my boys as retards… which honestly doesn't surprise me because that was his pet name for me when we were married.

Today is Sunday. I have the boys in my possession and they have to go back today. Radek cries and cries pleading with me not to go so they don't have to go back. PLEASE HELP ME!

I'm going to Edmonton today to look at a house so that I can move there before the new year. I will be leaving my husband and step daughter in Whitecourt just so I can fully protect my children from this monster called their father.

I have contacted a good friend of mine who is a police officer in Whitecourt. He advised me to contact your office. He also said that I should be able to just keep the kids from Corry until this is settled with a lawyer in court as their safety is at risk.

I will take the boys to Corry today. But, I told them that there was a process. I also promised them that after Christmas break, they would live with me. Please help me do this!!!

I will go to the police as well if need be. My boys have no problem doing an interview but only if they do not have to go back to Dad's house as they fear for their safety.

Look forward to hearing from you very soon. If you need anything else from me, please let me know. I can come any time to meet with you. Thank you for your time.

Sincerely A Very Concerned Mother
Tracy L. Stark

From: HS Edm Region [▓▓▓▓▓▓▓▓▓▓▓▓]
Subject: **RE: URGENT REVIEW**
Date: **Dec 6, 2016 at 6:09:46 PM**
To: **Tracy Stark** [▓▓▓▓▓▓▓▓▓]

Hello Tracy;

Thank you for your email and information. As I read through your email I can appreciate the concern you have for your sons; Ryder and Radek. I am forwarding your information to North Alberta Child Intervention Services (NACIS) for their review and follow-up. For your information NACIS is open 24 hours per day, 7 days per week and you can contact a caseworker there to assist you. I encourage you to call them directly as they will require further information and/or clarification regarding your information. The contact number is <u>1-800-638-0715</u> or <u>780-422-2001</u>. You can also contact the Spruce Grove Child and Family Services neighbourhood office at <u>780-962-7635</u> and an intake worker will be happy to assist you.

Thank you again for taking the time to write. If you have any further questions for myself you can call me directly.

Issues Resolution Coordinator
Human Services - Edmonton Region
Government of Alberta

Government

Notice of Confidentiality: This transmission contains information that may be confidential. Unless you are the intended recipient of the message (or authorized to receive it), you may not copy, forward, or otherwise use it, or disclose its contents to anyone else. If you have received this transmission in error, please notify us immediately and delete or destroy it from your system.

Reply from Human Services to Urgent Review

TRS to SYK: I called and left a message in the Spruce Grove office. A lady called me back a few days later and proceeded to tell me I was doing the right thing to protect my kids by moving to Spruce Grove. I asked her for help in removing the boys from their father's home. However, she didn't seem to think that was necessary. I told her if she couldn't help me, I would go to the police. She asked me why I would do that and I said, "Because I need help!"

The help I was so desperately seeking did not materialize so I changed my plan. I decided I hire a lawyer to change my order. I wanted Corry to have absolutely no access to my children until he was enrolled into some sort of help—anger management, effective parenting, or any counselling or other such program that would give him the skills to find discipline alternatives to the abuse he was laying on the boys. It would be hard to do in such a short period of time but I was going to try my darndest to get my boys out of Corry's clutches and into my care.

***

Once Tracy asked me to write with her, I attempted to piece together the information she had shared regarding her interaction with Child Services. I realized I was lacking a full understanding of what had transpired, so I texted her for more information.

SYK to TRS: Good Morning Tracy. Hope you are enjoying your laundry stint! Can you please explain what happened with Alberta Child Services that got you so riled up? Please, when you are writing this piece and you feel overwhelmed, do not hesitate to stop and call me. I am home today. We can do this together so we can go slow and do some self-regulation therapy when you feel too activated. Promise me that you will do that.

TRS: Good Morning Beautiful! I promise. But I am so ready to tackle anything you throw at me so don't hesitate to ask me ANYTHING!. Remember TODAY IS A GOOD DAY TO HAVE A GOOD DAY!

I smiled a small smile as I read our shared mantra. I was always teasing her about doing laundry often referring her Cinderella as she seemed to do a lot of laundry! It was a nice warm safe place where she could be in control washing, drying and folding when life as she knew it had been blown apart. I was hoping she would continue to have a good day after writing about her experience with Child Services. Her email arrived shortly, filling in the details.

Facing Off With Child Services

TRS to SYK: I have struggled with my experience with Child Services for many reasons. I believed there was a lack of concern for my children and a lack of understanding as to why I was contacting them, which I had made so obvious in my letter. Of course, this is still coupled with my feelings of guilt for not doing more and is still wrapped up in all of this. Sometimes the guilt is overwhelming, but as I write this, as you have reminded me over and over, I did not know my children were in the extreme danger they were in.

Firstly, NEVER in my worst nightmare did I ever imagine Corry to be capable of doing something this horrific. Secondly, as much as my children feared their dad and wanted me to take them out of his home, they definitely wanted to spend Christmas with him and his family. After all, as my Radek pointed out, it was Dad's Christmas!

When the lady from Child Services called me, she basically wanted to know what I wanted from her department. It was 9 a.m. December 8th, 2016. I was in the Dollar Store. I thought I had been quite clear in my letter. I found a place to have this conversation with the woman and kept telling her I needed help removing the kids from Corry's home. I suggested to her that if she followed up with him, he might think that someone from hockey had called in a report after seeing Ryder show up in a dress and then he would assume that was why Child Services was investigating. I told her I was in the process of moving to Spruce Grove and I would be taking my kids back. I explained my plan. I would let them be with Corry for Christmas but when I got them on the 29th, they would never be going back to him. However, I was asking for help in removing them from Corry's home and I needed to get everything in place to ensure he could not rip them away from me through some law or loophole.

She asked when I got my kids again. I told her Corry and I had just flipped schedules in September and noted that this had not been changed in the courts. Rather, it was a verbal agreement between Corry and me. I told her I would pick them up on Friday, December 16th after school and I was to return them to Corry on Sunday the 18th at 5 p.m. I let her know I would be taking possession of a place in Spruce Grove on December 14th and would be living there until school ended in June.

She said that if I was moving to Spruce Grove that I was doing my part to protect my children and wanted to know why I needed her involvement? I kept telling her that from past experience, I knew Corry would find a way to sabotage my plan. It would be so much easier if her department would go and remove them rather than me, because I knew Corry would lose it if I chose not to return them. I was not sure what she was not getting about that potential scenario.

She then asked if I were so concerned about my children, then why didn't I simply take them home with me on the Sunday night?

Like seriously??? WTF was this woman's job??? I then told her if she didn't want to help me, I would go to the police.

She asked again, "Why would you go to the police?"

Again, I said "BECAUSE I NEED HELP PROTECTING MY DAMN CHILDREN!!!!! Last time I checked, a parent should not be hitting his kid with hockey sticks or making a male child of 13 wear a woman's dress to hockey practice with a totally shaved head as a punishment for something he, as a crazy teenage boy, had done!"

She again suggested that I not return my children home on the 18th and that she would be closing my file as of that date having directed me not to return my boys to their father.

I read Tracy's email and texted her back.

SYK to TRS Thank you for the information. However, sorry to be a pain Tracy but I could still use more details. Will you please expand on what you have shared with me after taking that break I suggested?

TRS to SYK: You are right. I do need a break. I'll write you more details shortly.

Two hours later, the details arrived.

TRS to SYK: I reached out to Child Services for their assistance because of the information that my boys had shared with me. I thought that given this information, Child Services would do an investigation and they would remove the kids from Corry's care and return them to me. I needed time to get my ducks in a row to formally do this through the courts. I figured it would help my case if the boys were removed from the home by Child Services after hearing reports of Corry's abuse. Like many women charging inappropriate behaviours by children's fathers, I felt my concerns were not being taken seriously because I was the boys' mother rather than an impartial stranger. Of course, I was partial to what the boys had told me! As a mother, of course I wanted to protect my children. It was my hope that Child Services would remove the boys and conduct a home study that would insist Corry seek help for his anger and his bizarre disciplining techniques before having continued access. I was worried about my sons. I wanted them fully under my care.

I was afraid not to return them to Corry on Sunday. In my mind, Corry was crazy. We had been apart for ten years and he still blamed me for everything wrong in his life. If I took it upon myself to keep the kids on the 18th, I did not know what he would do. For one, we would both be at Ryder's hockey game together that night. I did not want to cause a scene in front of all Ryder's coaches, teammates, and other parents. Ryder didn't need that on top of everything else! I did not want my actions to affect my kids in a negative way. Besides, my history with the justice system hadn't really ever worked well for me. Corry always cited his parental rights. I was scared that the cops would make me give the boys back to him if I attempted to keep them Sunday night and then something bad would happen. Murder never ever crossed my mind, but I knew, deep in my gut that something bad would happen. I was particularly concerned because I now lived alone in Spruce Grove without my husband. I was afraid Corry might just randomly show up at my new place and do something if I did not return the boys. The man I had never feared was now causing me to rethink my bravado. My mind was in overdrive!

I still had legal custody of the kids and I should not have given the boys back to Corry that Sunday. If my kids requested to come with us, I was not going to return them that night but they were adamant about spending Christmas with Corry's family. I did not want to fight them on this. It was Corry's turn to have them for Christmas and they continually said they still wanted to spend Christmas with their dad despite what they had experienced with him. Besides there would be many people around Corry and the boys during the holidays so I figured they would be okay. There would also be piles of presents and plenty of fun activities with Corry's family. I was not going to deny them that.

However, I did think that if Child Services removed them, they would not have the choice of spending Christmas with their dad. They would be placed with me and ridiculous as it sounds now, the boys could not be mad at me! I would have time to do what I needed to do to get them fully in my care. They would be safe at home with me until Corry got the assistance his behaviours showed he needed in parenting my boys.

The more I thought about it, the more determined I was to get the kids under my roof and to get full-time custody of the boys following their Christmas with their dad. I would build a case that would allow me to keep my boys until I was certain their dad would not continue to harm them physically, verbally, or emotionally. I was hoping Child Services would help with this, but my frustration was rising as I did not feel the worker was understanding my grave concern.

I would go to the police and share my story. I would hire a lawyer to uphold my order and ensure Corry did not maintain parental rights until he got help. It would be hard to do so in such a short period of time, but I was going to do everything I could to protect my sons from, of all people, their father!

I never did meet with the lady in Spruce Grove in person. Our conversation was all done over the phone. As I said, she informed me she was closing the case on the 18th of December because she had told me not to return the boys to Corry once I had them in my care if I feared for their safety. However, she could tell me that all day long. Corry and I had been in conflict with custody for years, in and out of court, and she was not the one who had to deal with the fallout if I did what she was suggesting.

I guess the bottom line with me wanting help from Child Services was to build my case against Corry. From my experience and that of many women I have spoken to before and after my boys were murdered, biological dads always had their rights. My thinking was that if there was a file against Corry regarding his beating the hell out of my kids, then the courts would give me full custody. Since the boys had opened up to me, it had become very clear that he was abusive in his attempts to control the behaviour of his own boys. I felt strongly that having to get into counselling to learn better strategies for disciplining the boys and to deal with his own sh#t that was fueling his behaviour was more than essential. So many of Corry's behaviours that the boys told me about showed him to be an absolute bully!

Because of my past experiences with custody and access, though, I was going to do it by the law. I did not want to breach any court order because I did not want any files against me that would favour Corry continuing to share custody. If I took it upon myself to keep the kids from him on the 18th, I did not know what he would do. Mostly, I was scared of the repercussions my kids would face from their father if such a plan did not work. My mind was swirling in attempting to make the best decision.

It is easy to say in retrospect that I should not have given the boys back that Sunday. My heart continues to ache every time I think of the choice I made. To those who say I was blind, I have no doubt they never walked in my shoes. I had raised strong-willed boys. They were allowed opinions and their voices were heard in my home. As I said, murder was never on my radar. I knew there would be a fiery confrontation with Corry and with the boys if I attempted to insist the boys stay with me over Christmas. I wanted to build a case to allow me to keep them by following the law.

I went back and forth as I attempted to make the best decision. When I did not get the support I was needing from Child Services, I decided to tell Corry I was moving to Spruce Grove. Just maybe we could work together. I would be close and I could intervene if there was trouble.

SYK to TRS: What would you do differently now, Tracy?

TRS to SYK: Sandra, I guess in real life, my first reaction is simply just f*#k the rules and rule makers! Protect yourself and your kids because no one is going to do it for you. Is that harsh? Try finding your children dead after having been viciously murdered by their biological father in a situation that I believe could have been prevented. That … That … is harsh!

I feel for the worker at Child Services who turned on her radio that Monday morning to hear the newscasts informing her that the biological father of my two sons for whom I had been advocating just 10 days prior, ended up killing them. I wonder how she dealt with that. I wonder if there was any type of investigation, but then, how would I ever know?? There was no communication initiated by Child Services with this mama after the boys died. There was no inquiry involving this mother and stepfather of the slain children (aka Brent and me). None. I assume that was because they did not get involved. They were probably hoping that this case would find its way into a dead file box in some back room in a government office where it would lie dormant and covered with dust forever. Not going to happen. However, I have to be of clear mind when I contact the appropriate authorities and share my concerns regarding the handling of my case, not allowing my anger to interfere with my message. I believe that Child Services must take some responsibility for their non-action in the deaths of my children and change policies that allowed such a tragedy to occur.

Oilers Game December 17th, 2016

Chapter 31

THE LAST SELFIE

TRACY TOOK POSSESSION OF THE DUPLEX ON WEDNESDAY, DECEMBER 14TH, and fully furnished it to accommodate the two active boys. Except for their new beds, which would arrive on Monday, everything was in place. It was her weekend and she was excited to show the youthful hockey players their new Spruce Grove home. She and Brent had decided she would move to the boys' hockey community of Spruce Grove and have the boys live with her. Brent would remain in Whitecourt but they would manage the new situation. Tracy was adamant that she had to get her boys under her care again.

Radek had begun to share even more little pieces of information, and Tracy was extremely unsettled with what she was hearing about the boys' life in their dad's house. Ryder continued to say little in the typical "Don't ask. Don't tell" fashion of the male gender, but more and more often she would hear him say, "Mom. Just make the move happen."

On Friday, December 16th, Tracy picked up the boys from school. Each time she saw them they appeared to have grown even taller and more mature in their looks, even though it was rarely little more than a week between visits. She dropped Ryder and his friend Ty at the outdoor rink to play shinny. Ty was going to spend the night with Ryder in their new place.

Tracy and Radek watched movies that night while the older boys did their own thing. Saturday morning, Ty was picked up early and Brent arrived after lunch to take Ryder and Radek out to buy them their Christmas presents. The boys were revved when they learned they were each to be the recipient of a PlayStation 4 with accompanying games and accessories. When they arrived back at the duplex, they were excited to set up their new games.

Tracy and Brent planned to return to Whitecourt Sunday night after watching the first two periods of Ryder's 7:00 p.m. game at the Millwoods Recreation

Centre that evening. Tracy would be returning to Spruce Grove to get the boys in a little more than a week. After the Christmas break, Tracy would live in Spruce Grove with the boys. Brent would drive in as often as possible. But today, the couple was just pumped to have the boys for their weekend. After supper, they headed out to cheer on their hometown Edmonton Oilers to a win against the Tampa Bay Lightning. All was going well. Little Mama grabbed her boys for a selfie. It would be her last selfie with her sons.

The Last Selfie

Sunday morning, Tracy drove Radek to his hockey game. On the way home, they stopped and picked up breakfast fixings and returned to the new duplex. After breakfast, they planned out their day, deciding to take in a movie that afternoon and then come back to the duplex and get Ryder ready for his hockey game that evening.

Chapter 32

TEXTING WITH
THE ENEMY

TRS to SYK: I didn't know how the plan of taking the kids away would go down. When I got the boys in my care for my share of the Christmas holidays, I never ever wanted to take them back to Corry's place again. However, I knew I had to get some things in place before then. I wanted everything set up perfectly so there would be no glitches in getting Radek and Ryder under my roof again, full-time. After my exasperating experience with Child Services, I began to think more and more that maybe, just maybe, Corry and I could work together … somehow. I would be close and could deal with any outages between him and the boys. I texted him.

They were harsh texts, Sandra, but they were typical of how our relationship was.

TRS: So just a heads up…I think a meeting is needed! I'm moving to Spruce Grove.

CGM: Why?

TRS: Want to work out a better schedule with the kids. Children's Services called and said a parent from hockey called about Ryder wearing a dress and asked me if I knew and if there was more going on. This is serious Corry!

CGM: Yeah Right!

TRS: Yeah Right! I'm still the primary parent to these kids so either you can work with me or not! Your choice.

CGM: I know Tracy … your so much more of a parent.

TRS: Never said that did I?

CGM: Talk later. I'm busy today

TRS: I said I'm moving to Spruce Grove. I found a place already. I want the kids more. Not being a d*ck but I have the opportunity to be in their lives more and I'm taking it. I will deal with this on my end then or you can meet with me this week and we work something out. Your choice. You can answer me when you're not busy. I'm willing to work with you. Week on? Week Off? Just an option. Gives you more time to concentrate on work and I miss them Corry. Every second weekend isn't working for me.

CGM: I have a hard time trusting you from all your dirty tricks you pulled on me to keep kids from me

TRS: You talking to me about trust Corry?

CGM: So, you moving here full time or just when you have kids?

TRS: Full time. The new year I want it to be different. These kids are my life and I need to be with them more than every second weekend.

CGM: You can take them one night a week. You don't need to move here for that.

TRS: It's already in the works that I'm moving. And I want more than one day a week. Here's what I want … either week on and week off or same schedule as we had before.

CGM: Sorry. I'm not paying you and Brent child support for you to stick the kids with a nanny again. We have a good thing going on here and the kids are happy.

TRS: Pay me and Brent??? You better rethink that text Corry. He's basically raised these kids. Raised them financially. And I have no nanny. I'm moving here.

Well, the offer is on the table to settle an agreement between you and me and the kids.

CGM: LOL. The kids live with me by their choice. You owe me some serious apologies before I give up one second of time with my kids.

TRS: I owe you sh*t Corry. I want more time with the kids and I will get it. I was just going to have you on the same page and "work together" but once again you have a selfish agenda. Take care. I will be in touch.

CGM: I wanted the kids more too but you kept them from me out of spite.

TRS: You didn't live in the same town Corry. F*#k your impossible

CGM: I'm not being selfish. You can have them Thursday before your weekend and Wednesday the other week.

TRS: I'm moving to the same town

CGM: And they need to get to their sports

TRS: I'm done driving back and forth. I got a place in Spruce. In the new year I will live there full time. So, you have to think about this over the holidays. Deal

CGM: Maybe you should have helped me with the driving when you had the chance but you didn't do that out of spite either

TRS: I'm done here. You need to let go of the past or you will never go anywhere in the future.

CGM: In the future I will be doing the best for my kids. As I always have.

TRS: Me too! At least we agree on something lol

CGM: Sorry I don't think you do. You do what's best for Tracy and what's most fun for Tracy

TRS: That's what you think 'cause you hate me. Get over the past. You will see I'm a great Mom who will do anything for my kids.

CGM: I don't hate you. I hate that you took my kids from me. Plain and simple. I spend every second with them that I can and from the past I have learned that is all that is important to me.

TRS: That's what you think. You fail to remember you left them and went to Kelowna and lost everything because you were too busy trying to be a "big shot." … That's the sad reality of your life Corry. Stop blaming me for your silly decisions. I was there for my kids.

CGM: What the f#ck are you talking about "Big shot" You have mental issues. I think it is good you are moving here though

TRS: Yup! You question why I took kids away. I gave you a clear answer

CGM: I don't know what you are trying to say

TRS: I didn't take your f#*king kids away. You f*#king left Whitecourt. Holy F*#k!

CGM: You took them from me in 2008

TRS: You made poor family decisions. A reminder: A motorhome with strippers with your buddies? Your thousands of dollars and lying about strippers in Phoenix at the races? Every day in the lounge drinking? Leaving Radek in the crib while you ran off to the lounge? Oh Corry. You have a bad memory. And I wasn't a wife to sit around and be your personal servant. There's way more I can enlighten your memory with—shall I?

CGM: Bahahaha. Keep making sh*t up. And you were an angel!! And I never left Radek in his crib.!!!!!! That's your move! So now you can f*#k off!

TRS: Lol. I took Ryder to play school and told you Radek was sleeping in his crib. I called you and you were at the Gables Lounge. Remember now??

CGM: Go show your tits off downtown you f*#kin whore! You can justify in your own mind all you want you f*#kin' bar star. You left our kids countless times in the last eight years to go drink and holiday!! Raising your kids by a nanny and you not even in the country. The kids know it so you made your own bed. They chose me over you 'cause I spend time with them. I tried getting along with you over the last eight years and you can't stop f*#kin' me over. Get over it. You talk to me like a piece of sh*t so look around! I don't have to put up with your c*nt. mouth anymore. It was just one week ago you couldn't even show up to watch his hockey game. And two weeks before that you couldn't get them to their hockey cause you had to go party at the Wolverines' game? Nice dedication. And there is no such thing as primary parent. It's primary residence and I have that if you hadn't noticed.

TRS: Wow did I hit a nerve? Sad when you hear the truth about why your family walked out hey? Stop blaming me for your f*#k ups Corry. The kids miss me too. They want to spend time with both of us. You don't want to hear that 'cause you are a control freak but guess what Corry? I'm moving to Spruce so I can see my kids more. I don't have a nanny. I'm a mom who misses my kids dearly. I don't give a F*#k about what you think ***or want. You can either be ok with this and support the kids and what they want or I can go to a lawyer! So, grow the f*#k up and act like an adult. Your name calling doesn't hurt my feelings 'cause I have no feelings about you.so don't waste your breath

CGM: You brought it up Douche Bag.

TRS: I talked to Radek's coach and it was a fun skate so yes, we let the kids hang out with their friends at the Wolverines' game. Does that bug you? LOL Yes, I brought up seeing my kids more and I have a permanent residence in Spruce too

CGM: He wants to play but you don't give a f*#k what they want. Your too busy taking care of your pay check. F*#k off. I need to get ready for my grandma's funeral

TRS: My Pay Check? WTF. If you're busy I can keep them

CGM: Ohhhh! The truth. No. F*#k you. I'll be at Ryder's game to pick them up!

TRS: Not sure what you're talking about. Pay Check? Oh. You're not taking him to his game? Thought drop off was at 5 but ya I can take them. You can stop swearing.

CGM: Drop them off then. Ryder told me you were taking them. F*#k you!!! You swear at me all the time. So, f*#k off Tracy. I tried to be nice when the boys came to live here but you've taken every chance to call me down, call me fat and that I'll be alone my whole life!!! Swear and cuss at me so f*#k you! That's the last straw. You brought up shit from the past so you are the one who needs to get over it. Grow up and stop blaming me for your unhappiness

TRS: Unhappiness. LMFAO. What's wrong with you? I just moved to Spruce to have kids back more. My life couldn't get much better.

CGM: Good then. You can have them an extra day per week.

TRS: Not settling for less than half the time Corry. And I know a judge will give it to me. So, you may as well be on board. The kids love us equally. You don't need to make this more difficult. I'm sure when you were young you wished you could share your parents? No?

CGM: Sorry. The kids won't go for it. They like it here.

TRS: I think they will Corry, Do you blame them for wanting to share us?

CGM: This is nothing but a move to manipulate me and the kids' relationship. The judge will see that and the kids will say they want to stay. So, you can take your chances. I have years of neglect of you not even being in the country. So, if I were you, you better start talking to me with respect as I have to you until you start another fight.

TRS: You talk to me with respect??? Are you f*#king kidding me? And yes. Let's see what the judge says Corry. I will take my chances.

CGM: It doesn't matter what the judge says. It's what the kids say

TRS: I know and I told you four times already that they want to share us.

CGM: When you apologize to me, we will talk. I've made you an offer that the judge will accept. Looks to me like you're just trying to get child support. You have a house in Wct, Spruce & Phoenix. Do you really think the judge will believe Spruce is your primary? LOL. F*#k you you fuckin' gold digger. And another thing. I gave you 250K too and child support to raise these boys so any dollar that came out of Brent's pockets was for your spoiled ass!

TRS: Wow. You think I would move to Spruce for your f*#king $800 a month child support?! Get over yourself.

CGM: You've f*#k me over fir less

TRS: Lmao, right? My spoiled ass took Ryder to experience spring hockey in LA. LOL. See you in court. And you talk to me about giving you respect you f*#king clueless piece of shit!

CGM: F*#k you. You started it as usual. Like I said I don't have to put up with your mouth anymore. The kids chose me! I spent hundreds of nights away from my kids over the last eight years and you can't let me have one f*#king year you selfish piece of shit. F*#k you. I will be fighting for every single hour. Are you taking Ryder to hockey? Or dropping him off here?

TRS: You left them. Remember? So, stop with the pity party.

CGM: Who is taking Ryder to hockey? I'm at the house waiting.

TRS: I'm taking them. Maybe come early and we can have these words to our faces.

CGM: No! I'm dealing with a funeral and then Xmas. I'll talk to you in January. I've got nothing to say to you anyway. You can have them an extra day a week or if you have an event or if I work late.

TRS: I get the kids on the 30th so we will talk then. Pretty cowardly that you have no problem beaking off on text but can't to my face. Typical.

CGM: Are you getting Ryder to his hockey on the 30? And that week?

TRS: What week? 30th is a Friday.

CGM: I can say it to your face. It will mean the same

TRS: Easier to say such ignorant things on text. Pretty sure your lips would be slapped off your face if you said that sh*t to my face.

CGM: He has hockey 30, 31, 1, 2, 5, 7 & 8. Lol! Ya right

TRS: Well then obviously I will take him.

CGM: I'm not going to make a 'seen.' Obviously, you just want to fight. I have kids to raise. I don't care about your drama.

TRS: Nope. I'm just wanting time with the kids. Me too!

CGM: Ya that's why they spent the last four years with a nanny. You had your chance to spend time with them. Chose not to.

TRS: Holy F*#k! Drop the nanny. I spent every day with my kids.

CGM: Bahahaha you believe your own lies

TRS: I believe my own truth

CGM: Lol. Exactly. The kids know how often you left them. I have proof. See you in court.

TRS: Yes, we will. Courts probably don't take lightly to shaving your kid's head and making him wear a dress. But hey what do I know?

CGM: Nothing

TRS: 👄

CGM: Gross

Tracy continued her story in a future email.

TRS to SYK: The texting conversation with Corry ended. I breathed in deeply trying not to let him get to me. The movie was a good distraction and after it finished, we headed back to our new home. The boys rushed up to their rooms and set up their new Play Stations. Brent and I discussed my texting with Corry and we decided to have a family meeting to tell the boys I had told their dad my plans to move to Spruce. We would talk with them about options. I went to get the boys from their rooms.

Chapter 33

THE PRE-GAME MEETING

TRACY'S EMAIL CONTINUED:

Radek was all laid out on his bed excited to show me how cool his new game was. I asked if we could talk for a second.

He paused his game and said: "Sure Mom. What do you want to talk about?"

"Honey," I said. "I told Dad I'm moving to Spruce."

With the biggest look of fear I had ever seen on my child's face, he said, "WHHYYYYYYYYYY?????????"

I told him that I was worried about how back to school would go after the holidays if I just did not return him and Ryder to Dad's home after we got them for our share of the Christmas holidays. I made it sound as though Dad and I would be working together.

I said, "Dad will get fixed, Radek." I told him we would do a week-on and a week-off.

Radek looked terrified, in complete dread of what I had said. His body appeared full of tension. He put his head in his hands and started crying. I put my arms around him and told him I would never let Dad hurt him again. I asked him to come downstairs with me where we would talk as a family. I went to Ryder's room and asked him to join us as well.

Brent and I sat and talked about what was going on, reassuring them that everything would be ok.

"Mom now lives in Spruce," I said. "So, I will be here if anything bad is happening. I will be living close by if you need me."

We gave the boys the option of not going back to Dad's house that evening after the game. I said we would just keep them if they wanted to come with us.

Ryder piped up, "I'm not scared of Dad!"

I told him I wasn't either but it was very clear that Radek was scared to death.

After more discussion, they both decided they would go back to Dad's place that night as they wanted to spend Christmas with him and their cousins.

I hugged my younger son tightly and said, "Everything will be all right, little buddy." He seemed to settle and then returned to his PlayStation in his room.

Later, Ryder came downstairs again and slammed the pantry door after grabbing a snack. I asked him, "What the heck are you doing Ryder?"

He said in a surly voice, "Grabbing a snack!"

I asked, "But why slam the door, Ryder?"

"It's nothing!" he replied in a p*ssy voice.

I asked him why he'd told his dad I was taking him to hockey. In the same tone he said, "Well. Can't you?"

I answered: "Of course we can, Ryder. But what's with the attitude all of a sudden?"

"Nothing!" he replied and turned and left the kitchen.

This was the typical Ryder attitude so I just brushed it off, letting it go. Just those damn teenage hormones, I guess. Or so I thought.

Chapter 34

LAST HUGS

TRS to SYK: We loaded the boys up with their suitcases and hockey gear, took them for a bite to eat, and then headed to Ryder's game. We parked and after Ryder collected his equipment bag from the back of the vehicle, I gave my #3 a big hug. I told him I loved him very much and wished him a good game and a great Christmas as we were gonna leave after the second period and head back to Whitecourt. He said, "I love you too Mom," and promised he would text me later. My eyes followed Ryder's back as he walked to the rink and entered the building. He was getting so tall. I was excited to watch him play. That was the last time I would hug my older son.

Brent and Radek and I headed into the arena to wait for the arrival of our friends. We sat at a little round table in the concession area, sipping on soft drinks. Radek was soon busy scratching lottery tickets, hoping for the big win. I saw Corry come in and head to the concession. He totally ignored us and walked by, showing no emotion. He bought a drink and made no acknowledgement of Radek as he strolled back into the rink.

When the game started, Radek immediately went to sit with his dad, who had grabbed a seat on the opposite side of the arena from us. My boy took turns sitting with Corry and with me as the game continued. It was tough for me to witness this as I knew Radek did not want to upset his dad by only sitting with me during the game even though I would not see him again until the 29th. I was concerned that Radek had been uneasy and scared of his dad's reaction to me telling his father I was moving to Spruce Grove. However, I had a plan. If Corry would not work with me and get some help, he would never ever get the boys back in his home again. I had some work to do in the next few days until I, the custodial parent, would have them in my care.

The Joey Bouchard family arrived to watch the game with us and cheer on Ryder. Joey, a former Whitecourt Wolverine coach, was particularly interested in seeing how much Ryder's skills had improved since he had last seen him play.

Radek adored their little girl, Khyle, and was enjoying hanging out with her, but he made sure he split his time equally with his dad and me. I thought, *What a lot of pressure for a kid!* After the first period, Radek brought over his dad's truck keys to me and said he had to move his stuff over to Dad's truck. I assured my boy that we would do that after the second period. When we were ready to leave, Brent pulled his vehicle up beside Corry's truck. We moved the boys' things into the back seat and then drove Radek to the front of the arena where he and I both got out. I handed him Corry's keys, telling him in typical Mama fashion to make sure he did not lose them!

I hugged my boy tightly and said, "I love you very much Radek," reassuring him that his dad and I would work together. He started crying. I held him away from me and looking directly into his eyes, asked him what was wrong.

Attempting to control his sniffling, he said, "I'm just going to miss you so much."

I pulled him closer, reassuring him that everything would be okay. It was as though he knew he would never see me again.

I hugged him even tighter and said, "Honey, you don't have to go to Dad's. You can come home with me."

He shook his head vigorously, took the sleeve of his jacket to wipe his eyes, and sniffed through the tears as he stuttered, "Dad can't see me crying 'cause he will be really mad."

He sucked in his upset with a deep breath and said shakily, "I'll be ok." He appeared so torn. Afraid of disappointing his dad and yet, missing being with his mom. I swore under my breath as I comforted my son. My second boy wore his heart on his sleeve. He was so soft.

My eyes followed Radek as he walked back into the rink. I never knew that would be the last moment I would ever see my younger son. How I wish with every bone in my body that I had never let the boys go with their dad that night.

Later that week, she continued in another email.

TRS to SYK: After Radek's emotional reaction to my leaving and the fact that the text conversation with Corry didn't go so smoothly, I told Brent that we had to stay in Spruce Grove instead of heading back to Whitecourt. I wanted to be close by that night in case the kids needed me.

I remained calm as we drove to the duplex. I thought about the texting between me and Corry these last two days, knowing in my mind that since he'd refused my offer of shared custody, I was taking the boys back. I knew parenting young boys could be challenging, but I believed Corry's home had become unsafe for my kids. I was becoming more and more determined that Corry would not get them in his care again. I would find a way to remove them from his home. I went over my plan in my head. Everything would be okay.

Corry's Last Words

At 10:34 p.m. Brent and Tracy were settling in for the night at the duplex when a text from Corry came in on Tracy's phone:

CGM to TRS: I am willing to work something out but I want an apology for the time you made me drive from Red Deer to Whitecourt for Ryder's birthday weekend and you wouldn't let me take the kids and you told the cop it was because I didn't email you, just texted.[12] Also, an apology for when you booked your holidays two times on my week and I didn't see them for almost two months. Also, you will mind your own business when it comes to discipline in my house as I have for you the last eight years. And, I'm not paying a cent for child support. All holidays will be booked on our own time.

TRS: I looked over at Brent about to text Corry a "Go F*#k Yourself" message. Brent looked back at me and said: "Just leave it alone, Tracy. It's late. We'll deal with it tomorrow. He can have his f'ing $800 a month."

---

12   Regarding this incident Tracy explained in a later email: "The kids had begged me to not let them go with him!"

Chapter 35

FILICIDE

FILICIDE IS LEGALLY DEFINED AS THE DELIBERATE ACT OF A PARENT KILLING his/her own child. In December 2016, Corry MacDougall was guilty of the crime of filicide against not one but two of his children before he turned the gun on himself and fired, killing himself as well. Dr. Peter Jaffe, professor in the Faculty of Education at Western University who has done extensive research in the area of filicide reports there are approximately thirty cases a year in Canada where a parent has deliberately killed a child.* Often such acts of violence are meet with total disbelief that a man could actually kill his offspring. Too often such killings occur in the context of the parents' separation and are linked to an act of revenge when a mother has left the relationship [13] How can such tragedies be prevented? The authors cited in the research believe that paternal filicide may be preventable with better education about coercive control. Coercive control refers to the means by which to dominate individual women by using three equally important tactics: intimidation, isolation and control[14] Controlling and coercive behaviors are too often minimized and misunderstood by society where violence against women is only understood as physical violence. These abusive interactions may seem normal on the surface and may not even be recognized as controlling by the courts as controllers have subtle and unique ways of threatening their partners or ex-partners. Furthermore, male control of women and female subservience are normalized in our culture.

Corry MacDougall was a master of coercive control. He defied Court Orders. He did not return the boys as directed in such Court Orders or would

---

13   Lori Chambers, Deb Zweep & Nadia Verrelli, UBC Law Review Vol 51:3 Paternal Filicide and Coercive Control: Reviewing the Evidence in Cotton V Berry.

14   Evan Stark, Coercive Control: The Entrapment of Women in Personal Life (OxFord:Oxford University Press, 20070 AT 5 (Stark Coercive Control).)

no show or arrive late to pick up or return the boys. He intimidated not only his ex-wife but his boys as well. Tracy was afraid to do anything that would cause further difficulties for her boys when in their father's home. He humiliated Tracy in front of his friends and he continually talked down to the boys about their mother. Too often courts do not consider evidence of abuse or control of the mother as relevant to custody. There is a general societal belief that children do better when they have their biological father in their lives even when he is abusive to their mother. It is often thoughts that the two behaviors are totally unrelated. However, men who control and/or abuse their wives or ex-wives are not stellar parents and present a serious risk to their children if not physically, then psychologically.

A study published in the *Journal of the American Academy of Psychiatry and the Law* concluded that a majority of perpetrators of filicide were experiencing significant life stressors, socially isolated with few supports, and suffered a history of abuse during their childhood. Motivational factors for paternal filicide include personal feelings of inadequacy and a lack of parenting skills and coping skills.[15]

Too often, courts do not consider evidence of abuse or control of the mother as relevant to custody. While courts are urged to assess the risk of child abuse postseparation they often lack an understanding of coercive control and therefore, rarely consider the possible lethality for children in the midst of high-conflict separations.

The harm created by witnessing violence and control are often misunderstood and minimized by child welfare authorities and courts despite an extensive body of literature illustrating that children who grow up witnessing violence are more likely to perpetuate the cycle of violence in adulthood and have a lower level of academic engagement, social well-being and adjustment.[16]

The unfathomable crime of a parent taking the life of a child has historically rocked communities to the core as it did in the communities of Whitecourt and Spruce Grove. People are left to wonder what kind of man could do such a heinous act.

---

15 Bourget, Dominique, Grace, Jennifer & Whitehurst, Laurie "A Review of Maternal and Paternal Filicide, Journal of the American Academy of Psychiatry and the Law, Volume 35, Number 1, 2007.

16 Jaffe, Dr. Peter- General Information taken from articles and talks by Dr. Peter Jaffe (See information in italics above)

Information not cited specifically is taken from lectures, news reports and articles by Dr. Peter Jaffe, a psychologist and Professor in the Faculty of Education at Western University and the Academic Director of the Centre for Research and Education on Violence Against Women & Children. Dr Jaffe has completed extensive study in the area of filicide and domestic violence. For further information on Dr. Peter Jaffe and his dedicated work go to: http://.edu.uwo.ca-faculty profiles-peter jaffe to begin your search.

Chapter 36

REVISITING THE SCENE
OF THE CRIME

IT WAS JULY 2017. OVER SIX MONTHS HAD PASSED SINCE CORRY HAD KILLED his kids. Tracy was still tormented by so many questions. A few days after the murder-suicide, Corry's brother, who then had control of Corry's house, had called Brent and asked him to go into the home to retrieve any of the boys' belongings that Tracy might want. When Brent had entered the home, he was drawn to the many sticky notes all over the mirrors detailing goals Corry had set for himself along with ... a sticky note with Tracy's Apple ID scrawled on it. Old photographs of Corry and Tracy and the boys smiled from the framed pictures on the bedside tables in the boys' rooms. Then Brent came upon ... the shrine. There in Corry's closet was a vast collection of pictures of Tracy, Corry and Tracy as a couple, and pictures of their family of four from days long gone by. Tracy had left the marriage nine years prior.

In discussions regarding what Brent had found and had not found in Corry's home, the couple began to ask questions as they tried to piece the puzzle together. There were things Brent did not want to discuss with Tracy, protecting her from the reality of what he had seen that cold winter's morning. There were things he felt she didn't need to know, to hear, or to see. However, she was relentless in her pursuit of attempting to determine how her boys had died and other questions that would haunt her days, nights, weeks, and months after the incident. The questions included:

- Why were there so many pictures of Tracy in Corry's closet? If he hated her so much, why was he saving all her pictures?
- Why were there gun casings in Corry's bedside drawer?

- Why did Corry have Tracy's Apple ID on a post-it note on the bathroom mirror?
- Where did Corry get Tracy's Apple ID?
- Where was the missing iPad that Ryder had taken from the Stark household to his dad's house?
- Why was Ryder's cell phone found under Corry's body?
- Why was Corry obsessed with losing weight?
- Was this simply a rage-filled event or was this Corry's ultimate plan?

These were merciless questions, but not knowing what had transpired was perhaps as difficult as knowing what actually did. Like detectives, Brent and Tracy attempted to lay out the clues as they speculated on what had actually happened that night.

Tracy also had a list of questions for the investigators, who then questioned her questions! She wanted to know what kind of shotgun had been used in the murders. The investigators wanted to know why it mattered what kind of shotgun was used. The boys were dead, as was the perpetrator. Case closed.

She asked, "Why did it f*#king matter what kind of gun was used? It mattered because it might determine my older boy's experience that night. It mattered because they were my sons. That's why it mattered!"

As time went by, Tracy was furious that anyone would question why she wanted such information. She had birthed those boys into being and she wanted all the details of their deaths. Difficult as it was, she was glad it was she and Brent who had found the boys rather than Corry's dad or brother or a stranger or friend who may have stopped by in a day or two. She was their mom. She was the one, the one who should find them after their last breaths as she had been with each of them in birth when they had taken their first. And now? Now she wanted to know how things had unfolded in their deaths. She was tortured with only being able to guess what had gone on in Corry's home the night they were killed. She wanted more evidence.

The Medical Examiner

As Tracy shared her concerns in an email, I asked, "Tracy, in his report, what did the Medical Examiner surmise?"

TRS TO SYK: I have never read the autopsies of the boys. Brent does not want me to do so. Again, he wants to protect me, saying that it would be life changing. So, I do not know exactly what the Medical Examiner wrote. I only know what I know from Brent's having read it and his sharing of information from the report with me. I know Radek was shot in the head and died instantly while sleeping. Ryder was shot at numerous times with one shot missing him completely as evidenced by the bullet found in the wall behind his bed. He was then shot in the chest at the landing. That shot killed him. However, Corry then took the shotgun and shot Ryder one more time in the head. Just sharing this information blows me away as I cannot believe any father could be so heartless to his defenceless boys.

When I received Tracy's email, I thought, *God! This is too much for me and I hardly knew the boys! What must have been going on for her as she wrote this?* I was concerned about her state of mind in writing about the trauma. I sent her a text.

SYK to TRS: Can we meet tomorrow morning Tracy? I will come in early. We need to process this.

She agreed to meet. It was too raw. Too activating. We met the next day to slow down the process, working together, taking our time as we explored her experience regarding that night of chaos. We worked in small pieces of what she knew from the evidence of what had transpired. In our next few sessions, the template of my regulated nervous system[17] provided Tracy with the assistance she needed in letting go of the activation in her nervous system – in her trauma cup - drip by drip.

A Total Zombie

As we continued to work together, more of the trauma of finding the boys came up ready to be released.

Tracy breathed in the silence of the room as she sat in the blue chair of the AIM counselling room. "You know Sandra, the day the boys died, I was a total

---

17   Regulated nervous system: A balanced and healthy nervous system able to manage the unavoidable stresses of daily living. Once the nervous system is balanced, individuals are able to experience joy, closeness in relationships and vitality and resilience in the body (Dr. Lynne Zettl, CFTRE) Such is necessary in those working with individuals dealing with trauma.

zombie. I couldn't think. I couldn't breathe. I couldn't concentrate on any one thing. I was totally spinning. Sometimes I still have that weird feeling in my head."

"Can you describe it to me?" I asked.

She responded: "I felt dizzy for one and antsy as well and just wanted to run away."

I looked at her and said, "In your imagination, I want you to envision yourself running away from that day right here. Right now. What foot would you start with?"

She responded. "My right."

"So, Tracy, in your imagination just take off running away from the scene as fast as you can over hills and through valleys, beside highways and across meadows, feeling your feet alternating as you run and run and run far far away from Corry's house."

Her eyes closed.

On December 19, she could not fight and she could not flee from what she had seen that day, so today we ran away from it all, letting her body begin to thaw the freeze which had been locked in her body. We continued this imagining for a long, long time, running over hills and through valleys, on highways and in ditches, releasing more of the activation in her system. She was completely engaged and when she opened her eyes, she looked totally spent.

"Good work, Tracy. Just letting go of more of that activation." I waited as she recovered from the arduous release, and then I asked, "What are you noticing ... now?"

"I am totally exhausted, Sandra."

"Well, you have done some incredible work here. Just releasing more activation, more of the trauma in your system."

After such intense work over a few sessions, we took a break until she felt ready to rebook. Again, we met in the AIM office. She looked rested. She shared that she had been thinking a lot about her history with Corry after they split. "It had always been hard for me when the boys were not directly in my care. I would be missing their presence and sometimes I would be worrying about them being under Corry's roof. They were just little and he could be so tough on them."

"I can only imagine how difficult that would be, Tracy," I said. "What did you miss most when they were with Corry?"

"I missed simple things, like hearing their stories, playing with them, snuggling them. I missed kissing them good night, reading to them or with them. I even missed washing their hair and brushing their teeth and that smell that only little boys have when it's been a while since they have had a bath."

She laughed a gentle laugh and then sighed. "We did get into a good weekly routine after we split. When Corry had the boys, I worked long shifts at Boston Pizza just so when my week to have the boys came, I could be home with them. I was always excited to hug them tightly when we made the exchange and they were back in my care. For years I endured a husband who believed that he was the most important member of our family because he was bringing home the bigger pay cheque. Corry was not out of town for work much when we were together but was often gone at night or sledding on the weekends in the winter. I had always been independent, so I didn't mind Corry's lifestyle and his need for his male 'bonding' until we were raising two little guys and then the cracks began to appear in our relationship. I was working hard in the company along-side Corry as well as looking after the home front. Corry was obsessed with making money and spending it. He was a part of that oil patch culture."

I listened thoughtfully to her story as she shared her experience as the wife of an oilman.

She continued: "I learned early that I needed to earn my keep every day of the year as his business 'servant' as well as doing everything else to make our family run well. Oil was still flowing freely and so was money. Even in the later years, that culture had not shifted a lot. Corry's response to my take on things when we expanded our family was simple. 'Deal with it, Tracy! This is the way things are! Know your place in the scheme of things!'"

She continued, "By 2007, I was no longer willing to live that way. I wanted more in my life than simply giving my kids all the toys and trips that money could buy. Although he did not yet know it, my relationship with Corry was done, but when you decide to split up and still have children, you are never truly done. I thought and had hoped that Corry and I might be able to main-tain a friendship after the split. Unfortunately, once money becomes the issue on the table, friendship becomes impossible for many couples once alimony and child support and splitting the assets of a marriage move front and centre. It seemed particularly hard when it is the wife initiating leaving the marriage because husbands didn't get why a woman would want to leave such a 'cushie' situation and many were truly oblivious to the fact that something was wrong in their marriage!"

"Did you grow up in that same kind of environment as the one you lived with Corry?" I asked.

"Yes and no," she replied. "My mom seemed to do everything and my dad was always working, but he never worked in the 'Patch' and was home every night. We didn't live a high lifestyle like the one I did when Corry and I were together. In fact, in one of my rants, I wrote something on Facebook a while ago. I'll see if I can find it." She reached for her phone and began to scroll.

"Here it is," she said as she cleared her throat and began sharing the post.

Chapter 37

THE HOUSE THAT BUILT ME...

Facebook Post * Summer 2017

Tracy Stark

I was built in a home with family values. We weren't wealthy but we had each other. We were raised to have respect for each other and others. We ate supper as a family every night. Us kids grew up with a budget for clothing, sports, and extracurricular activities.

This didn't mean brand-name clothes, or sports such as hockey or dance ... this meant $100 at the Saan Store, school sports (although travel was NOT AN option), a bike to get around, and a swimming pool pass.

When I became a mom in 2003 ... I had a son, Ryder Patryk. This beautiful boy was raised to have everything. He rode a dirt bike. He rode a kitty kat snowmobile. He had a trampoline in the back yard. He had a new bike, and when he turned 5, he was enrolled in hockey. In 2005, when I had another son, Radek Stryker, he too would experience all of the above.

This was just the Whitecourt way of life in the early 2000s .... for what I knew anyway ... In 2007, although I had a great life for me and my kids, it was at an expense ...

The expense was: As a wife you take care of the babies, you do all the books, safety, and hotshots (with babies in tow), and prepare a "meat and potatoes" home-cooked meal every night while Husband goes out drinking (they call these business meetings) and went on boys' trips every second weekend.

This was the norm to me. I was just grateful to give my boys a great life … BUT I go back to the house that built me …

One day I was asked what I did for my new Jeep … besides the obvious of toting around two young boys and everything to make my family go round … I had no answer besides this … That was the day my life changed forever … See ya later Corry MacDougall.

In 2007 I left my kids' dad … it was a custody battle for the books … a custody battle that in the end … cost the lives of my kids.

I interrupted. "Hold on, Tracy, if that's okay. Just put your phone down for a minute and feel the support of the chair." I could feel her anger toward Corry rising to the surface and wanted to work with it for a bit to release more activation from her nervous system.

Time passed as we worked together going back and forth from the past to the present continually reminding her that the traumatic experience was over. We imagined scenarios that helped release the activation. I waited until she opened her eyes.

"Tracy," I said, reminding her of our first session when I had explained what happened when trauma occurred. "We have a part of our brain commonly called the animal brain and when in a situation where you cannot fight and you cannot flee, trauma gets frozen in your nervous system. You can't out-think trauma. It is frozen in your body. What is happening now is that you are simply releasing that freeze."

As time went on, her shoulders started to drop even more.

I continued, "If it is okay, just look around the room for a moment, Trac."

She followed my recommendation and after a minute or so, I said simply, "It's over, Tracy. I need you to breathe that in. IT IS OVER."

Chapter 38

NO LONGER A STRANGER
– HERE IN THE MOMENT

IT WAS MID-AUGUST AND SHE WAS BACK. I COULD SEE HER SORROW BREAKING off piece by piece—session by session, as she attempted to mend her fractured soul in the presence of a regulated nervous system, aka mine … I asked myself, *How can we turn this pain resonating in her body into power?* Some in my field called it activating post-traumatic growth. Firstly, we had to decrease the activation. Sitting with Tracy, I focused on my awareness of the changes in her physicality, paying attention to her breathing in and out, feeling the support of the chair, staying with her in the moment, wanting to find something—anything, to soothe the deep, deep longing within my own soul to ease her anguish. She was no longer a stranger.

I had lit a candle on the coffee table before she arrived, inviting the boys into the room to share time together with us. When she arrived, I administered my symptom check list. She reported she still had intrusive imagery and flashbacks, nightmares and night terrors, frequent crying, depression, feelings of impending doom, and the need for alcohol to relax. We still had a way to go in her healing.

We gently dissected her story, attempting to get it down into sizable chunks to work with, so she did not become overwhelmed and dissociate on me. We worked with little bits of activation. I attempted to work with the grief, but when she shared more of the story too quickly for her nervous system and there was too much activation, we came back to the present moment.

She had figured it out in her head. She felt that Corry had hated her and meant to destroy her, but regardless of her attempting to make sense of the tragedy in her neocortex, the trauma was in her body. That was where we worked. I was focused on noticing the pallor of her cheeks, the tension in her neck as we sat in stillness, breathing in and out, sometimes moving to have her track the breath or the sensations in her body she was experiencing. We were not back "there." We were "right here," fully present, in this moment.

She began to speak. "He was so angry that my life was going forward while he was stuck in his sorry story. He hated me for leaving him and building a better life with the boys. He wanted me to suffer. I …"

Again, I interrupted. "Come back here, my girl. Here! With me. Right now! Just feel the support of the chair and breathe."

She acquiesced.

"How have you survived?" I asked.

Her eyes filled with tears. She reached for a Kleenex and I waited for her reply.

"Well, Brent and I are constantly busy, so I don't sit around thinking about it all the time. The writing you have asked me to do has helped too. I have these angry headaches and sometimes, I just want to up and go. Anywhere! Driving is good and seems to be calming for me." Then she repeated, "But, as I said, Brent and I have been in a slump. We aren't exercising and I am feeling blah and totally unmotivated to do anything."

"Tracy," I responded. "It is critical that you look after the woman wearing your clothes and brushing your teeth even when you do not feel like it. Don't count on Brent to work out with you. That has to be his decision and honestly, if you can add a work out to a part of your day, it will help you to keep the anxiety and depression at bay. Such behaviour is one of the best 'medications' by far! It will even give your whisky a challenge!"

She laughed a quiet laugh as I continued my little lecture. "I think a positive routine first thing in the morning aimed at inner and outer well-being would set you up to have that 'good' day we talk about, my friend."

Tracy nodded and responded with, "Okay. I will think about putting a routine in place, now our new gym is finished. It's good to be in the new house. In a way, it's a new start. I am more of a morning person than Brent, so maybe I could try the mornings."

I sent her a high-five across the room.

She paused as our discussion moved to being in the new home in the country. "It is very different being out there. I do have so much more time to think and sometimes that's a good thing and sometimes, not so good." She smiled. "And sometimes it is very lonely. We miss people just dropping in. We had always had a house full of people and sometimes it's particularly hard for Brent to adjust to the quiet of our lives now. We do a fair bit of travelling, but right now, when we're home, I need the serenity of the country. However, I am afraid of the cougars and bears that frequent the area, so I don't go far from the house when I venture outside."

"What do you notice when you think about the predators just lickin' their lips waiting for you on the perimeter of your property?" I asked, teasing her.

She laughed. "Okay, Wild Woman of the Woods. Actually, I am terrified!"

I continued: "What are you noticing in your body, Tracy?"

She took a minute and then said, "My stomach is tight."

"Just notice that sensation, if that is okay," I remind her. "Remember trauma is in the body, not the experience. When we work with anything that disturbs you, we are emptying your trauma cup."

We worked with her fears, tracking the sensations in her body, and gradually she responded with the symptoms of release. We were back in the mode of decreasing activation.

Option B

Wanting to share a passage with Tracy, I reached for a recently-released book resting on my desk entitled *Option B*,[18] written by Sheryl Sandberg, CEO of Facebook and her therapist, co-author Adam Grant. The book detailed Sheryl's loss of her husband Dave while on a trip to Mexico when Dave collapsed and died after a run on the treadmill in the resort's gym.

Just two weeks after losing her husband, Sheryl had to find a fill-in for a father-child activity at the school of one of her children, and she cried out to a friend, "I want Dave."

Her friend had replied, "Option A is not available. So, let's just kick the sh#t out of Option B." Such an interaction led to Sheryl's book titled aptly, *Option B*.

I shared the story and then said to Tracy, "Of course, we know what your Option A is Tracy, but let's establish your Option B and then we too will kick the sh*t out of it!"

She breathed in as she pondered her own Option B. We created a list.

---

18 Sheryl Sandberg and Adam Grant, *Option B: Facing Adversity, Building Resilience, and Finding Joy* (New York, NY: Alfred A. Knopf, Publisher, 2017).

1. To maintain an amazing and healthy marriage
2. To watch Alesha and Shelby continue to grow up, get married, and have children if they so choose and have an active role in the lives of those children
3. To find ways to immortalize my sons and make a difference in the lives of other women and children
4. To share my story in hopes of inspiring other men and women both singularly and collectively to speak up about injustices in systems that are failing them and which failed me and my boys
5. To work to influence those in positions of power to change policies and procedures that do not adequately protect children
6. To accept that there is a greater plan for me that I do not yet fully know but once I find it, to work that plan to make every day a Good Day to Have a Good Day!

We had a vision statement starting to rise! The session ended and as Tracy rose from the chair, I handed her the new book saying, "This is for you, Tracy. Sometimes, another person's story of resilience can help too."

She smiled and gave me a hug, thanking me for the book.

I looked directly at her as I released her arms. "So, my friend, let's kick the sh#t out of your Option B!"

Later that evening, I sent her a text:

> SYK: After you left, I snuffed out the candle and thanked the boys for their loving presence today. Guess they just needed to know their precious mom was okay. Good work Tracy Stark!

Chapter 39

THE BAREFOOT BABE

TRACY CONTINUED TO DIP IN AND OUT, AS WAS HER PATTERN. IT WAS September and I hadn't seen her since August. She had left my office feeling more focused and I was hoping to continue our work together over the next few weeks. As she'd left our last session, she had given me a big smile and said, "I will call you to reschedule!"

She had booked but cancelled as Brent had surprised her with a trip to be a part of Dr. Phil's audience in Los Angeles. Then he had whisked her off on another adventure. He was diligent in making sure Tracy was constantly on the move, terrified of that depression kicking the sh*t out of her.

When I checked my schedule for November 07, 2017, I was happy to see the name Tracy Stark staring back at me from the 10:00 a.m. slot. Her beautiful smile again greeted me as I entered the waiting room. We walked together to the AIM office and once there, we settled in our chairs. She looked good as always, her bare feet caressing the floor.

"I see you are still wearing your favourite footwear even in this cold weather," I observed.

She looked down at her bare feet and laughed. "Yes. I would never wear shoes or boots if I didn't have to, but I did leave my boots at the door!"

I laughed with her again and watched as she sank more deeply into the blue chair. It was a free and easy conversation after not seeing each other for a while.

"So, my friend," I began, "what's going well?"

She paused and breathed in deeply.

I waited.

"Well Sandra. I am frustrated. Brent and the girls …"

"Hold on Tracy," I interrupted. "I will hear everything you have to say. We have lots of time but firstly tell me please, what's going well?"

She scrunched up her face. "I forgot you want me to think of something positive!"

I smiled at her.

She paused for a moment. "Well, as always, Brent continues to keep me very busy. We have been doing a lot of travelling. I do not know how I could have made it through this past year without him by my side."

"And what do you notice when you think of having Brent beside you on this challenging journey. That he wants to protect you and take care of you?"

Again, she breathed in and then responded, "He's wonderful in that way."

"Just notice as you reflect on that statement if that's okay," I say. I watched and saw her visibly relax, her shoulders again dropping away from her ears as she breathed in and felt the support of the chair.

She nodded before she began to speak. "But Sandra, sometimes I get angry with Brent and the girls. They still do not talk about the boys and sometimes I think if I talk about Ryder or Radek, they are uncomfortable. Brent is so afraid I will be sad, and I think Alesha and Shelby are worried that I will start crying and … I might!"

"Just feel the support of the chair, Tracy." I softened my eyes and leaned forward as she followed my directions. "It does sound like you have a good support team around you, but I am sure not talking about the boys is difficult for you. They were and will always be an important part of your life."

"I do have a great team, many friends and family, but sometimes I just want to talk about the boys with Brent and the girls. It's like no one in our little family wants to talk about them. Everybody is just focused on their own lives, their own issues. Never do we sit as a family and talk about Ryder and Radek. It's like they are forgotten. It's like they never existed. I am now just part of Brent and his girls, when before, we were all a family. That makes me feel so broken and alone."

I watched as she began tearing up and I addressed her frustration with her family. "You know, Tracy," I said, "One of the hardest things in families when someone dies is that each family member may process grief quite differently. Men have been socialized to take care of 'the women,' so they think they cannot show any vulnerability because they believe others will see them as weak. They may not allow themselves to get in touch with their feelings of grief and despair. They may have been taught that strong men do not cry and so unfortunately many unresolved feelings stay inside, and as I said before, these are the most dangerous feelings. For some people, getting in touch with those soft feelings is difficult. Be gentle with Brent and with the girls as they may simply be grieving in their own way."

I moved my chair closer to her as I began to speak again. "Moving through grief taxes both the mind and the body, and if you keep all the thoughts and feelings inside? Well, your body can react with all kinds of unhealthy symptoms or behaviours, which can distance you further from life. If it is okay, let's take a minute and again just feel the support of the chair and notice your breath as you feel that frustration in your body."

She breathed in deeply.

"That chair is a safe place for you to actively grieve, to talk about the boys, to feel your broken heart in the presence of someone who has no worries if you cry or rage or swear or … disengage. This is your personal 'inside' work to heal. Remember. Here we talk. We breathe. We titrate. We resource. We release. I hear your angst, but remember feelings are neither right nor wrong. They just are and, if you can allow whatever feelings you are experiencing to arise and sit with them a minute, honestly, they will pass through."

She sniffled as she nodded in understanding.

I added, "I think one of the most difficult things for families, aside from losing their loved ones, is that everyone may be grieving very differently. Remember there is no timeline for grief and no one way to do it."

"I should have been here last month just to vent!" she retorted. "I have been p#ssed at all of them!" Her voice became louder as she spat out her words of frustration.

"I hear you, Tracy! Just notice where you are experiencing that 'p#ssed off' sensation in your body now."

She took a minute to key in on the sensation and gradually she began to release the tension in her body. "Yes." She nodded; her eyes closed. "I am feeling more and more relaxed now."

"How do you know you are more relaxed?" I asked.

"Well, I could probably fall asleep now."

"Go ahead, Trac. I will hand you a Kleenex if you drool."

She smiled a weak smile and we went on—just two nervous systems breathing in and out in our little corner of the universe. She then inhaled a deep breath and opened her eyes. "Hey, that was pretty cool, Sandra. I actually do feel much calmer now."

"Right on. You know, Tracy, your family members and your friends are all doing the best they know of grieving the boys. They all just want the pain to go away too. And they do not want to see you suffer."

She began to break down again. "I know," she sniffled. "I am … just … so sad … and f"'in' p*ssed off! Maybe I just want someone to be angry at!"

The tears were again flowing as we sat together in silence. I kept my ground, witnessing her anguish as she continued to sob, releasing more of the activation in her nervous system. As her tears gradually stopped, I spoke gently to my client. "You have made it through one of the very worst incidents a mother could possibly experience, Tracy. You have survived the trauma of losing your boys in such a dramatic and terrifying manner. Now we must let your body know you survived."

"Okay," she said, catching her breath.

I reminded her of her survival of the December 19th incident, repeating over and over the phrase "You made it!" as she breathed in that reality.

"It is okay to survive, Tracy. No guilt. Your thoughts may go to 'I should have done something different,' but that does not mean you have to suffer until you die. Remember, pain is a given. Suffering is optional and the degree of suffering depends solely on how you chose to think about a situation. If you change your thoughts, you can actually begin to change your life. Thoughts are not facts, Tracy. They are just f'in' thoughts!

She nodded in understanding and then said, "I have been trying so hard to understand the whys behind Corry's behaviour. He was obsessive about things, but I continue to wonder if this was a premeditated act or simply a sudden attack of rage." She continued, "And why did he have guns in his home? He wasn't a hunter. And the gun casings in his bedside table? And the collage of pictures of me and him in his closet ten years after we split? And … why does mental illness become the excuse for all the raging behaviours of killers!!" Her voice was rising.

It's Over

"If it is okay, Tracy, just feel the chair underneath you. You have every right to be upset. In fact, if it is okay, let's work with this for a while."

She nodded again and then went on. "As I mentioned, Sandra, I was never scared of him when we were together. He would rage but it never phased me much. I was used to hearing lots of yelling growing up. Corry would swear and yell and call me all kinds of names but I would never strike him."

"Hmmm," I responded. "Did your boys witness these kinds of interactions between you and Corry?"

"Unfortunately, my Ryder saw and heard way too much," she said. "It scared him."

"Well, Tracy, you present to me as very resilient, but I can only imagine how tough some days are. You know, taking a pen and writing whatever comes up can be therapeutic in letting go of some of the angst you are experiencing. As well, if you write of your experiences, maybe you can help others who find themselves in challenging situations with their former partners and inspire them by telling your story. We can also use the information you share in such writing to release more of the activation in your body."

She cleared her throat and then said, "I hear you. Honestly, I do! Maybe someday, but not right now. It is too fresh. Too overwhelming."

As we finished our session, she rose from the chair. "I hope you saw I booked three sessions in a row."

"I did," I reply. "Good job today! Remember we are closing down old neural pathways and building new ones in your brain. You may feel a little upset, but it will pass. You did great work today. Call me if you find you feel too activated and I will see you before our next scheduled session."

She stood, as did I. "Brent told me I would feel better if I saw you," she said quietly, "and every time, I do feel better. I should have been here sooner! Thank you! Are you sure you didn't cast a spell on me?" she joked.

I laughed. "Today, Trac, we were simply releasing trauma. I save my spells for the weekend."

We looked at each other, eyeball to eyeball. "It's over, Tracy." I paused. "You made it through all that chaos. It's over."

"I have, haven't I, Sandra? It is over!" She rose again and exited the room.

I breathed in. It was over. I returned to my chair and felt its support. I was totally spent. Thank God my waiting room ... was empty!

Chapter 40

CRACKED OPEN

HERE IT WAS NOVEMBER 13, 2017. SHE WAS HERE! TWO WEEKS IN A ROW. WE were leading up to the anniversary of the death of the boys and it had to be constantly on her mind. I flashed her a smile as she settled into the chair in the meditation room of my log home to continue our work together. Because she found driving grounded her, we started to meet at my home thirty kilometres from town.

Sitting firmly in the leather chair, she looked at me as she crossed her legs. "I know. I know," she started. "You want to know 'What is going well?'" She formed the quotation marks with her fingers in the air and drew the word "well" out a little sarcastically.

"You're getting to be a regular now, Tracy. You know the drill very well! Soon you'll be taking over my chair," I teased.

She laughed. "Right!"

"So," I ask. "What is going well?"

"I really was thinking about this as I was on my way here. So many people have been so kind and so supportive since the boys died and that has been helpful. It has been very overwhelming sometimes, and yet at the same time, it is a wonderful feeling to receive such love and encouragement from so many people."

She adjusted her position in the chair as she continued. "The evening of December 16th, there will be an *R&R* Memorial Wolverine Hockey Game to honour the boys." She paused to take a drink of her Red Bull. "During the afternoon, people are going to be able to come to the rink and paint messages on the ice for our family in memory of Radek and Ryder. Anyone can come and grab some paint and a paint brush and write a message or draw a picture. I am going to arrive before anyone else and write my own message on the ice, and then I will stay for a bit as many of the boys' friends will be arriving to write their own messages. I miss those young boys and want to give them the tightest hugs as I know it will be hard for them too!" She paused again. "We are expecting a huge crowd, so I am a little intimidated but it is humbling to think of so many people coming forth with such caring and concern for our family."

I broke in. "And you have the Wolverine's Den to retreat to if you become overwhelmed. Right? To gather yourself ... if you need it. Right, Tracy?"

"You are right, Sandra." She sighed. "I do."

"What do you notice when you think of this expression of caring and compassion?" I asked.

"Well, it is absolutely wonderful and comforting but ..."

"Hold on, Trac. What are you noticing in your body right now?"

"I am trying to feel a little more relaxed."

"Take a minute if it is okay, but don't try to relax. Just notice what you are experiencing."

She breathed in again. "Yes. I am feeling more relaxed."

"What does 'relaxed' feel like today?" I asked.

She breathed in and said, "Not this again. Well, Sandra, I don't know! It just feels like, you know, relaxed!"

"Tracy, that's like saying an egg feels like an egg. What are you noticing that tells you that you are more relaxed?" I asked, trying not to sound frustrated with my client. We had been here many times before. I breathed in.

"Okay, I get you. I've been gone too long!" Her voice started to rise. "Okay. Maybe I am not relaxed. Really? When I close my eyes, all I can think about is the Memorial Game and I feel completely stressed! I can't do this today, Sandra!"

I needed to bring her back into this moment. Right now. "Okay, Tracy. Just come back here right now—just you and me. Two nervous systems just breathing in and out!" We breathe in. I paused on my in breath and continued "And then we breathe out. Right here. Right now."

I watched her for a moment following my directions. "Great. Just take a minute and feel the support of the chair, if it's okay." I see her sink more deeply into the chair, her head resting on the pillow supporting her neck. "Okay. What are you noticing now, Tracy?"

With eyes still closed, she responded, "My body feels looser, my shoulders less rigid. How's that?"

"Great!" I reply

We took our time and gradually I noted her calming down. I ventured in. "Now, tell me more about the Memorial Game, if that's okay."

She opened her eyes. "It is going to be absolutely fantastic. It is all about honouring my boys, which is wonderful but …" Her eyes suddenly filled with tears at the thought of the upcoming event. I again saw the tension increasing in her body. "It just makes it all so real, Sandra! It seems like my boys should be at the game witnessing this outpouring of love."

I noticed the colour rising in her cheeks. "And I know in some capacity, they will be there with me, but Sandra, I just miss them so much!" The timbre of her voice alerted me to the degree of difficulty she was having keeping it together. Tears began to stream down her cheeks and she let them flow freely as she grieved, speaking of missing the earthly presence of her boys and her very purpose for being.

We took our time allowing the feelings to pass through.

I asked, "How did you make it through this past year, Tracy?"

"Well. Honestly?" she asked. "Brent and my closest friends and many others have sustained me with their loving gestures. Initially, it was just too overwhelming and I drank much of the time. You were right about the whisky." She paused and reaffirmed her statement. "Seriously, it was the way I coped with all the feelings, the memories, and the flashbacks. My heart was totally broken. Being a mom had been my job, my passion! As I have said many times, there was nothing that made me happier than being a mother, even when I was challenged with the usual antics of two young, energetic boys!"

She breathed in again and continued, "I was and still am infuriated that Corry would do this. I felt I had lost my whole world. I was completely broken. I just checked out and drank from the moment we got home from that f*#kin' police station where no one gave a sh*t about what Brent and I had just gone through in finding the boys. No one was there for us at the crime scene or the RCMP station except those two poor women in the closet, who had no idea of what to do!"

She began to tear up again. "There was not one kind or caring word from anyone at the scene. Not one sense of understanding from those handling the case as to what we might be going through that morning! We were suspects, pure and simple."

She was raging.

"What are you noticing as you say that, Tracy?" I ask.

"I can feel the tears coming and my stomach is very unsettled. Very acidic."

I watched as she swallowed, sucked in a deep breath and continued, "I understand that the police needed to investigate, but where was there even a touch of humanity or compassion from those police officers? They knew so little about helping us deal with what we had just experienced in finding the boys! I would have thought they would have learned some kind of interventions to help traumatized people cope or have brought in appropriate resources to do so!"

The Arms of Love

And then, as the fire left her eyes, the tears began to flow again. Time passed as we did the work to move through the experience at the RCMP station. Then I said, "If it is okay, just take a minute to feel that love that poured into your very centre from your dear friends who arrived to rescue you from your experience at the RCMP station." I paused. "Just feel their arms wrapping around you that very morning as you left the building."

Her eyes closed as she reflected on folding into the arms of her dear friends. She stayed there for what seemed like a very long time.

"Just feel the support of the chair, Tracy," I said.

She took another deep breath and we waited as she regained her ground. "It has been such a rough year, Sandra. So, my greatest solace other than Brent and my friends and family has been … my whisky!"

I sat with this for a moment before I asked, "Has the whisky helped?"

She looked over at me, obviously surprised by my question. "Well, it would dull the pain for a while, but then I would become so emotional and write stupid rants on Facebook and wake up thinking, *What the hell did I write this time?* Then I would often feel upset at myself for sharing my feelings of rage and anger and sadness with strangers as well as with friends." She sat back in the chair and I gently closed off our session.

Chapter 41

BETRAYED

WE SAT AGAIN TOGETHER AS TRACY CONTINUED TO SHARE MORE OF HER experiences in the days and weeks following the death of the boys. She began, "For a while after the boys died, I would be getting over 500 messages a day from people all over the world and it was overwhelming. And then ... at one point after the boys' funeral, I was on Instagram and saw a number of Corry's friends all dressed up and obviously celebrating Corry's life while my sons were now ashes on a shelf. Ashes, Sandra, because of the selfish actions of their good buddy, Corry MacDougall. I could not believe that people, particularly those with children, could be so insensitive to not only gather together dancing and partying but then to ..." She choked up. "But then to post their carryings on ... on Instagram, knowing I would see it? Where was the human empathy and compassion there, Sandra?"

I quietly listened as she continued.

"The rage in me was so intense and unforgiving. Everyone had their opinions of me and of what happened and I was still reeling from Corry's brutal act of violence and then ... and then, I see someone post their celebration of Corry's life online as if to taunt me!"

I moved forward again in my chair and we took our time to process this until I said, "What a difficult scene for you to witness, Tracy." I paused. "What are you noticing in your body as you share this recollection?"

She breathed in. "In a way, I feel defeated. Helpless. Sad. Betrayed. Heavy, I guess. I thought some of those people were my friends, but when I saw them gathering together, laughing and carrying on, I felt very hurt that people could be so cruel."

"Tracy," I said. "It's over. You made it through that encounter. Just breathe that in now, girl. It is over."

She looked completely drained as she opened her eyes. I wanted to dislodge the power of the memory of the Instagram posting, and I softly repeated, "You made it, Tracy."

I waited and then repeated again. "You made it through all that, Tracy. Every minute of it! If it is okay, again, just breathe that in."

I paused and then said, "What do you notice when you realize you somehow have survived this past year? That you are still here, honouring your boys with a Memorial Game?"

She breathed in, nodding her head, as she settled further into the blue chair. "Yes. I know that, Sandra." Her tone indicated some irritation with her therapist. "I have survived but …"

I broke in. "You know that in your head, Tracy. Your body needs to know that you have survived."

She nodded as I continued having her breathe in the knowledge that she had survived the death of her children, the Facebook and Instagram messages that set her back, the vigils, the funeral, the unbelievable reality of what had happened.

She expanded on her sorrow. "Yes," she said. "I guess you are right. I have survived but the year isn't over yet, and the toughest part of this year is making it through the Memorial Game and the anniversary of the boys' deaths on December 19th and, of course, another Christmas without them!"

She struggled with the words again, breathing through the raw emotion and vulnerability she was displaying. "We are going to Arizona for New Year's Eve with friends, which will be good. The thought of being here without the boys during the Christmas season is hard, but we will stay here until after Christmas to celebrate with the girls and our extended families."

I slowed down our interaction with some wisdom I had garnered over the course of working with grief and loss. "Sometimes that first year is so challenging, Tracy, because there are so many firsts without the ones who have died. Birthdays, Valentine's Day, Easter, Mother's Day, end of the school year, start of the new hockey season, Hallowe'en, Thanksgiving, Christmas, anniversaries of their deaths, all which may bring forth the deep sadness because your boys are not physically here with you."

She nodded. "Yes. All of those days have been really hard."

I reminded her, "You have made it through all those events, Tracy."

She settled more into the blue chair. "I am feeling almost like a rag doll right now. I have no idea how I made it through this past year. Honestly, I don't!"

"But you have, Tracy Stark. You have made it through such a tough year."

We took the time to process the activation until I could see she was more grounded in herself.

The Grief Bursts

I went on, explaining what she might well be experiencing. "The grief bursts are hard too. Hearing a particular song that reminds you of the boys or seeing their friends and watching them grow taller brings heartache. Seeing a youngster on the ice reminding you of Radek's way of skating or a defenceman taking a wicked shot like Ryder, will often bring a swell of emotion forward. Walking behind a boy who seems to move like one of your boys or attending events where your boys should be physically present, all bring up a variety of emotion and learning to ride that wave and allow yourself to feel sad or angry or whatever is okay. Push those emotions away and they just come back even more intense. Sit with them. Breathe through them. Write about them. Walk with them. Talk to them. Whatever works to settle you."

She nodded as I continued. "Then there are the dreams, and waking up and finding out it was a dream, rather than reality, can be very challenging as well. All of it makes that first year so emotional and raw, so extra difficult! However, you need to know these are all normal emotional responses to abnormal events."

She shared some of the grief bursts she had personally experienced in the last year and we processed them slowly as they rolled off her tongue.

I said, "Many clients find it helps to change their usual traditions at certain times of the year to ease the pain of not having their deceased loved ones present at those special moments. Some clients set a place at the table on special occasions for those who have died to honour their memory, while others light candles or pass a 'talking stick' or a cherished item of the deceased around the table to have each family member share a memory of those who have gone before. These rituals can be very powerful, particularly for men who often find it very difficult to share the depth of their pain, but they can be pretty amazing at sharing stories. Those together times are opportunities to share very special rituals as family and friends cherish all the beautiful memories together, letting everyone take his or her turn … or … pass, both of which are equally acceptable."

She nodded and added, her eyes glistening with tears, "That's what I want at our table with Brent and the girls." We sat together, taking time to release more activation.

Tracy returned our attention to the Memorial Game. "I just don't know if I can handle seeing all the boys' friends and all the people who have been so wonderful without completely losing my sh*t!" She reached for a tissue.

I wanted to roll my chair toward her as I started to speak, but needed to give her the space to grieve rather than smother her as she got in touch with her emotions regarding the Memorial Game. Instead, I said, "You mean showing how much you care about the loving presence of those in the arena who have walked beside you this past year? Showing how much you miss your precious sons? Showing that you have been broken to the core by this tragedy?" My voice softened as I said, "Is that what you are saying, Tracy?"

She locked her eyes with mine and suddenly we were both here in the moment, gripped in the soul-splitting grief of a young, heartbroken mama mourning her children. Tracy's whole body was quivering, her face bearing the excruciating pain known only by mothers who have lost the babies they have birthed into being. "I just miss them, Sandra," she said quietly.

We sat in silence for a moment, breathing in and out. I moved forward, placing my hands lightly on the knees of her ripped jeans, wanting to make gentle contact with this sorrow-filled Little Mama.

I asked, "What do you miss most, Tracy?"

She paused, drying her eyes before she responded. "I miss all of them, Sandra. Their stinky socks. Their hanging around, their being annoying boys, their snuggling in bed with me, their making weird noises and bringing their friends over. I miss giving Ryder hell for some of his crazy antics. I miss finding his wad of gum everywhere but in the garbage! I miss Radek's hysterical laughter. I miss the smell of wet hockey gear, repulsive hockey bags. I miss their disgusting farting contests. I miss hugging them good night and then making them pancakes in the morning with their friends sitting around the table. I miss wrestling them for a kiss. I miss watching them play hockey and cheering them on! I miss … doing their laundry!" Her voice again broke as the tears fell.

I felt a physical ache in my heart for my client. We sat together, me wishing I had the power to inject through my fingers into her kneecaps the love, tenacity, and decorum that she wanted to manage the very public **R&R** Memorial Game Day.

We sat in the silence, connected physically by my hands resting lightly on the knees of the woman with the immaculately painted nails, stellar makeup, and the monumental sleeves of tattoos, now covering both her arms and imprinted into the skin. I noted the images of Radek and Ryder emanating from her right forearm as I listened to the pain of the unfathomable despair releasing its energy from my client, interrupted only by the occasional sound of the sniffling of the woman sitting in front of me. These were outward manifestations of the anguish ravaging her body. I could not see the inside where her heart had been shattered, but I felt the deep-seated sadness in mine.

I pushed back from her chair with my feet, "removing my hands from her knees, giving her space to continue her grieving. I kept on speaking softly. "If it is okay, Tracy, feel the stillness in the room, the peace that comes from letting go of the activation in your body."

I waited and watched Tracy breathing in and out, each breath a reverent testimony to the boys climbing the stairs to Heaven as evidenced in the image of the boys on her right forearm.

It was slow and steady work. She had again closed her eyes.

After a couple of minutes, her voice interrupted the silence. "I'm feeling kinda dizzy."

"Just let a little light into your eyes, and that will settle."

Her eyes opened slightly.

I looked at her. "You are doing amazing work here, Tracy Stark!"

Again, she closed her eyes.

I waited respectfully until she opened them and oriented to the room once more.

I smiled gently at the woman in front of me. "Remember when I said the most dangerous tears are the ones a person keeps inside?"

She nodded.

I paused. "My dear friend, I think we're both out of danger now!"

We again shared a little laugh, changing the energy in the room.

"What are you noticing now, Tracy?"

She took a minute. "I feel more relaxed ... more released and more—it sounds crazy—but ... more free."

"That's what we want, my girl. That is what we want."

The session ended.

Chapter 42

THE FIRST
MEMORIAL GAME

THE FIRST **R&R** MEMORIAL GAME WAS UPON US. I SENT TRACY A MESSAGE THE morning of the game wishing her strength and courage in her interactions with those attending the event. Following the game day, I asked her to capture, in an email, her experience of the first **R&R** Memorial Game 2017.

> TRE to SYK: That day was another hard day for me. Being the first memorial game and it being so close to the first anniversary of the death of Ryder and Radek, the media contacted us asking if they could do a story. I was all for them covering the story, but by no means was I going to do an interview with them. I still held resentment toward the media as I felt they gave us no space the day my boys died, and here they were again, right in our faces.
>
> Andrew Peard, our play-by-play sports announcer for XM105 and a good friend, had been my voice on many occasions since the passing of the boys. He offered to do the interview with the media. I felt very relieved.

The boys' Whitecourt Wolverines numbers #82 & #91

Our dear friend, Joey Bouchard, former Whitecourt Wolverine coach, posted a message on an arena flip board, which people could see as they entered the arena.

> One year ago, we walked into the Millwoods Rec Centre to watch Ryders last hockey game. I wish I knew then, what I know now. My heart is full of gratitude to have known and loved you. Ryder and Radek, your life was a blessing, your memory a treasure, you are loved beyond words and missed beyond measure. Brent Stark and Tracy Stark, there are no words for how much you mean to us and how fortunate we feel to walk this journey with you, even on the darkest days. As you navigate through the unimaginable, your strength and grace continues to inspire and heal us all. We love you, and we promise to be by your side and ignite the memory of Ryder and Radek for eternity. Tomorrow is never promised, tell those you love how much they mean to you.
> RnRForever. Joey Bouchard

Brent and I went to the rink an hour before everyone arrived to do our writing on the ice. We met our hockey team, the Junior A Whitecourt Wolverines, there as they were going to write their messages to Ryder and Radek with us. The day was so emotional. I wrote my message, wanting to get it done and leave before the public started piling in as I did not know if I could handle watching all our friends and family, as well as Ryder and Radek's friends, writing their messages to the boys. However, that plan was soon out the window as people started arriving early. I found myself on the ice, surrounded by so much love, much of it radiating from Ryder and Radek's friends.

Message on the ice

Radek's Spruce Grove Sabretooth coaches and a few teammates and their parents came from Spruce Grove to share their love for our boys and our family. With them, they brought me Radek's Black Sabretooth #8 jersey. Of course, tears were streaming down my face as I put on his jersey. The afternoon continued with hugs and gifts from Ryder and Radek's friends. The messages from all who choose to write on the ice were spectacular. My heart was full.

When it was time to begin the game, many of our closest friends and family gathered in THE WOLVERINE DEN to watch the ceremony unfold. There was a candlelit vigil followed by a beautiful video put together by Ryan Steinke, who had gone to Spruce Grove to interview a few of Ryder's friends there, and then came back to capture the words of close Whitecourt friends who shared their thoughts and their stories of Ryder and Radek. These young men spoke of their bond of friendship with my boys. The video was so touching and well done and probably the hardest thing I had ever watched. All of the boys present were so emotionally strong as they spoke from their hearts regarding my boys. Alesha and Shelbey met at centre ice to perform the puck drop. The first **R&R** Memorial Game was underway!

Puck drop by sisters Alesha and Shelbey

At the first intermission, Amanda Wilson, wearing a Wolverines jersey with the **R&R** heart with wings on the back, did a striking figure skating routine to the song "I Was There" by Paul Brandt. My emotions were running high.

Figure skating tribute by Amanda Wilson

Jerseys on the wall – tribute to #82 & #91

Then, former teammates of the boys shared a shootout wearing the boys' former Wolverine numbers. What an emotional day. I was so thankful for all the love and support we received from so many, not only on this day but on so many others.

Little Mama, surrounded by friends and family and others just wanting to be there for the Stark family, had survived the first anniversary of the death of the boys.

Chapter 43

A NEW YEAR 2018

A New Slate on Which to Write a New Story

January 05, 2018

I SAW TRACY'S POST ON FACEBOOK.

TRS: I dreamed of my beautiful boys last night. We were watching hockey and I was holding their hands. I remembered exactly how their hands felt the last time I held them. Ryder's were so cold as he didn't wear gloves and Radek's were warm and soft with hang nails. I started crying ... And Radek looked at me with sad eyes and asked me what is wrong ... I told him I didn't want this moment to end but I knew when I woke up it would be all over. He started crying too and he said he didn't want me to be sad. He didn't want me to cry. He said he and Ryder were always with me ... But it's only in my dreams that I can feel them and see them ... I just want to dream forever ... until I am where they are.

SYK: Saw your post Starkshine. They are ALWAYS, ALWAYS, ALWAYS with you Tracy! Feel those hands holding yours tight. Someone told me you had thumbprints of the boys ... True??

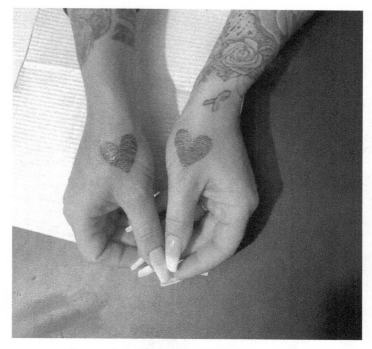

Thumb print tattoos

TRS to SYK: It is true! I got the boys' thumbprints tattooed on my hands because I have always loved holding their hands. Ryder's right thumb print is above my right thumb. Radek's left thumbprint is above my left thumb. Radek particularly always wanted to hold my hand, which I loved and now their thumbprints are forever with me.

SYK: Yes … ..Beautiful.

Chapter 44

WHITECOURT WOLVERINES LADIES' NIGHT SPEECH

Therapist's Perspective

The Elephant in the Room

IT WAS EARLY JANUARY 2017. TRACY AND I HAD BEEN WORKING TOGETHER for a while now and the bond between us as therapist and client was solid. When she began talking about this first Wolverines Ladies Night coming up, I asked, "Are you planning on saying anything?"

She looked at me, somewhat startled. "What do you mean?"

I just looked back at her.

"Well, I suppose I could greet everyone and say I hoped they have a good time," she said.

I continued to look directly at her as I began, "Tracy, I think it might be an appropriate time to talk about the elephant that will be in the room that night."

She tilted her head and looked at me. "I don't understand."

"You have been through hell this past year, but you've been surrounded by incredible love, much of it from women who will be attending your event. I think it would be wise to address the issue of losing your boys."

She crossed her arms and said quickly, "I can't, Sandra!"

As I looked at her, I saw stress personified, draining her face of colour. Red blotches appeared on her neck. I didn't crater to her fear of speaking publicly about what had happened. "Let's not worry about that right now, my girl. I promise you, we can have that fear under control before the first Whitecourt Wolverine Ladies Night. I guarantee it!"

She smiled a brave half grin, or maybe it was a grimace, and she started to get up, attempting, I was sure, to end this conversation.

I responded, "Just a minute, Tracy. Please sit for another minute or two." She sat on the edge of the chair as I began to speak. "I can't imagine anything harder than standing before a room full of women and sharing the deep despair of losing your beautiful boys. I wouldn't ask you to do this if I did not think you were ready to talk publicly about what you have been through."

I could see she was attempting to keep her composure as I continued. "Let me take what you have shared with me through our sessions and put something together and see if I can capture the essence of what you might want to say to this group of women. I know you continually tell me that women need to find the courage to speak up about important issues, so maybe it's time to find your voice in a way other than in a rant on Facebook."

I saw the defiance in her eyes. She was angry at her therapist. "I would suck at it!" she responded. I waited and she continued. "Speaking in front of people terrifies me at the very best of times, and you want me to bare my soul in front of a bunch of wine-drinking women out for a good time? Hmmm. Not in this century!"

She shifted her posture, withdrawing into the blue chair. Her voice had a f*#k you tone to it. Her arms remained crossed in defiance of what I had proposed.

I was actually relishing her resistance. She was showing some real strength in her opposition to my suggestion.

I reacted forcefully to her words. "Tracy, you have the 'real estate.' You've lost your kids in the most dreadful manner. You want women to find their voices individually and collectively to speak loudly about things that matter. You have a captive audience of 250 women. Finding your voice will encourage other women to find theirs. You told me, months ago, that was what you wanted to do!"

I was still getting the stink eye.

My eyes softened and I said, "Let me see what I can put together and then you decide if any of it resonates with you."

She had a second session scheduled the following week, so I crossed my fingers, my ankles, and my toes, hoping she would not cancel and end our counselling altogether. She was unmistakeably mighty angry with me, her therapist, for pushing her into something so foreign and abhorrent to her. I was taking a chance.

That evening I sat pensively in my home office putting together ideas, all the while thinking, *Am I pushing her too hard? Am I failing to follow her lead?* She had just survived the toughest month of the year: the **R&R** Memorial game, the anniversary of the death of her boys, and the Christmas season, and here I was encouraging her to attempt something terrifying and foreign to her. I breathed in, settling myself in my chair, and began to write the first draft of my thoughts to my client.

As I finished, I stepped out onto the upper deck and looked up at the star-filled night, up toward the north to where those "two new stars were brightly shining forth," hoping the spirit of those two kids would give their mother the mettle to give the draft I was about to send some consideration. I was concerned that maybe I was stretching her beyond her limits.

I checked in with my gut. I was taking a chance, but in my mind's eye, I again saw this same woman marching down the aisle of that restaurant in Calgary, her determination etched on her face, strength of character in her step. She could do this and do it well! I returned to my computer, breathed in deeply, and pressed SEND.

Speech Prep

TRS to SYK: You knew I was terrified of public speaking. Speaking in front of people was not something I felt at all comfortable doing. I thought what you were suggesting was an outrageous idea. Just the thought of it made me sick to my stomach! I wanted to get out of your office as quickly as possible.

When I got home, I told Brent what you had suggested. He asked me if I wanted to speak at the event. I shook my head vigorously.

He said, "Then don't do it!"

I breathed out a huge sigh of relief.

The next morning, I saw your email in my messages. I knew it would contain your "skeleton speech." I decided not to open it. But then I got curious and double-clicked to just check out what you have written. You included things I said in session, things I had shared regarding the tremendous support of so many, things I wanted other women to know. But I was still upset with you for suggesting I should say more than, "Welcome and have a good night!"

However, slowly I began to rethink your idea. Yeah okay ... Maybe I could do this. I reread what you have written. Some of it was DEFINITELY not me. However, I sat down at my computer and worked with it until it seemed to say what I wanted to say if I were ever able to find the courage to do so. I began to change my thinking. Maybe I can make this mine. I texted you back a brief "I might."

But the more I worked on my speech, the more anxious I became. What was I thinking? I could barely talk to my own family, especially on the topic of my beloved boys, without crying. My worst fear was 250 ladies seeing me crumble in front of them. I knew most of these ladies were mothers themselves. Some had walked beside me on this heartbreaking journey of "survival." Most likely, all had shed a few tears upon hearing what had happened to Ryder and Radek. I went back and forth—tenacious as that wolverine one minute and scared as a rabbit the next, asking myself, *Why did she put me in this situation? She was supposed to be helping me calm down, not agitate me!* Gradually, however, I began seeing the benefits of sharing my thoughts.

Then I said, "What the hell!"

You had convinced me I could do it. I began to believe I could too!

I told Brent I had changed my mind about the speech. He was concerned that it would be too hard on me. He was not worried about me failing, but rather, concerned about how difficult talking about our last year would be. But inside, I knew how powerful it would be for me to complete this task and say what was in my thoughts. To choose a platform other than Facebook was beyond my expectation of myself, but your belief in me gave me confidence and I began to become more focused.

I spent a few nights practicing my speech over and over in my head. I would practice until I was numb from crying through it. When I thought I had it perfected, Brent suggested I stand in front of him and read it aloud.

"What? Why?" I asked.

"You need to work on your body language," he said.

"My body language?" I asked.

"Well, Tracy." he replied. "It's not just what you say. It's how you say it!"

I got up, mixed myself a whisky/diet and did my speech again and ... of course I started to cry. DAMN IT! I was so frustrated! How the hell was I going to do this in front of a room full of women, when I couldn't even do it in front of my husband, who has obviously seen me at my very worst? I was not happy with my therapist. I was fragile. I decided not to go this route. I didn't need this damn stress! I would tell "her" tomorrow about my change of plans.

The next day I was scheduled for my last session with you before the big event. I was getting ready to tell you I was scrapping the idea of speaking but you "cut me off at the pass," gave me that big smile and led me to a different room than where we usually did therapy. You were toting around what looked like a pedestal.

I wondered what you were going to have me do now. Well, you asked me to stand in front of you with my speech resting on the pedestal. Actually, you called it a lectern and said it would make speaking easier as I could rest my speech on it, turn the pages easily and hide behind it! As if that slight barrier was going to help. Funny thing. It did!

You had me read what was on the page and it felt good to be able to hide a little behind ... something! LOL! I read it over and over and over again with you giving me tips and cheering me on until I (1) Stopped crying (2) Stopped fidgeting, and (3) Repeated most of it while looking into the "pretend" crowd that you said was in the room in front of me! I got the "body language" thing down pat! When you felt confident enough that I could do this, you sent me on my way with a hug, a big smile, a "You got this girl!" and ... the lectern. I was shaking my head as I walked out the door! I guess I was more afraid of telling my therapist I was chickening out than I was of 250 wine-drinking women!

The evening of the 1st Annual Wolverines Ladies Night arrived. I had practiced my speech in my head all night, getting probably two hours of sleep. The morning of the event, I received a beautiful message from you, and knowing you and your daughter, Kristin, would be there in the front row cheering me on ... Yeah. I got this!! Well ... maybe.

There were only three rules you had laid out for me regarding my speech in the text you sent.

1. No Drinking until your speech is done. *WHAT????? Are you kidding me? That's how I cope with everything. How will I calm my nerves without my loyal Whisky/Diet??*

2. Take off your stilettos and do the speech in your bare feet. *I don't*

know if this was because you feared me falling on my face, or that
you knew how much I loved being in bare feet.

3. *If you feel you need a shot of courage, look over at the pewter*
    sign I will be holding discreetly on my lap in front of you
    and BREATHE!

Once up on stage, I removed my shoes and felt my bare feet on the stage carpet. I was grounded. I was ready. I had my speech neatly printed out in large print as you suggested. My friend Carla, knowing me all too well, had the whisky/diet with lots of ice on the table beside me. Just in case … LOL. Well, being the rebel I have always been, I winked at you, took one sip of my drink, and started my speech.

"Good evening ladies and welcome to the 1st Annual Whitecourt Wolverines Ladies Night. I am privileged to stand before you this evening to celebrate not only our Wolverines hockey team but our great female fans and friends as well. Each and every one of you have been given the gift of the game …"

***

SYK: In the audience, I sat watching the "blonde bomb" weaving her own magic, thanking everyone who had been a part of making the Ladies Night a reality. She saluted the hockey moms, past and present, and those women accompanying their besties whom they lost from September to April because it was hockey season! She revered the volunteers, saying the Wolverine organization could not run without their incredible involvement at all the Wolverine events. She thanked the male "eye candy" at the bar, the inner circle of women who had come up with the idea of the Ladies Night, and all those who had worked to bring the vision into the beautiful evening of glitter and glamour. She was rocking it! The women in the room were having fun as Mama Wolverine set the tone.

I watched as Tracy paused. The next part would be the toughest. Her eyes shifted toward me and I watched as she took in the large pewter BREATHE sign I was holding upright on my lap. Then, her eyes returned to the eyes of the women sitting in front of her as she began the next part of her speech. I watched as she took another deep breath. As her coach, I too breathed in, waiting for my "star player" to make her next move to the goal.

Then she began: "Thirteen months ago our family was rocked by tragedy." The room turned deathly silent. She waited and then continued. "The support and love that I have received from so many of you seated in this room and many beyond the walls of this venue is unbelievable. Friends and strangers alike have supported Brent and me and our girls in the grief of losing our boys and in carrying the *R&R* symbol and thus the spirit of Ryder and Radek to destinations throughout the world. There is no possible way to express the complete gratitude to each and every one who has loved us through the last year with their words, their thoughts, their messages, their prayers, their gifts, their presence at celebrations and vigils for the boys, their support of the *R&R* Memorial Foundation, and their continual vigilance ensuring we were … okay.

"Tonight, I thank each of you for helping me and my family heal our broken hearts with such love and compassion. We have made it through a year of FIRSTS and we look to 2018 as an opportunity to continue to celebrate our *R&R*. Here's to my forever Wolverines … Ryder and Radek."

She raised her glass and the women in the room stood and followed suit, each woman raising her glass in honour of Tracy's boys. Then, everyone returned to their seats. The silence in the room was beyond deafening.

Tracy looked down at her speech and then out over the crowd and continued. "My life has been filled with the gift of girlfriends, whom I cherish very much. We women need to make time where we can get together to share our stories, our hugs, our laughter, our tears, our victories, and our challenges with other women in fun-filled nights like tonight and other more serious times as well. We need to work together with others who birth the babies to find ways to right the injustice of systems that failed my two innocent boys and others like them. We, as women, need to raise our voices to protect all children at risk because of angry, unstable fathers. We need to find our individual and collective voices to challenge situations that are simply unjust."

She went on, firing up for her finish: "Movements regarding the safety of women and children expand when we influence our men and boys to stand with us in our goal to stop the violence against women and children in both divorced and intact families. At each table there are quotes regarding inspirational women. I hope you will take the time to read them and … be inspired."

She looked over at me and continued, "I have a woman who gives me inspiration. This woman helps me catch my breath when I forget to breathe. She has helped me survive. She has helped me find my voice. She has given me courage. She swears, which is my favourite part! She is everything to me in my healing process. She looked into my eyes and gave me these simple yet powerful words to say each day when I wake up and wrestle with feelings of fear and sorrow that have rested in my heart since my boys died. The words are simple." She paused: "TODAY IS A GOOD DAY TO HAVE A GOOD DAY!

"In this moment, this evening, I say to each of you: TONIGHT IS A GOOD NIGHT TO HAVE A GOOD NIGHT."

She paused again before continuing.

"Finally, if you have not already guessed, I have always been terrified of public speaking. But tonight … I did it!! Another first. I found my voice because I am passionate and I am ferocious about women speaking up about things that matter! Remember, when you are as scared as hell to find your voice as I was tonight, shaking in my heels and then delivering this message in bare feet, may you stand extra tall and be a tenacious wolverine!"

The room erupted in a thunderous applause of appreciation for the woman delivering the message.

The Singer, the Coach, and the Mama Wolverine

***

Tracy's words continued as she debriefed with me in an email the day following the women's event. She was stoked!

> TRS to SYK: It was amazing, Sandra!! What a rush. When the room went completely silent, I could honestly hear the ice adjusting in my drink. I used my breathing to settle myself for sure, and when I forgot, I could look at you in the front row where you held your BREATHE sign! When I finished and all these beautiful women in the room were on their feet, wiping tears from their eyes and clapping loudly, I couldn't believe it! OMG! What a feeling!! I was thinking ... Is this what Michelle Obama feels like after she speaks?? Lol!
>
> When I walked off stage, I headed right to you and gave you the biggest hug ever! You did not stop smiling! I felt so strong inside! Three weeks ago, I did not believe I could ever pull this off but I did it! Thank you for believing in me. Thank you for pushing me beyond what I thought were my limits. This was truly a life-changing experience for me and I will be forever grateful to you for helping me to achieve what I had considered impossible.

Chapter 45

NOTHIN' GONNA
STOP ME NOW!!

AFTER THE LADIES NIGHT, IT WAS OBVIOUS THAT TRACY FELT TRULY EMPOWERED. Since challenging her greatest fear, she felt she could do anything. Her thought was, *What have I got to lose?* Nothing was going to stop her now.

As she sat in my blue chair the next week, her voice was strong. "I am not holding back. I am embracing all of who I am becoming and I am moving steadily forward. I know what a broken heart feels like. I know what intense anger feels like. I am excited about the rest of this journey. Of course, my deepest desire would be to have my boys back here right now, but I will continue to live this life on their behalf and speak about changes that I believe need to be made to protect other kids."

She again repeated. "Thank you for believing in me, Sandra."

I smiled and replied, "Tracy, you always had that scoring power in you! I just had to give you that pep talk in the dressing room. You dug that puck out of the corner, dipsy doodled across the blue line, aimed, and flicked that black piece of rubber directly into the net!!"

We laughed together at my bizarre hockey metaphor!

Tracy had indeed overcome one of her greatest fears. She said she still wasn't entirely comfortable speaking in front of a crowd, but she knew deep within that when push came to shove, she could do it.

After the high of the Wolverines Ladies's Night, I wanted to help her feel the power of moving forward in deciding how to best capture the attention of those in positions of power. To stand up for what is right and calling out injustices in systems that she believed had let her down. To bring forward her unsettling concerns of what had happened to her children. It was time to put a plan in place to bring full awareness of her story to those in positions of influence. She wanted to speak truth to such power regarding the necessity of instituting changes to protect kids like Ryder and Radek from an angry, vengeful adult. She wanted to shine a light on the RCMP procedures that had failed to assist her when, as a mother, she had found her boys murdered. She wanted to share her How should she proceed to ensure her voice was impactful?

Now that she was feeling powerful, I wanted her to use her voice well in educating others of her frustrations regarding policies and procedures that she believed had failed her and her children.

Hockey Alberta

Early in January 2018, Tracy had contacted Hockey Alberta to understand organizational policies regarding what a coach should do when a thirteen-year-old boy shows up at hockey practice in a women's dress and a shaved head, indicating he was unwilling to remove the dress because his dad would be angry.

> TRE: As you will see from the emails, Sandra, I was told there were no policies that relate to this sort of thing. I told them what happened to my son and those coaches had never reached out to me as a parent regarding my child. And that was basically it.

From: Tracy Ross
Date: January 9, 2018 at 10:59:39 PM MST
Subject: Urgent

Hello there
I'm not sure if you're the person I need to contact but if you're not maybe you can lead me in the right direction

What are the policies of minor hockey, when it comes to a child showing up to a bantam AA dryland In a women's Dress ??? What should a coach do ????

On Jan 10, 2018, at 8:46 AM, wrote:

Good morning Tracy.

There are no rules pertaining to the issue that you have highlighted, therefore how a coach deals with the specific situation would really depend on the circumstances around it. I might be able to provide more insight if there is more that you can tell me about it.

GROSS MISCONDUCT

From: Tracy Ross ▭▭▭▭▭▭▭
Subject: Re: Urgent
Date: Jan 10, 2018 at 9:08:36 AM
To: ▭▭▭▭▭▭▭▭▭▭▭

Well November 24th 2016 my ex husband put my 13 year old son in a dress and took him to hockey practice, to embarrass him for being suspended at school, no calls were made to me as the other parent, like maybe there's something wrong here?!
The coach had no problem suspending my son from hockey for the duration of his school suspension and he had no problem making my son write a letter to him telling him why he did what he did to get suspended and why he should be allowed to play hockey.

This was the start of a chain of events that ended in the deaths of my children by the hands of their father 25 days after the dress incident

There's nothing that can change what happened but I would like to know the policies cause I'd sure hate for another child to be over looked when things don't look right?! Does that make sense

From: ▭▭▭▭▭▭▭▭▭▭▭▭▭
Subject: RE: Urgent
Date: Jan 30, 2018 at 2:12:33 PM
To: Tracy Ross ▭▭▭▭▭▭▭▭

Good afternoon Tracy.

I'm sorry it's been a couple of weeks. In addition to the Provincial guidelines, I've been gathering as much data from the local MHA as I could to assist in providing information to you.

Within the hockey system we have many processes, procedures and educational programs that help prepare executive members and team officials for many different situations. Obviously, it is not possible to put a policy in place for everything, however through partnerships with companies such as Respect Group Inc. we do provide opportunities for volunteers and parents to be educated in risk management and common sense issues related to youth sport. The situation that you have outlined starts outside the realm of the minor hockey program and would not generally fall under the responsibility of a coach.

Hockey Alberta also has Conduct Management guidelines in place to assist our member MHA's in developing their internal processes regarding hockey related issues. This is where MHA's would refer to help them work through issues with the behavior of players and/or coaches within the scope of minor hockey. In particular, Spruce Grove MHA has a detailed process in place for teams and families of players to bring forth potential issues with registered participants (players or coaches) and ask that they be reviewed. If any coach administered disciplinary action, that is outside the scope of his/her authority, this would be the process to initiate. SGMHA confirmed for me that nothing has ever been submitted through their formal process asking them to review the conduct of the coaches involved with the team related to this situation.

Emails between Tracy & Hockey Alberta

SYK TO TRS: What do you think Hockey Alberta should do, Tracy?

TRS to SYK: I think Hockey Alberta should review their policies and include training for coaches to recognize possible child abuse in their players. In their training to work with kids, coaches should be educated as to possible situations that might indicate a child is at risk … a 13-year-old, new to town, new to this team, shows up in a dress … and this isn't a clear warning sign of some kind of abuse? What if this sort of humiliation had caused my son or any other child to consider suicide and even act on that thought? I believe coaches should be aware and accountable to report anything that appears to be "offside" not only to the hockey association's governing body but also to Child Services.

The death of my boys can provide the impetus for such increased awareness and assistance in providing children who may be at risk, a "safe person" to whom he/she could possibly open up about his/her concerns. I like the idea offered by Ryder's coach that each player be "interviewed" by the coaches to discuss his/her involvement in playing hockey. I also think questions could be structured and coaches educated as to how to conduct such interviews so that coaches can gain a true understanding of not only a player's hockey skills, but also of his/her challenges as a young person in general. Granted, coaches are not expected to be psychologists, but difficulties in a child's life could possibly be detected and appropriate steps taken to get a youngster the assistance he/she may need. Coaches have a great opportunity to be mentors to youngsters and can make such a difference in a child's life. Hockey is not just about hockey!

SYK to TRS: Good points Trac! You know, developmentally the task of teenage children is to separate from their parents. Having other healthy adults in their lives can be critical in their development. If young people are able to form trusting bonds with their coaches where they can share what is going on inside their teenage brains and within their lives both on and off the hockey ice, that could be helpful in diminishing their distress if things are out of sync at home, at school or on the ice. That, of course, means the coach himself must be self-regulated and can't be a ranting raving lunatic or a bully, which unfortunately is sometimes the case in minor as well as professional sport.

TRE to SYK: Hmmm. I wish my Ryder had been able to share with his coach or another adult what was going on in his life off the ice. Everybody kept their lips zipped so as to mind their own business, I guess. I wish people would keep this tight-lipped when they were gossiping about other people's jobs, marriages, and other personal matters which were none of their business, although suspected domestic violence or child abuse should be everyone's concern. In my case, my boy needed someone, actually any responsible adult, to notice and take action on what he or she had witnessed happening to my Ryder while under his dad's roof. The guilt I hold in my heart for letting my boys go to live with their dad will live within me forever. Hopefully, by my opening up and sharing my experience, such will be a driving force to increase the awareness of those in positions of influence in minor sporting circles to consider increased training by all sporting organizations to alert coaches and managers of what to look for in potentially dangerous circumstances for their players and definitely not turn the other way.

The "hockey family" also needs to increase its vigilance and take action, which may include further investigation when an event such as occurred at Ryder's hockey practice on November 25, 2016. Children too must be empowered in their own personal hockey family to speak up if anyone in their hockey life is abusive in any way. We need to protect these kids from such bullying in and out of the home. Radek and Ryder's father was a domineering bully and committed the ultimate act of terror. And … nobody anticipated this. The dress incident was my first clue that something was wrong in this situation. It kills me that the boys obviously felt they could not share what was happening in Dad's home until Radek finally opened up. However, if coaches were schooled in what may indicate child abuse was occurring in the life of one of their players, perhaps I would still be a mom "waving from the stands."

Finding Her Voice

It was obvious that Tracy was more committed than ever to speaking her mind after the great success at the Wolverine Ladies Night. In our next session, I felt it important to address her recent posting on Facebook of the letter she had sent Child Services on December 4, 2016.

Yes. She needed to find her voice. However, I expressed my concerns to her about her random post, fearing my client was at risk of just anyone being able to read the document she had posted. I was of the opinion that she needed to develop a definitive plan to follow up with those responsible for the action not taken by Child Services, other than with a random rant on Facebook. She needed to use her power to make a bigger societal noise... imagining an arena filled with the annoying sound of 30,000 cowbells perhaps, cheering her on to get the attention of those responsible for policies and procedures in cases of child protection. She was angry in her post, and I wondered if, after the high of the Ladies Night, she might be rebounding in the grief of the reality of the story she had shared from behind the microphone. I worked to ground her in order to have her make a real plan regarding how to proceed in her quest to address her concerns regarding what had ultimately resulted in the death of her children. She agreed.

> TRS to SYK: Sandra. As I said before, when I am feeling disheartened and, after having a couple of whiskies, I would post on Facebook and wake up the next day, angry at myself for my haphazard sharing. I promise I will refrain from such postings on social media but watch out! Now I will just send my tirades to you instead!

I laughed quietly. As she felt more powerful, I wanted to see her using her voice well, to achieve her goal of sharing her thoughts regarding her attempt to remove her children from an unsafe situation with a biological father. However, I could sense she was again fraught with agitation. The night before our next session, Tracy texted.

> TRS to SYK: Sandra, I am feeling very unsettled. My heart is totally broken.

I feared her rebound from the high of the Ladies Night. She had been so busy with the Memorial Game, the challenges of the one-year anniversary of the boys' deaths, and Christmas without her kids, and then preparing for the women's event... Now, there was a lull and she was floundering. I emailed her some suggestions.

> SYK to TRS: I remind you, Tracy, that this journey of grief is like a hockey season with many challenging moments. Many different strategies are needed at different times depending on your "opposition" and your own status. both physically and mentally. as well as your emotional/physical injuries and your mindset. During the season, a player may find different tactics that work at different times,

and some strategies need a place in your life at all times to be game ready for what life hands you. You choose what works for you. I am sending you some suggestions to ease the activation in your body and the despair that has taken control of your mind at this particularly gruelling part of this "season."

- ◆ *Go for a walk in the cold and kick at the snow in anger.
- ◆ *Rage at the sky!
- ◆ *Sit. Meditate. Breathe. Feel the support of the chair as we do in session.
- ◆ *Pet your dog Piper.
- ◆ *Write your boys regarding your speech and the success of the Ladies' Night.
- ◆ *Write your frustrations in your journal.
- ◆ *Write a timeline of the events and your involvement with the courts and Children's Services for the next step in your quest for justice.
- ◆ *Write a letter of anger to Corry.
- ◆ *Workout—HARD!
- ◆ *Curl up with your husband and watch a stupid movie.
- ◆ *Cry! Scream!
- ◆ *Get your game plan in place.
- ◆ *Brainstorm ideas for a daily ritual.
- ◆ *Meditate.
- ◆ *Fornicate! Lol!

TRS to SYK: I will do all of them!

Well … that wasn't exactly what I had in mind but … hey … she was focused. She was my first-line centre! She was ready and willing to do some more powerful work to settle the activation in her nervous system.

Chapter 46

LETTER TO CORRY

SHE ARRIVED AT OUR SESSION, BRINGING WITH HER THE LETTER I HAD SUG-gested she write Corry the previous evening. She again shared her experience of his controlling nature after they became engaged and detailed its escalation throughout their marriage as well as during their separation. She indicated she felt Corry thought she knew more than she did or would once the boys had opened up to her after her move to Spruce Grove. She also believed that his actions that horrible night were an indication of his inability to let her go. He was still attempting to be in control of both her and the boys. Once more, she stated that she believed it was Corry's inability to let her go that led him to hurt her by savagely killing those she loved most. Why? Because she had broken up his family. He had not been able to control the breakdown of his marriage simply by commanding it! This therapist wondered if Corry was reliving the story of his own childhood when his mother had left his father when he was but a youngster? But now…who would ever know …?

After we debriefed and processed some of the information she was sharing, I wrote the name CORRY in big letters on an 8.5" by 11" piece of white paper and propped it up against the back of the empty chair I had placed in front of my client. As she looked at the word CORRY, I asked her to close her eyes and imagine that he was sitting right there in front of her, listening to her share her letter.

She breathed in and unfolded what she had written. She looked down at the words as she held the letter in her hands. Her hands were shaking uncontrollably. She then looked up, again breathed deeply, looked directly at the word C*O*R*R*Y, and began to read the message she had constructed.

GROSS MISCONDUCT

C*O*R*R*Y

Corry,   January 30/18

Its been 407 days since I showed up at
your front door, banging my fists and constantly
ringing the doorbell, peeking in the side frosted
window, looking up and down the stairs.
Nothing seemed out of the norm, but when we
pulled up to your house, both your vehicles
were parked outside and the light above
your garage was on. So I knew you were
inside with my boys.

Never Ever in a million years did I think
                you were inside with my boys
                    DEAD !!!

Why? Why? Why? Why? Why? Why?
OMG how does a parent kill their own
children?

I looked down through the side window, and
I seen legs... Ryders legs.
With blood smeared all over them.
This is a vision that never leaves me.
My poor babies

What kind of sick mother fucker are you?
You wanted to hurt me in the worst way,
Why didn't you just kill me? Someone
your own size or how about you fight
fair you piece of shit coward?!!

You hunted your kids down, defenceless
and sleeping

WHAT THE FUCK IS WRONG WITH YOU??

I will tell you whats wrong with you ...

You are a definition of a coward
you are a fucking loser
Someone who had it all, but because
you think you're someone special, you
ended up losing everything.

You tried to be the big shot in Kelowna and
guess what? You failed .. Because
you're a LOSER!

You moved back, and tried business again,
but failed .. Because youre a LOSER

You belittle your own kids to make
yourself feel better, to feel more in contro
wow you're a piece of work!

The sad reality is that you tried to
brainwash your kids.
They finally moved in with you and
you couldn't keep your fucking pathetic
waste of skin hands off of them.
Did that make you feel more like a man?

When you hit them, called them names and
dressed them up .... Did you feel more
in control? Did you feel like God?

When Ryder looked you in your devil eyes
and screamed "moommmy!", as he ran
for his life, did you rebod angrily
because he was screaming for me?

You ended up taking his life at the front door, looking down at him, and giving him one more shot to the head. So I couldn't identify my baby at the funeral home.

How about when you started all of this ...
Poor Rader, asleep in your bed, which tells me he was scared..
His sleeping self... so peaceful ... so innocent...
You lifted your shot gun to his precious face and pulled the trigger.

YOU'RE A FUCKING PATHETIC EXCUSE FOR A HUMAN BEING.

YOU'RE A FUCKING MONSTER!

I tried to protect my kids from the day I left your sorry ass.
You just proved to the world what I was trying to protect my kids from

Don't worry NO ONE misses you

Your name is never mentioned, you're just the monster under the bed that ends up killing the kids.

I cant imagine what your mom thought when she greated Ryder & Rader at the gates of heaven.
Actually she would have watched you do it... YOU'RE SUCH AN EMBARRASMENT!

I wish my kids never went by the last name MacDougall. So many people shiver at the sound of that name.
And even more, noone can even say your first name.
I FUCCING HATE you!!

And the day I make it to heaven, I will have my boys again, FOR ETERNITY

So guess what? You didn't win.

Your soul will burn in hell forever, and if forgiveness is what brings you up to heaven...
I WILL NEVER FORGIVE YOU!

I monitored her physicality as she read, anger seeping, then pouring out in the words she had chosen to write. I continually reminded her to breathe as she spoke the words that had been written without censure. The shaking stopped. Tears of rage filled her eyes as she let go of what had been imprisoned in the confines of her mind. And then … it was done. We sat quietly for a moment.

I reached for my fire bowl, rested it on the floor in front of us, and asked her if it would be okay to burn the letter in the container. She nodded in agreement as she crumpled up the pages and placed them in the ceramic bowl

I handed her the book of wooden matches. Slowly and deliberately, she struck a match and caught a corner of a page. Smoke began to emanate from the words she had written. We watched as the pages became engulfed with the flame. We watched as the words on the page began to disintegrate in the depths of the bowl. I spoke softly of letting go of the trauma in her body, reminding her again that December 19, 2016, was over.

We focused on the dying embers in the bowl, waiting for the last cinder to lose its glow. She looked up at me and then down at the bowl again. It had been a painful exercise. When all that remained was the powdery resin of the letter, I asked her to take the bowl to the women's washroom down the hall, flush the ashes down the toilet, and watch their descent into the swirling waters, which would eventually take the residue to the bowels of the earth.

Bowl in hand, she left the room. I felt deeply saddened, but hopeful that the burning ritual would provide my client with a degree of peace. There was something about this ritual that has been helpful to many in releasing emotions trapped within, the result of relationship trauma, which has bruised and battered many in difficult life experiences.

Tracy returned, carrying the empty bowl, bent but not broken. "I'm glad the fire alarm didn't go off," she said, able to bring us back to the moment.

"Me too!" I replied.

We laughed gently, relieving some of the anguish of the moments we had shared in the process of releasing the agony of what Tracy has experienced in the loss of her boys.

It was over. "Oh God, my girl. You did it. Just letting go, one step at a time."

We were both emotionally exhausted. One more healing stride for my beautiful client on this forever journey.

Chapter 47

RELEASING ACTIVATION

APRIL 29, 2018. TRACY WAS BACK. WE HAD AGAIN SCHEDULED AN APPOINT-ment at my home. I saw the white Range Rover cruising up the driveway with the blonde at the helm. I was happy to see her. Tracy and I headed inside, finding comfort in the oversized leather chairs in the living room, the crystals in the front window refracting the sunlight and providing us with beautiful rainbows throughout the room. It was already magical as she shared her latest adventures, her thoughts, and her challenges. Two nervous systems again connected in the process of letting go of activation in her body. We inhaled and exhaled as she assumed her upright position, resting her head against the pillow in the chair as she reflected on the loss of her sons.

She began to speak. "I always thought I could never live through losing a child but somehow, I have survived the death of not one but two cherished children. Maybe I have been protected too. They are known for being involved in a tragic event that has blown my world apart. However, I did not have to watch them suffer through a fatal illness. I didn't have to see them behaving like imma-ture as*holes or driving drunk and killing themselves or one of their friends. I didn't lose them to a drug overdose or an alcohol addiction, and I don't have to be apprehensive about them being at their dad's anymore. They knew I was con-cerned about them at Dad's and yet they would always protect him. The worst thing that I never dreamed could possibly happen, has happened." She visibly shuddered. "I don't have to worry anymore because …" She stumbled on her words. "They are safely in the loving hands of God." She began to tear up early in the session.

She grabbed a tissue and continued. "Sandra, I am so proud of my boys and the memories I have of them. Memories I will have forever. I have been very lucky to be their mom. I want to take their memory and find ways to immortalize them, with their story being the push behind my work to influence those in positions of power to change policies, that in my humble opinion as a mom, were the reason my kids died."

I sat deeper in my chair, knowing I needed to allow her the space to let the material about the trauma come up naturally from my client. I wanted her more grounded. "Tracy, remember you have survived all of that."

She spat out her next words, that fire in her eyes, as she raised her voice. "Yes, I did, Sandra, but my kids didn't, did they?" The rage twisted her face until it disintegrated into the salt of the tears that followed, ripping an eerie sound from her soul like that of a female alpha wolf who had lost her pups to an errant hunter.

The frustration of her inability to save her sons pulsated from the hollows of her cheeks. I said, "Remember that you have survived and are carrying on the legacy of your beautiful boys to make this world a safer and kinder place for children and moms just like you. Breathe that in, Tracy! You have every right to be angry. You have no control over what has happened, but you do have a voice to speak up and share your story and your thoughts regarding what you believe could have been instrumental in saving your own boys. And thank you for being so real about what you are feeling in this moment." Just breathe Tracy.

With time, I visibly saw her beginning to let go.

She dabbed at her eyes, wiping away the smudges of mascara under them, but the determination in her voice was undeniable as she said, "I want to be strong and get my message out so this craziness of a parent bullying or abusing or killing children ends!" She lowered her head, indicating to me that tingling was radiating through her body. She was letting go of more activation focusing on her breath.

We sat quietly together until she leaned back in the chair and said, "I don't fully understand why God picked me to do this work, Sandra, but He did. You remind me to say to myself every morning that I am that 'Warrior Goddess' you call me and I will, on behalf of my sons, continue to speak up about how I was let down when I reached out for help."

I nodded and silently, we remained connected as she continued to release more activation.

"Well, Warrior Goddess," I replied. "I did give you that label, didn't I? However, remember a few months ago, I referred to you as a Wolverine. Actually, if I recall correctly, what I wanted you to say at the First Ladies Night was, 'When it comes to the safety of women and children, I am a F*#kin' Wolverine!' but you nixed that then. But now ... but now I see that sassy little gal who talked back to her mother has become that grown-up woman finding her voice laced with passion and determination in her quest to stand tall for what is just and important in the safety of children, particularly those children caught in the net of separation and divorce. I can feel it rising to the surface as I hear your sense of purpose in each word. You are really quite a tenacious woman, Tracy Stark."

"Yeah, right, Sandra. Look at me. I'm a wreck when I talk about what happened to my boys."

I responded gently, "Of course, you are, Tracy. You have been severely wounded, deeply traumatized. You are now simply releasing trauma that has been stored in your body. You will probably feel that 'offside' feeling again, so drink plenty of water when you leave here. You know how important hydration is for the players on the ice? Well, it is just as important in this therapeutic 'game.' You are releasing activation so you can become even more grounded in your quest to bring awareness to faults in the policies and procedures of the custody and access of children."

We continued working with the trauma in her nervous system. Once she had settled, I joked. "You don't need to catch a flight to Nashville tonight, do you?"

She allowed herself a little laugh.

"Well, really, Tracy," I continued joking with her. "It seems that you only come home to do laundry and then take off again."

She laughed again and I joined her as I continued to tease her, again lightening the mood. "Well. Sometimes it's hard to capture you to do this work with your busy schedule and all. What are you noticing now?"

"I still feel very shaky," she replied.

We worked together until the tingling throughout her body subsided.

She cleared her throat and started to speak again. "You know, Sandra, they had to leave together. Radek and Ryder, I mean. They have always been together and knowing they are with each other has brought me a degree of peace. Although, I can just hear Ryder, as he arrived in Heaven, suddenly seeing Radek up ahead of him and calling down to me, saying, 'Mom! Why does Radek have to be here? He's so annoying!'"

My eyes softened. "What a beautiful imagined exchange, Little Mama. You know your boys well!"

She gently wiped the remnant of a tear away with her right index finger. "Maybe Radek, Sandra, but Ryder always kept things to himself. I wish he had been able to share more of what was going on for him. Maybe if ..."

"Let's not go there today, Tracy."

She nodded, but ignoring me, continued to speak. "He learned well from his father that you just tough it out and in some ways perhaps, my boy was protecting me because he knew how upset and reactive I would be if he had shared what was really going on at his dad's place as it was happening."

I nodded in agreement with my client, saying, "That 'suck it up' or 'get over it' philosophy is all too prevalent in parenting young boys, particularly where crying is considered a weakness and only for girls. Actually, when you shared more of Ryder and Radek's lives and I was focused on getting to know them and their story a little better through your writings, I became even more mindful of the injustices that too many kids and vulnerable adults experience at the hands of another controlling adult. There are many kinds of abuse besides the physical abuse some people endure in their own families, which friends and neighbours in the outside world know nothing about. Many kids are not only scared but embarrassed by the conflict they are a part of or witness in their own homes, which should be safe havens for everyone in the family."

An *R&R* Law

Tracy replied, "That is why it is so important for me to tell my story. You know what I want Sandra? I want an actual **R&R** Law on behalf of my kids that states that biological parents don't just automatically get rights to their child or children in custody situations and I want all court orders regarding children to be enforced!" She shifted in the chair.

I listened as she gave voice to her inner thoughts and I did not interrupt as she went on sharing what was on her mind. "Corry's place was not a safe space for my boys and that is why I knew I needed to get them out of there. Ryder and Radek were reacting physically and emotionally from Corry's abuse. Something was amiss, but getting them to speak about what was going on was next to impossible until Radek broke the code of silence. Oh God, Sandra. How could I have possibly missed all the clues? Maybe those people who said I was blind were right. Why didn't I make them leave with me that last night?"

I intervened. "Tracy. Stop! Now! Don't go there!" I paused for emphasis. "No one. No one ever believed Corry would seriously harm his own kids. You know that! Your boys were tight-lipped for so long, like many kids from split families, particularly things that occurred when in the care of the other parent. It does you no good to wallow in what you might have missed. Your goal now is to tell your story and increase the awareness of others sharing custody, to prevent further instances of such happenings which, as we know, still occur."

She nodded.

"Your story is right here!" I pounded my chest with two fingers and then pointed my index finger at her. "Right there inside you and now you are sharing it!" I waited as she took this in. "What are you noticing now, Tracy?"

"I'm constructing my list."

"My list?"

"My list of what divorced and separated moms and dads need to watch for if they are concerned about what might be happening in the other parent's home."

"Okay. Good idea! However, you can do that later and send it to me. What are you noticing in your body as we discuss this?"

She sighed. "My chest is extremely tight as though it wants to burst open."

I continued coaching her. "You have a story to tell and you're gonna tell it, girl. I think your chest may be signaling you to break open and tell it!"

She settled as her shoulders dropped and she began to appear more and more relaxed during our session.

"Hmmm. That felt good and now I feel very sleepy," she said.

I follow her lead with, "If it's okay, just imagine the perfect place to sleep. It could be a beach in Mexico or resting on a cloud or beside a river, or sleeping in your own bed." I could see she was beginning to unwind the tension inside herself. We sat quietly until she opened her eyes and returned to the room.

Gradually she regrouped, extending her arms up toward the ceiling. "I hope I can make it home, Sandra. I'm always so exhausted after a session." She took a breath. "You know what else? I want to build an **R&R** Memorial Foundation to provide scholarships for kids who cannot afford to play a sport." Then she became reflective. "This is important to me but it is rather ironic because playing hockey was a large reason why Radek and Ryder were able to survive Dad's brutal way of loving them. Hockey was an obvious positive in their lives where they could forget what was going on at Dad's." She rose from the chair and put on her shoes as she prepared to leave.

"Sit for a couple of minutes in your car before you head out, please, Tracy. We did some powerful work here and remember the water. You need to drink plenty of water to move the energy."

"You mean water rather than whisky, Sandra?" she asked with the subtle playfulness I had come to expect and enjoy as she regained her ground.

I laughed. "Did I say that? And please, send me your list!"

Another monumental day in the life of a trauma therapist. Another session of letting go of the activation in the nervous system of my client. Another step on the healing journey.

Chapter 48

THE LISTS

WITHIN A FEW DAYS, SHE EMAILED HER LISTS.

TRE to SYK: Good Morning My Woman. The statistics you shared with me show that the majority of perpetrators of the filicide of older children and teens are fathers or stepfathers. I direct my suggestions for awareness to mothers, but such awareness may certainly apply to fathers caught in sharing custody with abusive ex-spouses. I have learned that such mistreatment is not necessarily physical and that it can be both "overt" and "covert." Good words, eh Sandra? I did some homework! LOL Here's my list. Where to start …

Twelve-Point Awareness Training for Divorced & Separated Parents Concerned About their Children's Safety when Sharing Custody

Things to watch for:

1. Children reporting unreasonable punishments being dished out in the other home by the other parent or step parent.
2. Children reporting a parent constantly calling down their other biological parent or being told they should not love that other parent
3. Children presenting as fearful of the other parent.
4. Children having difficulty sleeping or showing signs of anxiety after spending time with the other parent. Learn the signs!
5. Children reporting unsavoury behaviours by other parent—drinking/toking while driving, yelling, throwing things when angry, being drunk or disorderly. Learn to ask the right questions.

6. Children getting in trouble when they speak highly of the other parent.
7. Children lying to protect the errant parent so that parent will not be angry at them if they tell anyone of any physical, emotional, verbal or mental abuse occurring in their time in the other home.
8. Children erasing phone conversations with their mom/dad so the other parent will not see the messages.
9. Children having "accidents" in their pants/beds or displaying other stress responses including excessive anger, acting out, or becoming defiant.
10. Children blatantly refusing to spend time with the other parent.
11. Children losing weight or struggling with stomach aches or developing nervous habits or tics.
12. Children refusing to answer questions regarding "What happened?" Concerned parents need to learn to listen and become educated in asking the right questions.

Ten-Point Awareness Training for Child Services Workers

1. Pay attention and investigate parental reports submitted about children being disciplined with belts, fists, hockey sticks, straps or weapons of any kind including wooden spoons.
2. Review the files of previous incidents when a new report comes in.
3. Determine belittling, humiliating, and bullying tactics being used by parents on children by being trained in questioning children and noting symptoms of abused and frightened children.
4. Lobby for more workers becoming skilled at conducting home visits so that such are not prohibitive for those with few financial resources.
5. Establish a baseline for investigation erring on the side of caution in the safety of children and removing such children until investigations are completed.
6. Form focus groups with concerned citizens to gather ideas on changes needed in policies and procedures to stop violence against women and children.
7. Advocate for appropriate funding in Child Services so those in

the business of protecting children are not overburdened with the impossible task of managing too many caseloads effectively

8. Become fully trained as to the indicators of coercive control.

9. Become fully trained regarding the symptoms and methods of working with trauma and the impact of trauma on child development. Or... bring in those skilled in such areas for full consultation.

10. Form a STIC (Short Term Intensive Care) team of individuals involved in the life of an at-risk child to be on alert when reports of possible abuse are brought forward to Child Services.

Here's a start... from my experience as a mom and in talking to others who fear for the health and well-being of their children in custody situations.

Chapter 49

LIGHTING THE
FLAME OF LOVE

I HEARD THE SOUND OF HER VEHICLE DRIVING UP THE LONG ROAD TO THE Kolbuc Quarters. Today we would meet in the teepee. The sun shone brightly as she parked and exited her vehicle, bearing the bright and beautiful smile I have come to know over the past months.

She was carrying something and called out. "I have a gift for you!" She held up a wooden sign bearing the mantra, "Today is a Good Day to Have a Good Day!"

My smile widened. "Why, thank you, Tracy Stark. How thoughtful of you!" I gave her a warm hug. We moved inside the AIM teepee, where I rested my new sign against one of the poles before we settled into our seats inside.

She looked around and commented on her surroundings: "This teepee is incredible. I love it in here!"

I respond, "There is something very grounding about this space." I reached for another cedar shake and put it on the fire, watching as it caught the flame and ignited before us.

I began our session. "Before you came today, I was rereading some of the many messages you continue to receive on Facebook from your ever-expanding tribe. There is much love in those texts from so many who have been touched by your story and who want to walk with you on this road. It seems many are waiting to see what you're going to say, to do. They seem to be loyal followers who want to know how they can support you and your vision."

She moved her eyes from her focus on the fire in the centre of the teepee and, looking up, grabbed a stick and began gently stoking the fire. "I know," she said. "I am blessed to have had so much validation, particularly from women, which gives me even more courage to continue on this quest on behalf of my boys to make sure other youngsters do not go through what mine did while in their dad's supposed 'care.'"

"I hear you, Little Mama," I said softly. We sat breathing in the pleasant yet pungent aroma of the cedar as the fire burned in the centre of the teepee.

I turned from the fire, catching her gaze. "You know, Tracy, you light a fire in those who read your Facebook posts. I see the responses to what you have written. I know you say that you have trouble with the limelight, but if that were not your purpose, perhaps you could walk into the IGA store, buy your groceries, sneak out before anyone notices you, and go home and just cook dinner for your husband. But now, you have a different persona. Perhaps it is time to be even more seen and heard because now what you do has an even greater influence on your followers."

She sighed, continuing to stare into the fire. "Sometimes it seems like such a big responsibility, Sandra. My phone is constantly filled with messages!"

"Hmmm. I imagine it does feel that way, Tracy Stark. People look up to you and follow your posts. You need strength to manage all the interactions. I am impressed with how well you seem to be able to command such a following each time you post."

"Thank you, Sandra. Sometimes … it's hard not to just want to hide away from everything that has happened. Sometimes it's nice to go where nobody knows me or my story. Our counselling sessions help settle me, so I can go back out into the big wide world where everybody seems to knows my name and my story!"

She reached down and continued playing in the fire with a willow stick she had taken from the wood pile beside her.

"Well," I said. "Here we are, my friend, out in the wilderness where none of the moose, bear or deer know your name, but they did want me to ask you, 'What is going well?'"

She laughed. "Well, Brent has been great. He makes me laugh in the hard times and shows how much he loves me every day. He says, 'Tracy we have the means to go anywhere, do anything we want, anywhere in the world and plaster **R&R** stickers wherever we go. Let's do it!'

"He's very spontaneous, while I need routine. Most times, we do well and meet in the middle." I have her breathe into her gratitude for the man who had captured her heart and who has walked beside her through all they had experienced since that fateful December day. I knew that Brent was a strong character. He had shared with me that he simply wanted Tracy to be okay. He was not interested in sitting in my chair and that was okay too. I knew he would come when and if he decided it might be helpful for Tracy to have him by her side.

Today was a good day to have a good day with my client here in the energy of the AIM teepee. My golden retrievers, Saje and Sugah, entered and found places to rest beside Tracy. She stroked their fur as we talked and these, my co-therapists, provided the opportunity for my client to become even more grounded by simply stroking their fur. We processed the fear she had shared of losing Brent. We took our time to again decrease the activation in her nervous system. Each session, she was becoming more and more focused on her mission.

Chapter 50

A SINGLE VOICE

WE MET AGAIN IN THE TEEPEE THE FOLLOWING WEEK. THE BRISKNESS OF THE air of early spring was offset by the glow of the fire burning in the centre of the teepee, warming the counselling space. We went through our usual beginnings as she revealed to me sensations she was noticing as we processed what had come up for her since our last meeting.

I began. "I asked you to write an autobiography some time ago and you did a great job of sharing your history before and after Corry. What I want to know now is, if you have been able to find the time to take that second step and write about who you are becoming since you lost your sons?"

She suddenly glared at me. It was like there was a frigid chill coming from the north side of the teepee. "They are not lost, Sandra. They are right here in my heart!" She placed her right hand solidly over her heart as if to protect the boys from my errant remark. "Right here in my heart!" Her voice had risen considerably.

I responded quickly. "God! I am so sorry, Tracy! Of course, that is exactly where they are!" I could see that fire again in her eyes as I attempted to dial down her passion a little so we might continue in peace. I understood her reaction.

"Really, Trac, that was such a poor choice of words."

She was still rather intense but began to relax as she reached into a manila folder and removed a file she had brought to the session. She cleared her throat and asked, "So, are you ready to hear my 'Who Am I Now,' Sandra?"

"You bet I am," I replied, settling into my chair to hear what she had written. She cleared her throat and began.

Who Am I Now?

by

Tracy Stark

After everything I have gone through, I still consider myself a hockey wife and mama. Just as important, I now consider myself as the voice of many women and children who are silenced by broken justice and child protection systems built to be politically correct but not working effectively in the interest of women and children. Systems that believe a man can still be an excellent father even if he is abusive to his wife or ex-wife. I beg to differ.

I never imagined I would be the person I am today, shining a light on the issues I have dealt with in the death of my children on behalf of all women (and men) legally ordered to share custody of their children with unhealthy fathers or mothers. I never imagined that I would be at the mercy of the courts regarding the safety of my children. I never imagined that either of my boys would die before me. Nor did I imagine that I would choose a man in my life who would take away the breath of my children in such a violent way. I never imagined that I could survive losing my kids in the manner in which they died. I never thought I could ever live through the loss of my children without going insane, but then, I did go insane for a while after they died. I was certain that as a mother, I could never go on living if either my Radek or my Ryder died. Nonetheless, somehow, I have survived the death of both of my sons on the same day in the same year in the same ungodly manner by the same man.

My most important job was always to simply be a good mom: to walk with or drive my boys to the bus stop for school each morning, to dress them up for their Christmas concerts and Hallowe'en, to cheer them on in their hockey games. They were my boys and I felt so privileged to be their mom. Since the time I was small, I loved playing dolls and I was still playing dolls with my friend in Grade 8 when most girls were getting excited about boys in their lives. Hell. Guess I was what you might call a late bloomer. I had no great ambition to be a doctor, a lawyer, a massage therapist, a teacher or sell life insurance. I just wanted to be a mom. I wanted to watch my children learn new skills, to be good boys, happy in their lives. I wanted to watch my sons play, to hold them tight when they were sad or afraid. I wanted to hear them laugh with their friends.

When they were little, I wanted to get down on the floor and play with them even though my then-husband thought that it was … ridiculous. I wanted to joke with them, to hear them tease me, to tease them, and tuck them in at night. I loved chasing away the scary monsters that were ever-present, particularly under Radek's bed! I had imagined nothing different until it did not work with Corry. Then, after we separated, the hardest part of my life was not being around them during Corry's week. I was always wondering how they were doing and was helplessly missing my little boys who had been my whole world since they had been born. It was tough sharing them with Corry, simply because … I missed them and I worried about them without having me to protect them from Corry's anger outbursts and need for control.

Never did I imagine my quest in life would be to awaken in every reader the knowledge of how fragile life is and how it can change all your well-laid out plans in a heartbeat. Never did I realize the importance of taking a stand on what I truly believe and the importance of finding one's voice about things that matter and speaking up, loudly and clearly. Never did I think I would become an advocate working to protect innocent children caught in the crossfire of broken or damaged relationships by telling my story. Never did I think of establishing a foundation to help less fortunate children becoming involved in sport where good leadership could provide the possibility of a refuge for children whose homes may not be safe places in which to grow. Never did I imagine speaking about my sorrow and my vision before a room of 250 wine-drinkin' women and receiving a standing ovation!

Who am I now, you ask? I am but a single voice wanting greater protection for women and children in our society and wanting the strength to work to influence those who can change laws to increase such safety. That strength lies within me. Until my last breath, I will continue using my energy to bring awareness to the necessity of changing laws and attitudes regarding the protection of children.

I believe God knew if He took his children home, they would be eternally safe and my heartbreak would give me the strength to move those gigantic mountains everyone talks about when addressing a difficult task. God knew I have had a fire within me since I was a little kid. What do I believe, after much soul searching both in and out of your blue chair, Sandra? I truly believe that God knew that I loved my boys more than it is possible to imagine. He knew that if He breathed my boys' spirits into me to give me strength, I would do my part in making my corner of the world a safer, kinder place for women and children.

What about my day-to-day living? My days are simple. I relish routine. It is something I can control in my day. Every morning, I wake up and let the day unfold. I live more in the moment than ever before. Sandra, you taught me the importance of that and the skills that remind me of how I can be present in just this moment when I am overtaken by those grief bursts in my darkest hours. Those dark, dismal days are fewer and further between as the hours come and go, but until the day I am reunited with my sons, I know I will continue to experience such periods of grief and incredible sadness. Sometimes I miss them more than I can even say. My focus now is to ensure my boys did not die in vain. My work? To walk tall into challenges I never thought I could possibly take on. I now believe this is my path.

My task is no longer directly as a mom looking after the needs of my precious boys. God is doing that. My job is telling my story and our story as client and therapist in my healing journey. It is sharing the support of hundreds of people who have gifted me with their love and their own stories since my boys died. It is my purpose to gather those around me willing to join me in taking a solid position regarding the importance of limited, supervised access to those fathers and mothers with an obvious need for revenge against and control of their ex-partners.

Those who display unfiltered anger toward their own children and their children's other biological parent, as did the father of my children, need to be seriously reined in. Men, particularly those who still have access to their biological children without significant restraint despite their danger to women and children, must be kept in check by new and more significant policies, procedures, and laws.

Every day I wonder why God would choose me to do this work. My children were my whole world. I would have done anything to protect them, and yet they did not survive their walk on this earth. I was not able to save them. I spent my life as a mom protecting Radek from those monsters under his bed, never realizing that the monster to be most afraid of was his dad, lying right beside him in Dad's own bed, which should have been a safe refuge for my little boy.

I do believe in the power of God and yet often I still question why he took my children the way He did. What I now believe is that God knew that I loved my boys more than anything. He knew if he took his children into His forever care, that they would always be safe playing hockey on the heavenly ice as so beautifully described by L.M. Koziak in her poem "Heaven's Team."

My heartbreak gives me the power to work hard, so another mother does not experience the death of her children at the hands of an unhealthy father attempting to crush the spirit of his ex for leaving him and "destroying" his privileged life. I will not be crushed. Instead, I will team up with others willing to join me as well as other women whose ex-husbands with deep pockets contract the most expensive lawyers in their fight to undermine their ex-wives and gain access to their children in unfair financial and custody settlements.

My heartbreak gives me the mental and physical muscle to battle in the corners with those not in alignment with my vision of safety and security for all women and particularly, because of my experience, all those women and children of separation and divorce. I am willing to work diligently with those in positions of power as I pursue justice in the name of my sons for any and all children impacted by separation and divorce custody issues when emotions run high. I am willing to give my all in this effort even when I feel there is next to nothing left to give.

God knows I have the strength to work tirelessly and be ready for every encounter and let no one or nothing defeat me in taking my concerns in the direction of the goal of changing the rulebook governing custody and access. God knows I have the tenacity to work hard and handle myself with finesse, provided I learn to keep my anger under control and use it properly when I talk about what I believe could have saved my boys. When I speak about what I believe is needed now so other children and their mothers are protected which iinvolves not only changing laws but bringing awareness to the need for a shift in thinking. Do I believe all men are bad news? Far from it. However, I do believe we need fathers modeling for their children respect and kindness in their interactions with the mothers of such children.

When I was in my last days of pregnancy with Ryder, my baby boy's heart rate was drastically dropping and his birth became an emergency C-section. He was only 4 lb 8 oz, so he had to be placed in the NICU.[19] He was having a hard time and we were initially separated. During those first few hours, his nurse sent me a Polaroid picture of my newborn baby. Ironically, in that picture, it is

---

19   Neonatal intensive care unit.

Corry's hands holding Ryder for the first time. This message was written neatly across the bottom of the picture: "Are you ok, Mom? I am. Love Ryder."

I want both my boys to know their mom is okay.

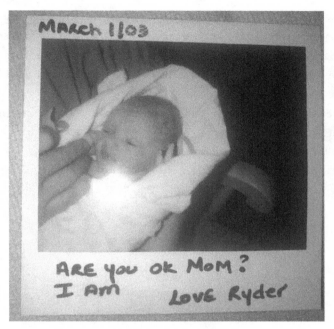

"Are you okay, Mom?"

* * *

I was spellbound, totally silenced by the beauty and power of her writing.

She looked up at me and smiled, her eyes wet with tears.

"Wow, Tracy Stark! That was amazing!"

She closed her notebook. "And that, Sandra, is who I am becoming … now and rest assured, when it comes to wanting to make a difference for other children, I am becoming what you called me that First Wolverine Ladies Night when I descended the stairs and gave you a big hug. You are right. I am becoming … that F*#ing Whitecourt Wolverine!"

The fire was almost out in the teepee but I could see the eternal flame of the passion and the power within my client.

"Oh Tracy. You have such a story to tell. You are a model of resilience and strength. I know some days are really tough. Just taking that pen and writing whatever comes up can be therapeutic in letting go of the angst you experience on those tough days. Bit by bit, those words, those sentences, paragraphs, and chapters will move you toward your goal of getting this story into the hands of those you want to join your team and moving this story into the mainstream."

"Yes, Sandra. I hear you. I am just learning how to tell it." She rose from the chair as we finished our session and smiled. "It felt good to write what I did and then share it with you!"

I looked at her with admiration. "I am the lucky one, Tracy. Thank you for sharing."

She exited the teepee, returning to her world.

I spoke quietly, half to myself, "*Yes, Ryder. Rest assured. Mom is doing OKAY.*"

Chapter 51

THE MOVE BACK "HOME" 2018

I SAW HER NAME IN MY ROSTER AND AS SHE ARRIVED ON A BEAUTIFUL APRIL day, I was delighted to see her again.

"So, my friend, what is going well?" I asked as we settled once again into the confines of the teepee, listening to the ping of the spring raindrops on the canvas.

"I'm ready for this one," she said. "I thought about how to answer your question all the way here! What is going well are many things but I think the biggest one is that we are moving back to our old house!"

"Are you kidding me?"

She shook her head. "Nope!"

"Wow! How did that happen?"

Tracy sat taller in her chair. "Well, it's actually pretty lonely out there in the country sometimes. Brent tells everyone he is rotting out there." She laughed softly. "If we are out with friends in town, we have to take a taxi home and people just don't drop by like they did when we lived in town."

"What do you notice as you think about moving back to your old house, Tracy?"

"My toes are already tingling!" she replied.

We breathed in and breathed out in sync, taking the time to allow her nervous system to release the activation.

I watched her settle in the chair. "So, tell me, how did this move back come about?" I asked.

She began: "Well, although Brent denies it, before we made the decision to move back to our old place, I am sure he secretly got Lindsay and Cory Mercer, good friends and renters of our old place, to invite us over one evening so that he could lure me back to where he felt most comfortable. It had been exactly seven months since I had even been on our old road. After we moved to the country, it had been too hard for me to drive down that street where we had lived. The memories of my boys playing street hockey, riding their bikes, playing basketball in the front driveway … it was all way too much.

"But that night, as I walked through the front door of our old home, crazy as it sounds, it was as though my boys were greeting me, hugging me warmly, welcoming me home. Amazingly, it felt right. There was a sense of comfort that I had not experienced for a long time."

She shifted in the chair and continued. "When we returned to our country home after our evening together with the Mercers, Brent and I talked long and hard into the night. As I said before, I had been too afraid to walk the perimeter of our acreage because of cougar and bear sightings, so I felt somewhat confined to our yard. It was so quiet out there. Unless we planned an event at our home, we were too far out of town for people to just drop by, and our home had always been a place filled with people. Poor Brent was going insane because he feeds off that 'people' energy. The serenity of the place had been good for a while, but I think we both recognized that, though the death of the boys had changed us, we were still Tracy and Brent and our lifestyle needed to involve other people.

"We missed our friends and family dropping by, now that we lived out in the wilds! It had been what I needed for a while, but as we talked, we realized we have so many great memories with the boys in our old house. Brent had said continually, 'Tracy. Don't blame the house. The house did not do anything to us!'

"It took a while, but after my shedding more than a few tears, we decided to move back to town and do a renovation on our old place. I knew I could handle the memories. That was all I had! We still owned the house and the Mercers' new house would soon be finished.

"We are going to make a number of changes in the house before we reclaimed our space. Obviously, we wanted to do something with the boys' bedrooms. I would not be able to handle walking by their rooms that were simply turned into a couple of guest rooms with the boys' beds and furniture still intact for visitors. No! That space is far too sacred to be simply guest rooms. The renovations will honour their spirits that live in the walls and … honestly … I can hardly wait to get started. I want to create a special space to honour the boys in that bedroom area."

I noted the excitement in her voice as a smile spread across her face.

The Zen Den

She expanded on her vision for the renovation: "Once we made the decision to move back, time could not move quickly enough! I had been thinking of the possibility of creating a meditation space and in mentioning my idea to Brent, he was all in. We would call it 'The Zen Den.' It would also be a special space for all the beautiful gifts we had received when the boys died, heartfelt gifts, filled with the loving energy of the givers.

"It didn't take long before Brent was on the phone hiring a contractor. Our neighbours, who have lived down the street from us for the past ten years, said they would be proud to contract to do the changes we wanted. Our kids had been like family to them, particularly Radek, as he had gone to school with their daughter since they were in kindergarten and had ridden bikes and practiced lacrosse with their son. The endearing energy that would go into creating that space was also a blessing. Nothing like living in a small town with friends down the block putting their caring energy into manifesting my Zen Den, fully engaged in creating a transcendent space to honour my sons. The room will give me a true centre where I can simply be in my boys' energy, explore my own thoughts, engage in my Pinterest addiction, or read or watch TV when I need the distraction."

"Well, Tracy," I replied, "in some ways, it can be particularly gratifying as you think about renovating the area that had been the boys' rooms in a way that still celebrates them."

"Right," she said. "The hardest part for me has been knowing that the contractors will be tearing down their bedrooms. Rooms where I would tuck them in at night." She stopped as tears welled up in her eyes. "I just miss them so much sometimes, Sandra. Particularly when things are quiet."

"Of course, you do, Tracy. Let those tears fall." I waited a moment. "Just take a minute to focus on the love you continue to share with your sons."

I paused as she closed her eyes.

"What do you see and hear when you close your eyes and remember your boys?"

She took her time, breathing in the energy of the teepee, and then she shared the images. "I can see Radek with his stuff all over the place. I can hear him giggling!" She took another breath. "I can see Ryder heading up to his room with his friends or I can hear him slamming his bedroom door when he was mad at Radek!"

Her eyes remained closed as she shared the remembrances.

"Would it be okay to tell me of some of the most memorable moments with your boys, Tracy?" It was again a "Hello before Goodbye" moment.

She breathed in, sighing and opening her eyes as she continued to share what was coming up for her in our conversation. "I think often of the last time I saw them. Our last hugs. Waving to Ryder in the player's box as we left the Millwood's Recreation Centre that last night and Radek saying goodbye and telling me he was going to miss me as he wiped his tears on his sleeve."

She hesitated. "They died doing what they loved and that still comforts me. However, sometimes it is still like a dream I am going to wake up from and then, I wake up and it is not a dream. It is real and that ... that is the hardest part, Sandra." She became emotional again as she touched into the reality of her boys' deaths.

I grabbed the box of Kleenex but removed a tissue that I handed her directly. She dabbed her eyes.

I continued stirring the coals in the fire with a cedar stick as I shared my thoughts. We breathed in the silence together, the crackle of the fire amplifying the intensity and the beauty of our healing work. "I know I can't 'fix' what happened for you, Tracy, but I want to make sure this space you share with me allows you to feel whatever you are feeling right here, right now and be okay with that. I hand you a tissue not to stop the tears, but rather so you feel safe enough to be fully present to all the feelings arising within you."

She accepted another tissue, wiping her eyes as tears continued to fall. "Sandra. What you said just now ... about feeling safe enough to be in touch with all my feelings. You created that space in our first session. I have learned to accept all my feelings, both dark and light. I do sit with them and allow them to move through me as you have suggested and I have found that it really does help. I thank you for creating this safe space with you where I can use all your Kleenex month after month!"

I smiled gently at the woman sitting beside the fire, embracing its warmth as she shared what was going on inside of her.

We remained silent until I asked, "What do you notice as you think about your Zen Den, Tracy?"

She breathed in, remaining silent.

I am reflective as I wait for her response. I add, "A room called The Zen Den where you can be in the forever **R&R** energy sounds like a beautiful idea."

She smiled, gently drying her tears as she nodded and said, "I already have the vision in my head. Now if I can just relay my ideas to my renovators!" She shared her decisions regarding the memorabilia she wanted to place in this space. We processed her vision until our time was up. Our session ended.

Tracy returned to her world to proceed with actualizing her Zen Den. Deconstruction was soon underway. She knew they were building something that would still represent Ryder and Radek, which made the tearing down of their bedrooms much easier to accept. Later in the month, I received a text telling me everything had gone extremely well. On June 21, 2018, the Starks moved back home, just in time to host a beautiful graduation celebration for Brent's younger daughter, Shelbey. What a party! What a celebration!

Shelbey's High School Graduation

Chapter 52

WHY WRITE?

The Purpose of the Story

SYK to TRS: Refine for me again, please. I need to make sure I've got this clearly in my mind. What would be your purpose in writing this story? What are your key messages?

A few days later, I received her completed assignment.

TRS to SYK: You are truly relentless, Sandra! I thought I had covered this … but how's this? The purpose of sharing my story and that of my sons would be to eventually see laws changed! No biological parent deserves rights to his or her children if those children are being raised in a unsafe environment while in that biological parent's care. Such should be earned by being a competent, caring, mentally healthy adult and not given, in many cases, to a father simply because he had planted the seed of life years before or … because he pays child support.

SYK to TRS: Funny, isn't it, Tracy? A person needs a licence to fish in the rivers or hunt in the forests or drive on the highways. A person needs specific training and examinations to become a teacher, doctor, lawyer, welder, power engineer, social worker, or therapist but funny thing … there are no restrictions, no guidelines or tests, no requirements necessary to raise children. Do we just assume parenting is instinctual in human beings? NOT! What do kids learn regarding parenting and other life skills on the road to becoming a competent, healthy, kind, and caring human? Is learning to balance an equation more important than learning skills to be a good partner or a good person or a self-regulated human being? Kids learn their emotional intelligence by what they see in their own families, their own parents who have learned to parent from how they were raised and when there is dysfunction, such negative behaviour is often passed on to future offspring. And that is scary. Increasing awareness of such abuse is certainly a good start. And sometimes, that is very scary! Increasing awareness as to what constitutes abuse is important because abuse is not always as outrageously blatant as it was in your case. But you telling your story is powerful.

I received Tracy's response in an email.

TRS to SYK: I hear you, Sandra. In my mind, people in the business of protecting children need to become even more alert, more curious when they see or hear of possible instances of parental abuse or reported concerns regarding changes in a child's behaviour or appearance. Self-reports by children and mothers must be followed up in quick order! Why was this not done in my case? Because it was … December? Because the case worker was overloaded with far too many cases? Because bureaucracy takes time? Because people who are unfair have the rights to a "fair" trial and load up the court system? Individuals in positions of authority must create opportunities to check in with a child or perhaps a child's coach or teacher or relative without delay when a report such as mine is submitted. It is very unlikely that a child, particularly a young teenage boy like Ryder, would tell anyone directly what was going on in his home. I think kids in situations like mine learn early that silence is the best way. Caring and concerned individuals cannot be afraid to report such instances where immediate investigation is needed for the safety of children. Has everyone forgotten the slogan "It takes a village to raise a child?" Where was my village?

In many of my "could have turned bad" situations, the authorities (aka the police) told me over and over that Corry had a right to his children simply because he was the biological father. Corry continually threw that in my face. That to me was absolute bullsh*t. I find it unbelievable that someone in a decision-making position who did not know our history could simply justify Corry's rights by the simple statement, "because he is the biological father," and put the onus on me to remove my children from an unsafe environment without assistance from a government department or a legal system supposedly committed to protecting vulnerable citizens. Who is more at risk than our children? Should police officers and our justice system not be more focused on keeping innocent children safe rather than the 'rights' of all biological fathers. This makes for maintaining a culture advocating for those who make it difficult for kind and caring fathers to have access to their children because such biological 'bullies' do not model good behavioral standards for their children. Why do we need adversarial systems rather than honoring the couples who work in the best interest of their children rather than the those who model resentful attitudes toward their ex-partners?

I know that many of Corry's antics were simply done to cause me distress. In two incidents when I went to the RCMP in regards to the safety of my children while they were with their father, I was denied any kind of help, any kind of compassion or direction, any kind of acknowledgement that my concerns might be valid. I guess three times a charm because the third time, it was a murder-suicide and the police had to answer the call for help.

When I discovered that my children were at risk in their father's care, I felt I needed help in removing them from his home. As I have stated many times, I was never ever afraid of Corry. However, I was afraid for my children because I knew they would always suffer the repercussions of my actions from their father if he was upset with me. I had to be smart once I went to the authorities and Corry learned I knew what was going on. I would have taken all the bullets for my kids if I had ever suspected what was going to happen. Perhaps, had I not returned them on December 18, 2016, a raging Corry would have hunted us all down—Brent, me, and my boys, and murdered all of us. But then, what I am experiencing as a grieving mother is far more painful than my dying, which I am sure is what Corry would have wanted. It was the ultimate revenge he could have inflicted on me.

However difficult losing my sons has been, I am not curled up in a ball on the floor as you thought initially that I might be, Sandra. I promise you … that will never be me! I will continue to stand my ground and be an advocate for women and children in the name of my children. Radek and Ryder are my forever teammates and we are on a mission to ensure that there are serious consequences for offenders when court orders regarding children are breached.

Policies and procedures of Child Services must be revised and written in CODE RED when children are reported at risk in the likes of a letter such as that written by me, Tracy Stark, and sent on December 3, 2016. Children must be removed immediately from unsafe circumstances until a full investigation renders a biological parent fit to access his/her children or requires supervised visitation to ensure their safety. It is my desire and my hope that such laws will be done in the name of my beautiful "gone too soon" children. They are my reason for pushing through the pain of losing them to create a different story for others.

SYK to TRS: I am with you, Tracy Stark. To expand on your disappointment with Hockey Alberta, I want to tell you about a movement in Canada called the Responsible Coaching Movement.[20] On its website is an excellent section on Ethical Decision Making, which is designed to be useful to any coach in making decisions regarding difficult situations with players or parents. The Responsible Coaching Movement is a call to action for sport organizations across Canada—on and off the field, court or ice.

TRS to SYK: Thank you for that info. I will definitely check it out. That call from the other hockey mom meant so much to me when Corry was humiliating Ryder in the dressing room, when my boy was playing on her son's team a few years ago. That was so wrong and I would never have known if she had not called me. It prompted me to get Ryder some additional counselling to counter his dad's influence.

SYK to TRS: I become very passionate when I see or hear of supposed "adults" abusing youngsters with humiliating taunts or engaging in their own tantrums when they are interacting with their own kids or other kids within their sphere of influence as coaches, teachers, or parents. What was Corry modelling for his boys? What was he trying to achieve with his meanness to them? And his denigration of you as a woman? A mother?

TRS to SYK: I have asked myself that question a hundred thousand times! Did I ever think December 18, 2016, would be the last time I would hug my children? Never! Did I ever think Corry would resort to such violent behaviour in disciplining and then destroying my sons? Never! But I needed support and when I reached out for such back up to remove my boys from Corry's home, no one was there. I want people in the justice system and in child services held accountable for their part in what happened to my boys. Corry was allowed too many liberties in parenting my sons. He was never taken to task by the authorities for not following court orders. I want those in decision-making positions to know they failed me and they failed my boys.

---

20   The Responsible Coaching Movement (Coach.ca) is an organization invested in improving practices that ensure the health, safety, and well-being of all participants.

However, they turned their backs on the wrong mama! I will die fighting for the rights of children to be protected and treated fairly in the name of my **R&R**. But my concerns as a mom go beyond the issue of children in separated and divorced families, Sandra. It goes beyond what happens on the ice or in athletic dressing rooms. It goes beyond sport. How many children cry themselves to sleep because they are scared of a parent's rage or ache for that hug at night when such actions are not forthcoming because Mom and Dad are too busy with their own lives to take that time to be present to their kids? How many kids are terrorized by what may be going on in their own homes and are petrified of telling anyone? How many moms turn a blind eye to such things going on in their families in their own need to avoid conflict with the man in their life or simply out of their own fear for themselves and their children? How many tender little boys learn early that tears are a sign of weakness and that to be a real man means never showing tender feelings, never telling his own sons how very much he loved them and … that a little boy's precious teddy bear named Baby belonged in the garbage!

SYK to TRS: I hear you, Tracy. I chose to talk about sport specifically because your boys played on a team, but it does go far beyond hockey or any other sport. What concerns me as a woman and a therapist is that we need so many family violence shelters in our province and country. This is beyond a travesty that such domestic violence cannot be reined in within a supposedly civilized country where many bullies like Corry who abuse their wives or who torment their own children are not brought to serious justice. Where domestic abuse continues in a supposedly enlightened society. Where we need to actually raise money to fund shelters to protect women and children from abusive men. The stress of the pandemic has clearly brought even more women and children into requiring safe places to escape domestic violence. Shelters are having to turn away victims or scramble to find additional accommodations. What does that say about our values as a society? What does it say about our culture?

Another email arrived in reply. Two women on a rampage!

TRS to SYK: What are we teaching our boys? What are we doing to our boys? My boys loved Corry and they wanted him to be proud of them. He was their model for a man. They did not see him as the bully he was until the very end, but that is exactly what their words and his tactics showed me he was, long ago! And then, for too long, my boys were too damn afraid to tell me what was going on. Oh God, Sandra. Now I am getting hot. I see it all now!

I cringed when I received her email. Maybe this writing back and forth was not a good idea. There was no titrating her experiences here, no lessening the impact of what she was sharing. She was in full-blown anger. Maybe I should have just listened instead of projecting my concerns regarding the raising of young males onto her. Maybe ...

SYK to TRS: Please shut it down Tracy and call me!

TRS to SYK: I am on a roll Sandra, but I'm okay. I will call when I am finished.

Hmm. I had just been told.

Mental Health Issues

TRS to SYK: Let's talk about mental health issues. It is so easy for people to say, "Oh, Corry must have suffered from a mental health issue" as if that's a valid excuse for such totally abusive behaviours when the boys were in his home. To me, he was just a spiteful human being who couldn't get over the fact that his wife left him ten goddam years before because he was a total control freak. He could no longer control me, so he tried to control me through the kids, and when the kids got smarter than he was? When he thought the boys might tell me all that was happening in his home, he had to pull the ultimate control and kill them. The Medical Examiner said he was not drunk or stoned when he committed such a hateful act. However, there was evidence of long-term alcohol and drug abuse. My opinion in this matter may differ from yours as a therapist, Sandra, but I feel badly for those suffering from mental illness who are lumped in the same category as a monster who murders his own children because of the manner in which he believed young boys should be raised and because he finally realized a way to hurt me beyond belief.

SYK to TRS: As a therapist, I have learned that there is a strong link between childhood trauma and adult dysfunction. Trauma itself can come in many forms. Abuse, neglect, loss, and bullying fall under the category of interpersonal relationships, but trauma also includes the categories of accidents and falls, difficult medical and dental procedures and surgeries, and global activation (near drowning, electrocution, natural disasters, and growing up in a dangerous environment, amongst other traumas) that end up filling an individual's trauma cup from the time they are in utero with their mother. There is also more and more research on the impact of intergenerational trauma that is passed on to the offspring of parents and grandparents severely traumatized in their own histories. Such can be very activating and contribute to filling up that susceptible trauma cup that we all have since before we were even born. These childhood traumas often contribute to the basic tenets of many psychiatric disorders. There are countless individuals who have crossed the door of the AIM office who have faced many adverse childhood experiences, colloquially called ACE. I can send you more information on this if you like. You sure you are okay?

TRS to SYK: I'm good. Actually, felt good to share what I have been feeling inside.

I settled once again into my office, reviewing our interchange. I sent a quick text sharing my concerns regarding my fear of her being retraumatized by writing about the past trauma surrounding December 19, 2016. She replied, admitting feeling unsettled in revisiting the events surrounding the death of her sons. She mentioned that Brent too, was often frustrated with her after she wrote her remembrances of those painful days. He told her that she changed when she wrote about what had happened and was hard to be around. I spoke about this with Tracy, stating that she was no doubt retraumatized by revisiting some of the scenes she was sharing. She promised to meet with me more regularly after writing more segments of her story. I breathed in a sigh of relief. We scheduled a meeting the next day where we processed what she had written. She continued to release more of the activation she had been experiencing.

Time passed before she tackled sharing her memories of saying goodbye to the boys. Eventually I received her next writings and we scheduled another meeting to again decrease the activation in her system. She was always the expert on what was going on within her, and I, but the consultant. We worked continually to be in the present moment, here and now. As always, she templated off my regulated nervous system. I made sure I was grounded in the now, not back in her past experience with her. She began to release more and more of the activation. She began to become more regulated.

Sorry I Couldn't Save You

I visited Tracy's Facebook page on the second anniversary of the death of the boys and read what she had written. I guess she forgot she was just going to send these dramatic posts to me. I read the hundreds of beautiful replies. The support of so many people was a most important resource for my client.

Facebook Post

December 19, 2018
Tracy Stark

Two years ago, at this exact moment, I was standing outside of the home where my boys were supposed to be sheltered and safe. At this very moment my breath was wiped from my body. My heart felt a hurt that can never be fully described. My only sons were murdered by someone they loved and trusted. I relive this moment every single day. What I saw at the door that December morning will never escape my mind.

That day could have been prevented if people had done their jobs. From the day my son showed up at hockey in a dress and not one person stepped in to ask why. Not one parent. Not one coach. I never even heard about it until Radek told me the following weekend.

How about the letter I wrote to Child Services ... Telling them about my children being beat with hockey sticks, Ryder forced to wear a dress to hockey, getting his head shaved against his will, plus many more disturbing incidents ...

All I wanted was help getting my kids out of that house.

But nope, I guess it was not enough to protect my sons.

For the past two years ... I have one word ... Why????

I'm so sorry, Ryder and Radek. I'm so sorry I could not save you

MOM

Chapter 53

THE BLUE DIAMOND - FEBRUARY 2019

WE WERE EMAILING BACK AND FORTH AGAIN IN THE NEW YEAR AND TRACY shared with me one of her recent experiences.

TRS to SYK: In the peace and tranquility of my Zen Den, Pinterest has become a safe place for me to explore. It was a calming experience to look through the many ideas that were displayed on the website and to connect with those who had found my boys' story on the site. One day, I was looking at ideas of what people did with the ashes of their loved ones and I came across a picture of a diamond made out of such ashes. The very idea of creating a diamond ring with my boys' remains resonated strongly with me. I contacted the listed company. The co-founder of the company answered my call. I could tell she had a passion for what she did. She was very kind in answering all my questions. A week later, I received a kit from her in the mail, which would enable me to send my boys' ashes to her company and have them made into a diamond.

Feet & Inches

One evening, shortly after that, my friend Carla and I were visiting at my kitchen table when I told her about the kit, mentioning how hard it would be for me to go into the boys' urns. I had never seen the ashes of human-remains before. I remembered Fran from the funeral home telling me that if I ever wanted to remove ashes from the urns, I was to take the urns to her and she would do it for me. My understanding was that the urns were locked shut. Carla said, "Let's check them out right now and see if we can get them open."

We were living on the acreage then and I had the urns on a shelf in my office. I got up and went to retrieve them, returning with one urn under each arm. I placed my sweet boys on the kitchen table. As I set them down, I took a deep breath. I did not know if I could really do this. I had seen those necklaces with gold-trimmed vials of ashes of a loved one featured, but … a diamond? A diamond, forged from the ashes of my sons, that I could wear forever on my finger? A diamond that would catch the sunlight and sparkle? Sparkle like my boys had in their short lives? Sparkle as I wandered the globe, placing the **R&R** stickers and giving my sons new opportunities to see the world. I looked at Carla and she at me. My dear friend was with me. I breathed in the nerve to do what needed to be done. I turned the lid on Ryder's urn. It opened! Immediately I felt sick to my stomach as I regarded the ashes inside. I was hesitant and teary. I breathed in again and turned the lid on Radek's urn. It opened as well. I still did not know if I could really do this. I looked again at Carla. She was right there beside me, giving me courage. We would do it together

I referred to the instructions sent inside the containers enclosed in the return package. The instructions said to send a half-cup of ashes for each of the boys. I held back. It sounded so crazy. I used to measure my boys in feet and inches and now I was measuring them in cups??

Carla undid the twist ties while I grabbed a measuring cup. We proceeded with the task at hand. It seemed so unreal. Once we had their ashes in the appropriate containers, I reverently carried their urns back to their resting places, caressing them gently with my fingers all the way down the hallway to their resting place. I dug out their Death Certificates, wrote a card to my new friend whose team would be constructing my diamond, attached pictures of my beautiful "gone way too soon" sons and added a few **R&R** stickers to the mix. The next day I addressed and sent my priceless parcel.

When she received the package, my new friend messaged me to say the boys had arrived and the office was overflowing with tears as she shared their story with her staff. She promised to take good care of them and send updates along the way. She also informed me she was going on a trip to South Africa where she would take **R&R** stickers and place them in beautiful places. While she was away, her team reported working with great care and love to turn my boys into a forever diamond. They emailed me pictures of the diamond. I arranged for delivery.

As my angels would have it, it arrived on Ryder's 16th birthday right to my front door! With all the sadness surrounding Ryder's birthday, it was a beautiful way to feel close to my boys. Its sparkle radiated through the package before I even opened it. Within days, I was on my way to Independent Jewellers to have it set in a sturdy custom band, so I would never lose my precious diamond.

The Touchstone

By Sandra Young Kolbuc, Therapist

It was over a month after the arrival of the diamond that Tracy was knocking at my front door for our appointment. We hugged and then she backed away and extended her right hand. She was wearing the gorgeous gemstone. I had the privilege of seeing her treasure glistening on the fourth finger of her right hand. The sun, shining through the stained-glass window of my entranceway, brought forth its radiant lustre, reflecting the love of the woman stretching out her hand. She touched it and looked at me, saying, "This blue diamond ring, forged from the ashes of my sons, represents so much of their love for me and I for them."

She paused. "It already feels like it belongs on my finger! When I touch it, Sandra, it calms me and reminds me of my commitment to them." Her eyes clouded as she continued to allow the sun to reflect the beauty of the ring in all its radiance.

The blue diamond

As I led Tracy to a chair in my meditation room, I reminded her, "The spirit of the boys is always with you, cheering you on one day, sometimes one moment, at a time. And now, you have a special touchstone to remind you of that very special mother-child bond between you and the boys, every time you touch it."

She continued to regard the sparkling jewel on her finger, caressing the diamond as she spoke, "It really does represent the forever connection I have with Ryder and Radek."

I regarded this irrepressible woman. The phoenix had arisen from the ashes and that was what was going well! She settled into the chair and we began once again further decreasing the activation in her nervous system and celebrating the beauty of her new gem.

How Have You Changed?

We sat for a bit until I asked, "How has the death of the boys changed you, Tracy?" She took a sip of water. As I waited, I interjected, "Hey Trac, I have whisky in my liquor cabinet if you need a stronger kick to answer this question."

She laughed at my ridiculous joke. "No thanks, Sandra." She looked at her watch: 10 a.m. "That would be my amazing Gramma Lorraine who I told you about! She would take you up on that. You know I don't actually drink until after lunch!"

"Oh right," I replied, lightening the mood. "I forgot! Actually, Lorraine sounds like a pretty cool gramma!"

"She is," Tracy replied. "I think sometimes I am a lot like her!"

She pondered my question. "How have I changed? I explained some of this when I wrote the piece 'Who Am I Now?' but there is more. The loss of my children has changed me on so many levels. It has made me stronger than I ever thought possible. I have a fight within me to protect kids who live in the same fear as did my kids. I want parents to hear me. A parent's main job is to keep their children safe and secure and to make an even louder noise when systems let them down. Perhaps I needed to make a more resounding noise, although I thought my letter to Child Services was very clear."

I nodded and Tracy sighed. "I know I am a broken record, but I will keep playing the same tune over and over again until things change. F*ck the biological parent bullsh*t. Changes are needed to protect kids. I am not afraid of anything now! I have nothing to lose. My voice will be heard and will continue to resonate with the voices of my sons who will always be the driving force behind my actions."

She again touched the blue diamond on her finger. "My boys and I have always been a team and ..." She leaned forward in her chair. "And when I get discouraged, I need only touch this blue diamond ring to be recharged!"

She breathed in deeply. The session had ended. The gleam of the blue diamond on the fourth finger of her right hand filled my meditation room.

Chapter 54

THE *R&R* MEMORIAL FOUNDATION

rnrmemorialfund.com/donate

Spring 2019

WE AGAIN SAT IN MY MEDITATION ROOM, AND I LIT THE CANDLES TO BRING the spirit of the boys into the room. We began with our usual formalities, and then I asked about the *R&R* Memorial Foundation.

Tracy's face lit up. "What began as a beautiful gesture of love and friendship when the boys died in December 2016 has grown to a wonderful charitable organization to honour Ryder and Radek. The idea for the foundation came about after the boys' funeral. So many generous people wanted to help in any way possible and giving donations to our family was one way people did this. Months after the funeral, as I was going through a box, I came across a bunch of envelopes filled with cash and cheques from individuals and companies as well as donations from large organizations, such as the Edmonton Oilers, which was one of my boys favourite NHL Teams. Brent and I did not need the money, but the kindness of the gestures of people wanting to support us, could not go unheeded. Initially we started out by directing people to send donations to Whitecourt Minor Hockey. At least then, the funds would be going somewhere. As my mind cleared, I wanted to put the money toward something in Ryder and Radek's memory. Brent and I talked and came up with the idea of starting a memorial foundation in their names. This foundation would raise money to help kids in our community needing financial assistance to play the sport my boys loved most, which, of course, was hockey."

I heard the passion in her voice.

"I initially chose to support the sport of hockey for a number of reasons. Hockey is one of the more expensive sports and I was unsure of how much money we would raise. Hockey was the reason my boys moved to Spruce Grove. Being on the ice gave Ryder and Radek the chance to forget the difficulties they were having in Dad's home. As Ryder had said to me, 'Mom, my team raises me up when I am feeling down.' I wanted other kids to have the opportunity of being on a team where they felt 'raised up' when things were going sideways in other aspects of their lives. The idea began to manifest.

"We registered the organization and established a board of directors. We developed the **R&R** website. Through fundraising efforts and good promotion, we were going to give some children the gift of hockey. We would begin with children in Whitecourt, Alberta, where my boys first explored their feel for the game, which grew into their desire to move beyond the confines of our community. Of course, in retrospect, I wish they had not moved into a situation that caused their deaths, but I, as a mother, would never have denied them following what was solidly etched in their hearts at such a young age. Their thirst for hockey was similar to that of many Canadian youngsters, maybe not quite so much in Radek as in Ryder, but my younger son was going to follow his brother wherever he went. This was not my dream nor was it Brent's. It was their dream to participate in hockey at a more intense level of play.

"Were they too young to pursue such goals? In my mind, never did I ever expect that they would not be safe with their biological father; that he would take their dreams away. They both wanted to try life with their dad. Often, though, on this journey, my mind has gone to self-blame. Why didn't I know better? My decision to allow Radek and Ryder to live with their father has broken my heart into a million pieces many times over. However, perhaps in some small way, the establishment of this foundation can assist other children in following their appetite for the great Canadian game and my boys will have helped other kids follow their aspirations."

Chapter 55

PSYCHIC READINGS

FOLLOWING THE DEATH OF HER SONS, TRACY HAD BEEN DRAWN TO THE world "beyond the veil." She had been to a few mediums to have some readings shortly after the boys passed. She shared her story in an email.

TRS to SYK: I was looking for something for me and a girlfriend to do for her birthday. My friend had also lost a son, and I thought it would be a good "bonding" date for us to have a day to communicate with our boys, with lunch together to follow. I was hunting online when the name Naomi Mailhot came right up. I read her reviews and I booked each of us a half-hour reading. Naomi was different from the others I had seen as she was the only medium I went to who had connected to two male figures ... two children ... my children. Right then, I knew my boys had somehow brought her to me.

Since that day in the fall of 2017, I have seen Naomi over a handful of times. Each connection has been ... more. More emotional. More real. More needed. Soon I was realizing the power in healing and connection. She knew things I did not tell her. She knew places we had travelled. She knew of upcoming family vacations. She knew of gifts I had bought loved ones. She knew about the Zen Den and the stickers being placed throughout the world. She told me Ryder had connected with the security of his "Baby" teddy bear! She knew I would find the boys dead that morning.

Now of course you say, 'Well she could have just been following the news stories regarding the boys.' True, but she knew other things as well. She told me things that happened when they were crossing over. She shared what the boys said about their sisters and my family. She quoted the things I said or was thinking when I was in my vehicle alone before our meeting. She knew the last songs I had listened to. She knew about our pets, the hockey bench made in their honour, the messages on the ice at the Memorial Games. She knew that every time I saw a Ryder truck, I said hi back to my boy …

I asked her why I felt Ryder so strongly and not Radek, and shedding tears, she said, "Because Ryder carried Radek across that morning and has been carrying him ever since." She said they come as one big, beautiful angel. When she sees them, she said it is always Ryder coming first and Radek following. She reported that Ryder has owned his new position and was a leader, which was no surprise to me! Naomi told me that my boys had taught her so much. She told me they were very active and had lots to say. Knowing my struggles with missing them, she said my boys wanted to ease my heartache as much as they could. She confirmed that Corry was not with them. She told me that they had forgiven Corry for what he had done, which confirmed for me that they were far better people than me. Maybe that is what happens when one becomes an angel! Ryder spoke of that last night, saying that, although it was scary, he felt protected. He wasn't alone. He didn't feel pain.

I have been blessed to have Naomi in my life. I believe we will forever have a bond through my sons. She also has two sons and had lost a son as well. I felt like our boys brought our paths together.

In subsequent sessions she told me that my boys would be sending me kids. Boys would be seeking me out. Such interactions followed shortly. A friend called to tell me her son had been signed by the Drayton Valley Thunder Junior A team. I connected with a Warrior Sister who lost her 23-year-old son. A couple of friends of Radek's stopped by, asking if they could have a sleepover at our house.

Naomi said my boys were evolving. I believe I am evolving as well. I heard of a woman who has lost her husband. In the past I probably would have avoided her, not knowing what to say. Instead, I took her for lunch and talked with her about my own grief as well as hers.

Naomi told me my boys said I was happy, in a different place.

SYK to TRS: And … what do you say, Tracy Stark?

TRS to SYK: I say I am in a good place. I know it is okay to be happy. I am no longer feeling guilty about having good times. As I said, I know life can change in a heartbeat and I am cherishing every beat! Actually, I am loving who I am becoming. Stronger. More passionate about what I believe. Very proud to be

Radek and Ryder's mom and helping them see the world! Excited to be helping other kids through the **R&R** Foundation. Naomi no longer charges me for my sessions as she says she is honoured to do them. So, in return, I put the money I would usually pay her into the **R&R** Memorial Foundation in her name. It is a win-win situation.

As well, I am finding that processing what I have written to be helpful in discovering more of who I truly am. Thank you for helping me get to know and love and be compassionate with the woman, who, as you say, is wearing my jeans and brushing my teeth. I like that I am growing as an advocate for positive change and excited about finding ways to immortalize my sons.

SYK: to TRS: This is the woman you always were, Tracy. I was just able to help you bring her forward. Listen to this quote, my friend: "And one day she discovered that she was fierce and strong and full of fire and not even she could hold herself back because her passion burned brighter than her fears."[21]

Sounds like someone I know ...

---

21   Mark Anthony, *The Beautiful Truth*. Taken from Goodreads.com

Chapter 56

THE BUFFALO

Spring 2019

TRS to SYK: On a bike trip to Sturgis, North Dakota, on one of our day rides shortly after the boys had passed, we came upon a wild buffalo just standing right there on the side of the road. Brent slowed down so I could take a picture as the beast was so big and beautiful. I had never seen a live buffalo up close. This magnificent creature did not move and stared directly into my eyes as if he was looking into my soul. I took his picture. Honestly Sandra, I know, without a doubt in my mind, that that summer day in 2017, the Sturgis Buffalo carried the spirit of my boys.

Then, in the spring of 2018, I attended the Butterdome Craft Sale in Edmonton, Alberta. I was powerfully drawn to a beautiful photo of a buffalo taken by Brandon T. Brown, a photographer who took pictures of wildlife in their natural habitat. I absolutely fell in love with the photograph and when I got home, I told Brent about this picture and how I felt that the gigantic beast was staring right back at me and how attracted I was to it. He said, "Buy it!!" That is always his answer!

I searched out the photographer and found the picture and purchased it. It is titled *The Protector*. How fitting. I felt it was meant for me to give me strength and courage. I hung it in our front sitting room, and when I need that extra courage, it is there you will find me taking in the magnificence and power of this beautiful creature.

The Sturgis Buffalo

In a subsequent email, Tracy shared the following story.

TRS to SYK: In the spring of 2019, my friend Carla and I flew to Phoenix, Arizona, to retrieve and drive one of Brent and my vehicles back to Canada. On our return journey home via USA Route 89, we placed the memorial **R&R** stickers all along the way, making Ryder and Radek our focus. We were diligent in finding both beautiful and interesting places so the boys had wonderful views to behold from new vantage points along the route. We put the decals on things that we thought would make the boys laugh or places to which I felt particularly drawn. Determining where to place the stickers was an interesting quest and as synchronicity would have it, we came upon a buffalo sculpture. Of course, we placed a sticker on it and once again I felt this strange connection. Then, once we hit Alberta, we stopped at Head-Smashed-In Buffalo Jump and placed another. Again I felt the strong attraction to this stunning beast.

As Tracy spoke further about the buffalo in a subsequent session, she was pensive. "When I place the **R&R** stickers somewhere in my travels, I feel very connected to my boys at that moment, and it is almost like they are hugging me. When I placed them on the buffalo sculpture and at the Head-Smashed-In Buffalo Jump on the trip home, honestly Sandra, it felt as though the boys were actually beside me at that exact moment. Known as 'the protector,' maybe that is a part of my attraction to the majestic animal."

She cleared her throat. "I always attempted to be the protector for my boys and maybe now, they are mine; protecting me from falling to the ground in my grief of not having them physically present in my life. Maybe that is what the buffalo symbolizes for me." She stopped and again sipped a drink from the glass of water I had set beside her. "I was always wanting to ensure my boys were safe when they were with Corry, but sometimes, I felt so powerless because of the laws and the lack of enforcement that occurred." She settled more deeply in the chair as we grounded and reflected on what she was noticing after our discussion regarding the buffalo. The relationship with the animal felt so very real. So vital. We stopped and continued to reflect on the puzzle of her strong connection to the buffalo.

The Mystery & Majesty of the Buffalo Connection

Chapter 57

HIS "DONE ME WRONG" SONG

A FEW WEEKS LATER, TRACY WAS AGAIN SITTING IN MY CHAIR. "YOU KNOW, one of the cruelest things I heard after my boys died was that someone had said I drove Corry to do what he did." She took her time as she shared her thoughts. "That stung. It seemed so unfair and unkind. Few people know what actually goes on in another person's life. I knew Corry badmouthed me to his friends. Of course, there were always rumours flying around, but often somebody only hears one side of the story.

"After Corry and I parted ways, few knew of the roadblocks he would put in my way in parenting the boys. He was all about teaching the boys how important it was to be tough, when what my boys also needed was the loving tenderness of their mom. He would constantly attempt to sabotage my efforts to protect them from his wrath and physical discipline or the bizarre punishments he believed were important in the raising of young boys. He always believed in being a man's man, rarely allowing the softer feelings to surface with me or the boys, even when we were all together. My boys, like all little boys, deserved and needed tenderness from both of us. He was a control freak in our home and his word was law. There was no negotiating."

"What do you notice when you say that, Tracy?" I asked.

She breathed in, taking a few moments to ground herself. "I take exception to the comment that it was my fault Corry killed the boys. The privilege and arrogance, the rudeness and ignorance Corry showed me as his wife, and then as his ex-wife, in his attempts to still control me even after we split, were totally inappropriate. Corry still wanted me and our kids to know I had done him wrong by leaving our marriage, while in fact, his behaviours had been the cause of my leaving. His ignorance with the boys and his desire to still control my life with them after I left our marriage was the cause of my having to continually go to court and have so many court orders put in place—court orders which he seldom observed and which were never enforced." She paused and took another drink of water.

"What do you notice in your body, Tracy, when you tell me this?" I ask.

Again, she took a moment to check in with her body. We processed the body sensations she felt as she shared her thoughts, letting go of the activation our discussion had brought forward.

The Character of a Man

TRS to SYK: "Corry made that choice to abuse and subsequently kill my boys all on his own. He wanted revenge against me so badly and for so long. In 2016, I gave him the opportunity to be the dad he said he wanted to be by allowing Radek and Ryder to live with him. He could have been the everyday hero in their lives. I had given him two beautiful boys, who, despite his meanness to them, still loved him very much and still wanted him to be proud of them. But he wanted to be in total charge of their every move. He also wanted them to hate me. Above all else, I think he simply wanted to hurt me. When he asked me for $60,000 when we met to discuss the boys living with him in Spruce Grove, I began to think his financial situation must have deteriorated considerably. He needed money. He was obviously hurting inside himself to murder his children and then put the gun to his head, but in the long and short of things, what does that say about his character as a man? What does that say about his values as a human being? What does this say about what he had been modelling for my sons in how to treat a women and children or so many years?"

We again worked with the activation that arose when she shared what was on her mind as she sat in the blue chair. It was long and hard work going back and forth but release came as we processed her thoughts and she began to feel more settled, recognizing the importance of her own truths rather than those of others sitting in judgment. I was proud of the strength she was showing as we continued on her healing journey.

Chapter 58

THE GAME PLAN

IT WAS APRIL 2019 AND TRACY'S SESSION WAS ALMOST OVER WHEN I NOTICED she was not getting ready to exit my blue chair.

She cleared her throat. "Before I go, I have a question for you, Sandra."

She gathered herself to speak again. "After the boys died, I knew I needed to write. What had happened was resting so uncomfortably in my soul. I wanted to free myself by writing about what I was feeling and thinking. However, every time I started or every time I even thought about writing, I felt sick to my stomach and wanted to throw up. I didn't want to revisit what had happened. It was too overwhelming to think about, let alone write about. So, I just pushed it away. Then, I began to share with you what was in the deepest part of my soul. I have been able to open up and actually allow myself to be vulnerable with you." Her voice trembled. "You created for me a presence of acceptance and love and compassion as you listened. You must have many of my words in the notes you take each time we meet."

My face softened as I watched her bravely sharing what was on her mind. Her eyes clouded over as she spoke. "I want you as my therapist to …" She paused and then spoke quickly, "… write my story. I have thought a lot about this since our last session. I am totally serious. I want you to write my story and that of my boys from your perspective as my therapist."

I sucked in my breath, taking a minute to feel the support of my own chair. I sensed my stomach clenching, but I held her gaze as she continued. "You have gotten to know me better than anyone, maybe even Brent."

I attempted to interrupt and again, she stopped me. "Please! Wait!" she said. "You always say you want to teach people about trauma. What better way than this? I know that, as a mom, you could take my words and tell my story in a way that would radiate the love I have for my sons onto the pages of a book.

I know you would make my story as real and ..." she hesitated, "as piercing as it has been. I am fanatical about telling my story and you could make it come alive! You have always said writing was your passion so here is your opportunity to write!

In concentrating on what she was saying, I was silent on the outside, my gut totally unsettled on the inside as I listened. I closed my eyes as I breathed in, attempting to absorb the fullness of what she was asking. I pondered what to say and looked up at the blonde who had been sitting across from me for over two years, working so hard today to maintain her ground.

Gently, I said, "But Tracy, this is your story, not mine and, I think you need someone more experienced in writing professionally to tell it."

She shook her head. "No Sandra. I need you. You have been walking with me on this healing path. I thought you could tell it from your vantage point as my therapist. I want other women to learn from my story. I want other people to speak up when they see things that are, as you say, 'offside.' Do you remember when you told me that the smartest person in the room is not the one who has learned from experience, but rather, the one who learns from other people's experience?"

I smiled and nodded.

"That made sense to me," she said. "That is what I want. To help others learn from my experience. I cannot leave what is in my heart unspoken. I want you to help me find my voice on the pages of a book." She was endeavouring not to break down.

She was quiet. I waited. She forcibly grabbed me with her stunning blue eyes. "You are my woman, Sandra. You gave me the courage to stand up and speak from my heart and talk about what I thought impossible at the first Ladies Wolverine Night just a year after the boys died." Her eyes were glistening with the intensity I had come to know. "You gave me the confidence to share, not just the facts, but the feelings I was holding inside regarding the death of my boys and the incredible support I had been given by many in that room! Never did I ever imagine ever being able to do that!"

She just looked at me, and I, her. Right here. Right now. She had taken my breath away. Why? We sat frozen in time, definitely fully present to each other. The intimacy of the moment was intense as I regarded the blonde whose life as she knew it had been shattered into a million pieces on December 19, 2016.

I addressed her directly, saying. "I am truly humbled that you are asking me to write your story, Tracy. It would be a privilege to work on this with you, but I really don't know if I am the best person to share in the writing of your story."

"Sandra, I need your help to make this story told in a way that will hold the attention and influence those who can change the laws that allowed my ex-husband to take a gun and murder my children in cold blood!" Her eyes were ablaze with fury. "He wanted to hurt me so badly that he did the worst possible thing he could do in his attempts to destroy me!"

My heart was truly breaking as I witnessed the excruciating pain of the Little Mama sitting in front of me. I can't recall how long we stayed that way—me working to keep my own ground as Tracy released some of her despair. We sat, our nervous systems in tandem, releasing more of the activation that had plagued her since the death of her sons. Finally, I said, "Just feel the support of the chair, Tracy and notice your breath."

Her body began to tremble as her tears flowed down her cheeks. Again, I witnessed this extraordinary woman letting go of the continued pain of grief, the price one paid for loving those who might someday leave this earth before you. Children definitely weren't 'supposed 'to die before their parents.

After a few moments, she managed a weak smile as she asked, "So after all that … Are you saying you will join me in writing?"

"Let's go with 'I'll think about it,'" I responded.

She sat quietly, her eyes closed, inhaling and exhaling the molecules in the air between us as I reflected on the journey we had taken thus far. I was deeply moved by her confidence in me, the potential unknown writer. This would be unknown territory for both of us. I wheeled my chair back from her, increasing the space between us.

Suddenly her eyes were wide open as if she had discovered her second wind. "So … when can I have your decision?"

I started to laugh softly as she looked like she was expecting an answer. "You are pretty funny, Tracy Stark." I looked at my watch. "Listen. We are half an hour over time already and there is a lot to think about in such a commitment."

She continued her pitch as she wiped her eyes. "Listen Sandra I thought you were planning on retiring from doing therapy and becoming a full-time writer! That is one of the reasons I am asking you. You can ask me any questions you want and I will answer all of them. I am so ready to tackle whatever you throw at me. Honestly, I will answer anything! Anything! You have told me, since the beginning, that I needed to write and … "

"But Tracy, that is because getting your thoughts out of your head and down on paper is aiding in your healing. You have also indicated that you want to leave a legacy for your sons. Write so that their story can help change laws that allow unhealthy parents to gain access to their innocent children. Write to ensure the story of their deaths will empower other moms to speak up and share their stories and concerns. Write to create a following of people you awaken with your story and who will support you in this effort for social justice in divorce and separation if that is what you still want to do!"

Her voice became even stronger as she said, "That is precisely why I want you to help me, Sandra. Maybe, together, we can muster up a strong enough readership to lobby for a review of systems and examine policies and practices that did not work for me and my boys!" She was getting feisty again, eyes enflamed with a burning desire for the task she wanted me to undertake with her. "Isn't this something a woman in your profession would want to do? Help women tell their stories and encourage men to call out abusive men for their behaviours?"

"I hear you, Tracy," I said quietly , and I watched as she settled and began to regain her ground.

She once again had found her voice as she badgered me! "So, will you or will you not write my story with me?"

I felt like I was in court. "Oh sure," I responded. "Ask me when I am vulnerable and my heart is aching for you!"

I sighed as I reflected on her plea. My creative mind was already in overdrive, starting to think of possibilities. I attempted to slow my thoughts and come back to the moment. Writing was my passion.! My goal as a woman had always been to help other women find their voices and speak their truth. Part of me so wanted to say yes. What an incredible mission to share with my client. I could feel the expansion in my chest as I considered her appeal to my nature. However, I also knew the right thing to do was to take some time to think through her request and talk to my "logical sequential" husband before making such a huge commitment.

"Sandra," Tracy said, "You have convinced me that my story is bigger than me. That in telling it, I can perhaps help prevent a replay of what happened to my children. Please don't abandon me now, Sandra. We are just beginning …"

"God, Tracy! Now you are using guilt! Of course, I am not going to abandon you! But I am not a professional writer. I have never published anything other than newspaper columns and blogs." Now my voice was stronger. "It's just not a path I would ever have considered taking, Tracy. So I need to consider all the ramifications of doing this."

Again, she just looked at me. "Sandra, I have so much more to share. We have dealt with some of what you have labelled as post-traumatic stress. I have been actively grieving, as you say, but now, we get to share 'the rest of the story.' There is much more to the impact the death of my boys has had on me. In many ways, I am now a different person. A different person … with a vision and a mission! I know we could do a great job of this together. Think of all the women we can perhaps influence. Think of all the people you can educate about trauma and the importance of self-regulation in one's life.

I remained pensive, thinking about possibilities. Suddenly, she interrupted my reverie. "Sorry, but," she looked at her watch. "I have a nail appointment at 5 p.m., so I had better leave now." She stood, as did I.

In the time we had worked together, I had never noticed how much taller she was than me. I wondered if she was trying to intimidate me as she stood so tall, making eye contact with that look of dogged determination in her eyes. She leaned in, gave me a hug, and left my office, closing the door gently behind her before I could lodge any further reservations about writing with her.

I returned to the comfort of my chair.

Suddenly, the door burst open once again and I saw her red Wolverine claws, soon to be mauve for Easter, clutching the door frame as her blonde head poked around the corner and she said with conviction, "And thank you, MY WOMAN! We will make an incredible team! See you next week!" And then … she was gone.

I sat transfixed in my chair, wondering … *What the hell just happened?*

The Acceptance

SYK to TRS: Good Morning Tracy Stark! I have given your proposal a lot of thought since we spoke last week and I talked it over with my family and they all agree this is a most important story to tell.

Been up half the night thinking of possibilities. So … this is my official "**YES.**" You got me on your team girl! Actually Tracy, my mind has been on fire as to how impactful your story can be and to be a part of its delivery will be a privilege. We will now continue to share the many pieces of the story through texts and emails as well as content from our live sessions. I will bring forth the life blood of your experiences, Tracy StarK. I just hope I can do it justice … ….

Here's the thing. The essence of Radek and Ryder that has been breathed into you will hold you up even when you share the replay of the events surrounding the earthly death of your little hockey heroes. Your boys will give you the energy and the fortitude to gain strength with each page in the telling of their story and yours as their mother.

In the quietest of the quiet, ask the boys what they think of Mom telling their story and listen closely to the responses that will come through to you. It is in silence where we will receive the clearest answers to our questions. The boys need to know how much their story can change and has already changed the lives of others in a positive way. Maybe, after reading your and the boys' story, some dad will look in the mirror and quell some of his own behaviours that follow the same pattern of control as Corry displayed. Maybe just one dad or mom will reach for help to work through his or her own anger or fear. These actions alone would indicate victory in our quest. And yes. Readers will begin to learn some basic tenets about how trauma impacts an individual. We will be a great duo!

Your boys need to know that their mama is still being their mama and what a brave 'Warrior Goddess' she is to share with the world the intricacies of her life with not only those who stand beside her but with those who will judge her/us harshly for our insights. Some will stone us both as we challenge society's status quo in our writing.

The skills I bring to our team is as a strong caring and compassionate woman, a wife, a mother, a grandmother, a teacher, a friend, an athlete, a therapist and a teller of stories. When I saw you striding down that aisle in the restaurant in Calgary to be with my devastated niece the day after Trevor died, I knew you and me -we were going to do something very special some day. I think I know now what that is. Can we do it Tracy? Can we f'ing do it???

I press SEND and receive an immediate reply

TRS to SYK: YES WE CAN SANDRA YOUNG KOLBUC! YES WE CAN! Let's get started!

Chapter 59

A BETTER WAY

WE WERE IN MY OFFICE AGAIN. SHE SETTLED INTO THE BLUE CHAIR AND began to speak before I even had a chance to sit down.

"Sandra, I know you are going to ask me, 'What's going well?' and I want to answer that question before you even ask it!" She withdrew a paper from a file folder she had brought to the session, looked up at me and said, "What is going well is that I have put together a list of questions for decision makers and those in positions of influence that need to be addressed because of my specific experience with Alberta Child Services and the Alberta Justice System as well as those accounts from other women whom I have heard from since the death of my children."

She handed me a copy of her document and sat straighter in the chair.

QUESTIONS FOR DECISION MAKERS
by
Tracy Stark, Mother
of
Radek Stryker MacDougall (Oct 08, 2005-December 19, 2016)
&
Ryder Patryk MacDougall (March 1, 2003- December 19, 2016)

1. *What laws, procedures and systems need to be in place so divorced or separated women are fully aware of their rights in custody issues without having to fork out thousands of dollars to lawyers to ensure such laws are followed in custody situations?*

2. *What needs to be done to repair the legal system to serve those in custody and divorce situations and prevent continued coercive control or*

filicide? Many women are terrified of leaving abusive situations because of the coercive control of their partners. And, what about others, who in the best interest of their children and themselves, leave relationships where they are abused physically, mentally, verbally, or financially and who then live in fear of reprisals for their children or themselves from the men they have left.

3. *What laws or practices need to be enacted so women and children will be protected in their hour of need in custody confrontations or threats from an angry ex-partner?*

4. *What action needs to be taken to ensure social workers are not over-whelmed with caseloads too large to deal appropriately with cases of custody and access?*

5. *What are the danger codes for social workers when dealing with reports of abusive or threatening partners or ex-partners? Are perpetrators charged and punished appropriately or do many receive a mere slap on the wrist?*

6. *When Child Services goes to remove children from an unsafe environ-ment, what are the procedures when there are fears of or indications of potential violence? What are the indicators for action to be taken by the authorities?*

7. *Is there an unwritten rule that social workers are not to touch custody issues "with a ten-foot pole" and if so, what are the options for those in conflict with their ex-partners in custody situations?*

8. *What changes are needed and what options are available when women leave relationships where they or their children are being abused physi-cally, mentally, verbally, or financially?*

9. *What procedures are in place when a parent fears a child will be or is at risk physically, emotionally, or mentally when in an ex-partner's care when inappropriate behaviors by that spouse were the reasons a woman has left the relationship*

10. *When are those who share custody and are abusive to their ex-spouses in separation/divorce relationships mandated to address anger or control issues in counselling session before being allowed access to their children?*

11. *Why are court orders not enforced and how can such enforcement become a reality?*

12. *Why Is coercive control not treated as a criminal offence in Canada? Why are those who exhibit violent, threatening, or coercive control behaviours to their ex-partners still allowed access to their children and deemed to be a good parent when displaying abusive behaviours to an ex-spouse?*

I regarded the woman in my chair, sharing her thoughts, her strength oozing out of every pore as she spoke. There were no tears this time. There was only resolve and great passion in her voice. I listened, riveted to my chair, as Tracy shared the questions with which she had been wrestling since her boys had died.

As she finished, I said, "I think you have put together some excellent questions for both research and discussion, Tracy."

"Well, it's basically a summary of my concerns, Sandra."

I said, "What do you notice today as you think about sharing your concerns with a larger audience than those who read your rants on Facebook?"

She laughed and then sat quietly, obviously considering her answer. I observed any changes in her pallor, her body movements, and her demeanour as I monitored her stress level.

Then she spoke. "Well, it is a little overwhelming to see the questions together in a comprehensive list, but I feel lighter and more focused. I am excited at the thought of working together and hopefully inspiring others to bring forward possible solutions and other concerns that need to be addressed in regard to the safety of women and children."

I was feeding off her passion as I said with conviction, "We will share the *R&R* story, Tracy, and in doing so, bring awareness to anyone ready to be 'woke' about such issues." I smile a little as I say, "God, I love the energy of that word 'woke' as it applies to social justice. Our book will create opportunities for people to read and discuss such questions in venues where both men and women gather: people who are willing to ask questions and appeal for answers from those who can influence the process of change."

The session was about to end when Tracy finished with, "Women and children who live in fear of an angry ex need to know someone, some law, some system will protect them from the rage and behaviours of any man who is attempting to continue to exert power or coercive control over an ex-spouse. I heard quite clearly the passion in her voice.

I was thinking, *This session isn't over yet! She's too revved up to leave here in this state.* I responded, "I hear you, Tracy. Just take a minute and if it is okay, just feel the support of the chair as you think about what you just said."

She did not blink as I went on.

"Remember, trauma is in the nervous system, not the event, and it is very activating." I reminded my client. "We will handle this, but let's slow it down a little."

Tracy again settled deeper into the chair, closed her eyes and breathed in and out as I said to her. "Trauma is too much! Too soon! We have touched on some very difficult content today—procedures that could perhaps have saved the boys if they had been in place. I want you more grounded before you leave here. Talking as we have can be retraumatizing as you relate your experiences regarding the points we have been discussing."

We went back and forth between activation, titration, resourcing, and releasing activation. Over the course of our work together, she was becoming more regulated. Then ... finally we were done for the day.

I locked the door of the office building and we walked to our vehicles in the parking lot. As we each went our own way I commended my client on the list of questions she had formulated. She smiled and waved as she headed off to her Range Rover, which sported the **R&R** sticker on its back window. I moved toward my Volvo SC60, where the sticker on my back window read, "**Changing the World ... One Nervous System at a Time.**" Today? A good day in the life of a trauma therapist in the business of regulating the nervous system of a brave and daring client who was definitely finding her voice.

Chapter 60

BOYS! BOYS! BOYS!
WERE MADE TO LOVE!

FRIENDS OF RYDER AND RADEK HAD ALWAYS BEEN WELCOME AT THE STARK home. Youngsters loved being invited into Ryder and Radek's world. It was a fun place to hang out. With the death of the boys, Tracy missed the kids who had filled her home with uproarious laughter and all the insane behaviour of young boys. Even after the boys died, Radek's besties still called for sleepovers.

Part of Tracy's personal battle was watching these little boys grow up, knowing that her boys would not be experiencing these new "growing up" adventures with their friends. She loved hearing their stories, but knowing she would never be able to be the proud mom at such events was heartbreaking. She would never be dropping off her own boys at their first day of high school. She would never see their smiles at passing their learner's permit tests and then getting their driver's licences. She would never be able to tease them about their first love. She would never witness them drinking their first beer (that she knew of) or being a rookie at the Junior A Wolverines tryout camp. She would never buy them their first legal drink of liquor in a local lounge. She would never attend their high school graduations and be a part of such revelry. These never-to-be events in the lives of her boys carried a huge degree of sadness for Tracy, although she loved to celebrate these milestones with the boys she knew.

She enjoyed visiting with the friends of her children and the children of her friends, young boys who had breakfasted at her table or were a part of the street hockey games when her boys were alive. She loved hearing of the events in the recent chapters in their lives and their memories of their time with her boys as well as laughing with them at their latest escapades. She listened intently to their plans for the future. Many of the boys continued to stop by or give Tracy big hugs when she would see the grown-up versions of her kids at the rink or around the town. Her relationships with these kids were still very important to her.

A Grocery Story Conversation

SYK: In casual conversation with a friend whose daughter had graduated from Hilltop High School in June 2019, I developed a greater awareness of the special bond Tracy had with such friends of her boys and their families. While in the aisle of the No Frills Grocery Story, in discussing the wonder of her daughter's graduation, my friend shared a very special highlight that had included Tracy Stark, who she said had attended the Hilltop High School Graduation in a very special way. At home that evening, I texted Tracy.

> SYK: Quit keeping secrets Cinderella! I want to hear about your attending a very special event: Grad 2019 with a very handsome young Prince! Thank God for small towns, Tracy. I might never have known!

Tracy sent me a laughing emoji and then emailed me the story.

Going to Grad...At Forty
By Tracy Stark, Mother

When I say I went to Grad at 40, I don't mean as a supporter, a cheerleader, or a proud auntie. Nope! I went as a full-fledged escort!

Back in January 2019, Chase Wheeler, a young man of 17 at the time, offered to give me and my girlfriend a safe ride home after the Whitecourt Wolverine Ladies Night. This was a task he had done on previous occasions as our designated driver. On our short trip up the hill to my house, I made a cocky comment that I was available to be his grad escort if he was still looking! Chase politely said he would love to take me to his graduation. Thinking he was just going along with my joking with him, I never really gave it another thought.

A few months passed and Chase's grad plans came up in casual conversation between Brent and me and Chase's parents, our good friends, Kevin and Sharon Wheeler. We were talking about who was to be his escort.

I laughingly said, "Well, I volunteered to go with him!"

Brent piped up, "You're not going with Chase, Tracy! You're too old!"

We continued joking and laughing when Sharon said, "Oh, she better be going with Chase, because he is telling everyone that Tracy is his escort!".

Instantly I felt butterflies in my stomach. OMG! This was really going to happen?

I had known Chase since he was a chubby little baby still in diapers. He was born in June 2001 just a year before his younger brother Cruz. A year after that, my Ryder arrived and then two years later, along came Radek! Sharon and I had raised our boys together.

Growing up together; Cruz and Chase Wheeler with Ryder

Chase would be the first of the boys to graduate high school. Since graduation was never going to happen for my sons, I felt privileged that Chase would actually want me to be part of such a big day in such a big way! I could not believe that he really did want me on his arm at his Grad but, as it came closer, I discovered, he was totally serious!

I was more nervous than I had been at Brent's and my wedding! Here I was going to the Hilltop Grad with "a bunch of kids"—handsome young men and stunning young ladies! I didn't want to look stupid. I didn't want people laughing or pointing fingers at me. My God, it had been 21 years since I had graduated high school! But you know what? I decided I was going to rock this special day with my date—my "nephew" connected, not by blood, but rather by heart. I told Brent I was taking the Bentley so at least that might make me look a tad bit cooler to these high school kids! LOL! I bought the great outfit. I got my hair and makeup done. I matched my "wolverine claws" to my outfit and showed up at the Forestry Interpretive Centre just in time for pictures

My heart raced as I parked "my baby," aka my Bentley. I looked up and saw Chase walking toward me with a corsage in his hand. Was this what it felt like for a parent when your child graduated? I should have known this feeling because both my stepdaughters had graduated and I was very happy to be part of their celebrations, but something about this was different. Perhaps it was because the Wheeler boys were in so many of my memories of when my boys were alive. They had been little together. They had grown up together. They were friends of my boys. Perhaps it was because of Chase's kindness in wanting me to accompany him. I wasn't sure, but the feelings inside were very special. As this tall, handsome young man walked toward me, I choked back the lump in my throat and gave my "date" a big smile and then a huge hug. We carried on with family photos. Chase asked for an **R&R** sticker, so we could include the boys in the pictures. Oh, my heart.

Being a part of Graduation Day 2019 meant the world to me. To be so involved in such an important day in the life of a young man I had had the pleasure of watching grow up with my boys was beyond incredible. My heart was full. Walking in the Grand March in front of the school on the arm of my handsome escort and seeing the looks on parents' faces—the tears in the eyes of other mothers, with dads' eyes close behind—was extremely touching. I could tell many parents were in complete awe that this young man would take as his escort the mother of two boys who would never get to do this walk. The mother who would never stand with pride on the sidewalk and watch either one of her sons in the Grand March. The mother who had watched most of the graduates grow up as friends of her boys and … the mother who loved this boy on her arm almost as much as she did her own. It was a day filled with gratitude and love! A day I will never forget. I am forever thankful that Chase took the plunge and had an "old lady" accompany him to Grad 2019. I swore we would start a new fad … but … nope! Didn't happen! LOL! However, we did make the yearbook!

Hilltop High School Graduation 2019

Chapter 61

THE HAND IN THE SKY

By Sandra Young Kolbuc, Counselling Therapist

IT WAS AN EVENING IN JULY 2019. I WAS PROOFREADING MATERIAL I HAD written as I wished to share it with Tracy tomorrow. My iPhone beeped, indicating a text. It was from Tracy.

> TRS: Hello Beautiful. Just throwing this out there. Would you want to come and do our appointment tomorrow in my Zen Den? Just an option.

> SYK: That sounds lovely. I will see you at ten in the Zen Den!

> TRS: Yay! I am excited. Been feeling all day that my boys wanted me to invite you.

> SYK: Thank them for the most gracious invite. I am getting to know your sons so well as I write about them. It will be a privilege to sit in their energy with you. It will be … a Good Day to Have a Good Day!

> TRS: I agree. See they're so connected with you, they want you to come over. LOL. See you in the morning.

Tracy and Brent had completed the conversion of the boys' old rooms to a space honouring them. Tracy would speak of the peacefulness she sensed in her newly christened Zen Den. I would be happy to have the opportunity to sit in the beanbag chairs in the area where Radek and Ryder had had Little Mama tuck them in.

The next day as I drove east down our driveway to head to town and Tracy, I noticed the clouds directly in front of me. I stopped to fully regard what I thought I was seeing in the cloud formation. The glare of the sun was directly above the cloud I was looking at, so initially it was difficult to be a hundred percent certain of what I was seeing. I exited my car, cell phone in hand, to capture the image. There, at the bottom of the gathering of clouds, was the definitive shape of a giant hand. I snapped a couple of pictures, wondering if the image would be visible on the phone as I was looking directly into the sun.

Returning to my car, I regarded the pictures. There was no doubting the cloud formation. A giant hand! My heart started to race as the words flashed before me. "The Hand of God. The Hand of God. The Hand of God!" Tracy always said her boys were safely in the hands of God. It was as though that the Creator of all things was about to ride shotgun with me on my journey to Tracy's home. There was the hand reaching out to me as if to say, "Come. I will guide you on this journey with Tracy and her boys." I breathed in deeply, my eyes wide with wonder as I drove silently to meet with Tracy, afraid to turn off my phone for fear the image would evaporate by the time I reached her home. I was filled with the essence of the phenomenon I had just captured on my cell phone.

Hand in the sky

The Zen Den Experience

Tracy greeted me at the door and walked with me up the stairs to her Zen Den. I felt the sacredness of the room as I entered. She gave me a tour and explanation of each piece of memorabilia that filled every corner of the room. Every item had been so personalized. People had contributed in such creative ways of honouring the boys, fashioning many beautiful remembrances of Ryder and Radek for their mama. Throws made of their t-shirts, quilts of their blue jeans, works of art depicting the boys, and photographs capturing their smiles surrounded me in this space. Their hockey jerseys lined the walls. So many people had taken the time to create and design such treasures with love in every stitch of their needles, in every stroke of their paint brushes, in every screw in the beautiful bench made from their hockey sticks and in every work of art displayed. The room radiated the kindness and love that immortalized two innocent boys. It was truly an **R&R** Hall of Fame.

We each settled into our individual bean bag chairs, central to the space. I looked around and breathed in the loving energy, palpable in the room. Before we began, I leaned toward Tracy's chair and handed her my phone, wanting to share the picture I had brought so carefully to the Zen Den. She brought up the image.

I asked, "What do you see as you look at these clouds, Tracy?"

She peered at the photo and immediately said, "It looks like a gigantic hand."

"I thought so too, Tracy! Remember how you continually say, 'My boys are in the hands of God?'"

She nodded.

"I believe that hand may be guiding us today, my friend," I said. "Let's get started."

We clicked off our phones and I began to read the manuscript aloud to her. We both commented and corrected as I continued to share what I had put together from our interactions. The time passed quickly, so engaged were we in the content. I looked over at her. We were but a third of the way through. For three hours, we had been totally focused.

It was the first time I had read out loud what I had written, revised, and organized. I felt relief, not having realized how nervous I had been to share the manuscript with her.

Her French Bulldog, Piper, and Tabby cat, Rikka, then joined us, knowing intuitively that we were done ... or maybe it was simply their meal time! Both appeared thankful as Tracy turned her attention to her animals as they each attempted to reclaim her.

I was concerned that perhaps reviewing so many of the events that had occurred would be too taxing for my client, but she appeared to be okay and was off to a meeting regarding the **R&R** Memorial Foundation as soon as I bid her farewell. She said she was happy with what had transpired in her Zen Den.

I, on the other hand. was totally exhausted. There was the challenge of my two roles, as therapist and as writer. However, I was seeing how they could work well together if we continued interspersing self-regulation therapy to release the activation in her nervous system after her revisiting particularly difficult aspects of her story. I was always concerned about retraumatizing her as we revisited the past, worried that she would begin to feel overwhelmed. I was glad she would not be alone tonight. Brent would be returning that evening.

The Following Morning Text July 17, 2019

SYK to TRS: Just texting you to ensure you are doing okay. That was a heavy load yesterday. Remember the importance of our touching base after our review of your writings to process some of the materials we are detailing.

TRS to SYK: Okay My Woman. But know that right now I am good! No worries. Maybe the 'Hand of God' was a protective factor in our meeting. Gotta go and do some laundry. LOL. Thank you for your concern.

A couple of weeks later I received a text from Tracy.

TRS: Thank you for taking this journey with me, Sandra. I am so blessed. Just want you to know I am trying to make an effort to eliminate my small i's as you asked me to do when I was writing about me and am incorporating capital I's into all my emails and texts now too. Did you notice?

SYK: LOL. You bet I did! Good work! Your "I" always deserves a capital letter girl. Would you be kind enough to expand on the **R&R** stickers? I know… more homework! When are you heading south?

TRS: Tomorrow. So, I will write it up in the hot Arizona sunshine beside the pool!

Chapter 62

THE R&R SYMBOLS CONTINUE TO SCORE BIG TIME!

STILL STICKING! THE **R&R** SYMBOL AND THE ACCOMPANYING #rnrseetheworld continue to take centre stage. Tracy and her team created black, white, and grey bracelets with the symbol as well as **R&R** hats, waterless tattoos, T-shirts, and hats in memory of Radek and Ryder.

The R&R heart

TRS to SYK: July 18, 2019. Good Morning My Woman! Here is my homework! People across the world have been so kind in requesting **R&R** stickers and placing them all over our province, our country, and the world and then letting us know where they have placed a sticker. You would not believe the emails and letters I have received from people asking for stickers or telling me where they have seen them or placed them. Even many rednecks were feeling the burn and tearing up when we connect.

Many of the emails and letters I receive say things like, "Dear Tracy: Can you send me a couple of stickers for my old Chevy pick-me-up truck?" or "Dear Tracy: I have a fleet of trucks here in Nova Scotia and I would like to place **R&R** stickers on every one of them! Can you send me ten?" It was so heartening how respectful people were of the stickers, placing them on their vehicles, on their hockey helmets, in restaurants and monuments around the world and then on their Facebook pages on special days in my kids' lives and treating them with such care and concern. I cannot tell you how much that has meant to me. I have attempted to reply to every request personally as I am so taken by people invested in wanting stickers to help my boys to see the world! As you know, Brent and I travel a lot and take many **R&R** stickers with us on every trip and place them where my boys can see the sights. Doing so brings me both joy and peace. I place each sticker carefully so my boys can have the best view of the world in places they have never been or where they had visited with us on our holidays. When I see a sticker somewhere, I am deeply touched and delighted that someone has taken the time to give my boys a chance to see the world. Then to hashtag to let me know makes it even more special. Such action seems to bring forward the very best of people, some of whom I know and others I have never met but for whom my boys' story has resonated.

All the stories I heard have meant a lot. One particularly beautiful story has emerged and expanded **R&R**'s opportunity to see the world. In 2014, when Brent and I were planning our wedding, we met a woman who managed a boy band in Phoenix, Arizona, called Promise to Myself. When she heard what had happened to my boys in 2016, she shared our family's story with the band. The band immediately wanted to do something to help share the **R&R** memory. Brent and I flew down to Phoenix, met the boys in the band, and provided them with stickers, which they wanted to sell at their concerts and have the profits go to the Memorial Foundation. At the beginning of their concerts, they let those who had purchased stickers know that the goal was to place each sticker in a special location to let our boys see the world. The band was about to embark on a tour in the USA and would be taking many stickers to sell at their concerts. They then created crested t-shirts to sell at their concerts, which also had the **R&R** logo as a part of the design. A portion of the profits would also go to the Memorial Foundation. They were simply a great group of young men who had been touched by the **R&R** story and wanted to be a part of celebrating my boys.

Radek and Ryder continue to be immortalized by the love and concern of each person peeling the tape from the back of an **R&R** sticker and placing that heart with great reverence in locations across the globe where these two young boys continue to follow their mother's vision of **R&R** seeing the world and the world hearing their story.

Promise to Myself & Tracy

Chapter 63

THE TUCK-INS

TRACY'S SOJOURNS TO PLACES FAR AND WIDE WERE SHORT BUT REFRESHING for her. For the next little while, I did not hear from her. When she returned to meet with me after her adventures, it was always with a big smile and that definitive determination to continue working together on our project. We met in the teepee where I had lit the fire that particular day as there was a crispness in the air. She shared with me her postings of **R&R** stickers on her travels. Then, I shared my daughter Kristin's and my latest adventure of attending an evening with the indelible Oprah Winfrey in a packed Roger's Place in Edmonton, Alberta, in June 2019.

I started: "We sat transfixed in Oprah's positive energy. The vitality in Rogers' Place was electric as each woman present breathed in the feminine energy of the venue, grasping at the many crystals of wisdom Oprah shared from the stage. I do not think there was a man in the building other than a few of the ushers! I was absolutely riveted to my chair, scrambling to take notes on the scraps of paper I had resting on the back of my purse, which I was using as my tablet in the darkness of the venue. We were front row, in the highest section of the arena! LOL"

I recounted a significant sharing from our experience that evening. "On stage, Oprah told a tender story of playing the role of a mother in the film, *Beloved*. She recounted one scene in the movie where the director asked her to tuck in her child. She performed the task. The director said to her, 'Not military style, Oprah!' Oprah took a minute to process what he had said and then began to tear up, recognizing that, in fact, she had never been tucked in as a child and never having mothered a wee child herself, how would she possibly know how to do it? The director then said, 'Think of tucking in your dog, Sophie,' who he knew was a very precious critter in Oprah's world at the time. Oprah immediately got it and performed the 'tuck in' task admirably. The man was obviously a very intuitive director!"

My client listened to my sharing and then she said, "I miss tucking my boys in at night. I thought those nights were never going to end but … they have." Her voice had shrunk to a whisper. "When they were here on earth, it was always so good to know they were upstairs safe in my home. I never knew what went on at bedtime at Corry's place, but I am pretty sure he never did tuck-ins or read to the boys before bed or sat at the end of their beds listening to their stories or worries or highlights from the day. He was only into the 'boy' things, as he called them. Tuck-ins? In his mind, that was women's work and entirely unnecessary."

I interrupted, "Many kids whose parents share custody are tight-lipped when it comes to sharing what happens in the other parent's home. Often, they just don't want conflict between their mom and dad."

She shifted in her chair and continued. "Yes. Sometimes I knew the kids just wanted to protect their dad and didn't want me being mad at him. They loved him! They just didn't like it when his anger exploded around them."

"So, how did you like to tuck in your boys, Tracy?" I asked.

She took a minute before responding. "I had a ritual, particularly on school nights. They would have some time to settle before they had to turn out their lights. I would go in and sit on the side of their beds, push their hair back from their foreheads, pull up their blankets under their chins, kiss them good night, and tell them how much I loved them. I always tucked them in when I was home. That's just how it was. If I were late getting home, I would creep into their rooms, make sure those blankets were in place, and then kiss each of them good night on the cheek before tiptoeing out. I never shut their bedroom doors as Radek was always so scared of the dark. I would usually leave the laundry room light on for him. That had always been a part of our routine since they were tiny."

I replied, "Tucking children in is so much more than 'tucking them in,' isn't it?"

She said, "You know what I think? I think parents are often so exhausted by the end of the day that lots of kids do not get tucked in or they are tucked in by their iPad or their iPhone. Once the kids are older, many parents stop tucking them in altogether. I think that is sad because bedtime can be such a special time. At least it was for me and my kids."

I nodded. "I always tell parents in my sessions that bedtime can be a time for connection like no other as is the time when a kid is in the car alone with you. At night is often when kids' fears or concerns come up and parents have the opportunity to reassure their kids of their presence and their love with a simple tuck in. Even as my own kids got older, that ritual continued to be important as a way to end their day and stay bonded with them. Hell, I still do it when my adult kids come to visit!"

Tracy laughed and nodded in agreement. "Sometimes, since the death of my boys, when I talk with other women, I get frustrated with those who complain about how much trouble their kids are. Sometimes I just want to scream, 'Give me that chance!' I would do anything to have my boys driving me insane each and every day instead of bemoaning the fact that parenting teens is tough or that parenting responsibilities are interfering with other parts of their lives."

Her eyes were again full of that fire as she took a deep breath and shared what she was thinking. "I have to watch because I can get pretty intense! I do understand how busy everyone is these days and how hard it is to get teenagers to bed and off their phones at night so one's parenting responsibilities are done and a parent can have a chance to take a breath before turning out the lights! And, of course, many teenagers stay up longer than the parents too! However, I think coming together with your kid in some way before you go to bed is important. But then ..." she shrugged. "What do I know?"

I looked at her, sensing her dejection and said simply, "I think you are rather astute about kids, Tracy."

"Sandra, I guess I am just jealous of my friends who still have the chance to tuck in their kids. I have said before, being a mom was my greatest joy, even when my boys were challenging. I did get breaks from parenting, which many of my friends do not. When the boys were younger, Corry was in their lives, initially sharing custody 50/50 until he moved to Kelowna. Then, when he returned to Alberta he still had them five days a month, so I had a bit of a break from parenting each month. Raising kids in two homes had additional challenges, but when they were with me, they were definitely tucked in."

She mused: "I had everything I could possibly want, except the law stated I had to share my sons with a man whose primary objective seemed to be to make my life hell for destroying his little family. But you know what, Sandra? The one thing my boys did know was that they had a mother who loved and cherished them totally. That I made sure they understood very well!"

We engaged in calming her nervous system as she spoke of what was on her mind.

"There were times when dealing with the behaviour of my boys was difficult even when they were just at the cusp of their teen years. Ryder's hormones were raging at such a young age. When he seemed to find his place amongst his new group of teammates and friends in Spruce Grove, I was ecstatic to see him shine! As I contemplated letting them go with their dad and how focused they were on, as Radek would say, 'Giving Dad a chance,' I thought that maybe having Corry more involved in their lives would be a good thing. In hindsight, I should have listened to my gut and been a stronger force and said no! Unequivocally NO! Sadly, I revisit that decision over and over and over again."

I sat, bearing witness to the pain in her eyes and the agony of her guilt as she shared her thoughts.

"I should have known that it would take a lot before my boys would reveal what was really going on at their dad's. Ryder would have been so afraid that I would remove them immediately from his new life in Spruce Grove where he was becoming so self-assured. His world would have cratered! It is so hard to let those thoughts go, Sandra!"

"Just feel the support of the chair, Tracy, and notice your breath as you think about Ryder keeping everything inside." She knew the drill and we proceeded.

"What are you noticing, Tracy?" I asked as I continued to stoke the fire.

She took her time as she checked into what she was noticing in her body. "I feel some sadness in my chest right now, missing the chance to watch Ryder drive, I guess, as I hear of his friends all getting their driver's licences." She teared up. "How that boy loved speed! I am sure if he were still here, I would be having endless sleepless nights worrying about him being on the roads and then be mad as hell at him when he arrived home late or found myself having to text his friends to find him at two in the morning! I know that would have been my life! That was just Ryder."

She continued to talk about the boys, remembering some of her favourite times together with each of those memories bringing them to life again as we both laughed and cried at some of their antics. The session ended with Tracy feeling lighter after sharing such positive recollections of her connection with her sons.

Chapter 64

COURT ORDERS & SHARING CUSTODY

SYK to TRS: Good Morning Little Mama! Hope the Arizona sun is shining on you today! When you have a chance, I need you to tell me more about the court orders you sent me to review. You certainly had enough of them!

Before long, the following email arrived:

TRS to SYK: Yes, unfortunately they were a big part of my life Sandra. I received more of those pretty little green pieces of paper than I care to remember. I always wondered why a judge would hand out court orders when such decrees were not going to be enforced. I think this is a travesty in our justice system. I am sick of paying for those in positions of power to live the good life while helpless kids and parents pay the ultimate price because of laws that do not adequately protect women and children.

There will be many women or men who have heard or who will read this story and relate to my challenges with my ex-husband. So many people reached out to me after my kids were murdered, saying they were living the same kind of life as I had lived. They were afraid for the safety of their children when the law said that the other parent had custodial or parental visitation rights to see his/her child/children without supervision even when his/her actions deemed that parent unsafe or extremely troubled.

I refer specifically to fathers as I write because that was my experience but such reference could surely apply to mothers who display abusive or dangerous behaviours with their children. Interestingly enough, though, it has been mainly women who reached out to me with their stories of their uneasiness and frustration in sharing custody.

From what I have heard, many women live in fear when their child/children are with their dad or are terrified of what may be happening at their father's place. Some women shared that they were concerned that their children would not make it back home alive and safe—either physically or emotionally. They feared that Dad or his new girlfriend or wife would be mean to the children or ignore their needs. They worried that Dad would not watch out for the kids because he was too busy partying or working or looking for a new woman. What happens when his "new woman" becomes the "primary" caregiver of his children when he is at work during his custody time and she treats the kids poorly? They were supposed to be visiting with their dad! What happened when Dad continues to be so full of rage at his ex-wife for leaving him that he takes that anger out on the kids? What happened when a parent tells lies to the kids about their other parent? Or how about when he becomes Disneyland Dad and buys outrageous gifts or lets the kids do dangerous activities on his watch? How do these behaviours affect the children? These were just some of the concerns I experienced or heard from moms opening up to me.

Other women told me they were anxious the whole time their children were at their ex-partner's because they had lived with the instability or rage or moodiness or addictions of their former spouses. Some feared that Dad would drive drunk or be stoned with the kids in his vehicle. And how about those kids waiting at the window for the likes of an irresponsible parent who said he would pick them up at three p.m. Saturday and then never comes or is continually late or making excuses for the no-shows. What does that do to the heart of a child? When does a parent have to show responsibility in working together with the custodial parent before he or she has continued access to the greatest gift of all … his children?

SYK to TRS: You and I both know there are unstable moms out there as well and great dads involved in their kids' lives, but you are right. The statistics show that it is unequivocally the men who pose the greater risk of abuse and violence and filicide toward their children. We must call on all those concerned about domestic violence to gather together and become a voice loud and strong regarding the safety of children. Those in decision-making positions need to hear our collective voices of concern.

In a few hours, I received a text.

TRS to SYK: Right My Woman! Why do parents have to fill the pockets of lawyers to see which parent can get the best deal when separation and divorce occur or when another court order is required?

SYK to TRS: In my experience working with individual clients going through a divorce and trying to reach a settlement with their spouse, many thousands of dollars are spent and an adversarial system is created, involving each lawyer attempting to get the best deal for his/her client. There always seems to be a winner and a loser, particularly when children are involved. Many adults do not realize that separation and divorce often include trauma for everyone involved in family breakdowns. There has to be a better way to end relationships with the least amount disturbance to the children when living as one family in one house is no longer an option.

TRS TO SYK: I want to answer another important question you posed a while ago when you asked, "Who is our audience for the book?" I want to target everyone to read my story. Lawyers, judges, police officers, child protective services workers, social workers, deadbeat parents, worried parents, perfect parents, hockey parents, stepmothers and stepfathers, grandparents, neighbours, doctors, therapists, teachers, coaches, stay-at-home parents, the garbage man and the lady selling coffee at Tim Horton's. I want everyone to know that my Ryder and Radek should be here and other children involved in unsafe or unstable situations should be immediately removed from such circumstances.

SYK to TRS: I agree. Both parents need to be held accountable to find healthy and mature ways to cushion the major change of separation and divorce for their children. Continual conflict and calling down the other parent seriously impacts the children in a profoundly negative manner. After all, each child is half mom and half dad and hearing one parent speak negatively not about the poor choices or behaviours of the other but about the actual character of the other parent is in effect crushing that child's own self-esteem. Parents working together to ease the tension, which can result in serious dysregulation for their children, is a strategy needed to save kids from future mental health issues. We know that childhood trauma yields adult dysfunction. Divorce is a traumatic experience for children and the more parents can work together in finding solutions as mature adults, the less impact the separation will have on the kids. Sharing Ryder and Radek's story is an opportunity to hopefully influence all those involved in the process of separation and divorce to work on behalf of children to prevent such future travesties as you have experienced and bring greater awareness to parents as to the impact their behaviours have on their children.

Coercive Control

From Tracy's writings, it became very clear that the behaviour known as coercive control had been evident in her life and that of her children when Tracy and Corry were together, as well as after she left the marriage. Coercive control[22] is defined as an act or a pattern of acts of assault, threats, humiliation, and intimidation or other abuse that is used by a perpetrator to harm, punish, or frighten his/her victim(s). Coercive control is a pattern of behaviours that enables someone to exert power over another person through fear and control. It may involve monitoring activities, isolating the other person, using insults to undermine a person's self-esteem, breaking household objects to scare others, intimidating others with threats, or defying rules as set out in the court orders. The controlling behaviour may also be designed to make a person dependent by isolating them from support, exploiting them, depriving them of independence and regulating their everyday behaviour. It may involve behaviours that negate a person's confidence by acts of personal or public humiliation or degradation. This may involve name-calling, highlighting a person's insecurities, or continually putting them down. It may also involve threats of committing self-harm if a partner attempts to leave the relationship.

Because coercive control is a plethora of behaviours, it may not have the acute and blatant symptoms like that of physical violence, as it may create invisible constraints on its victims and a sense of fear that may pervade many elements of a person's life. Although Tracy indicated that she had never been afraid of Corry, she reported his need for control was a serious determent to the well-being of her children and herself throughout the time they co-parented.

Given that coercive control is not an offence under the Criminal Code of Canada,[23] there is an important gap that impedes the ability to address the

---

22   Women's aid.org.uk

23   Victimsfirst.gc.ca

harm it causes to victims of intimate partner violence. Despite the difficulties of the legal system in prosecution, coercive control is still abuse and it can cause long-lasting psychological trauma for those who experience it. In much of the United Kingdom, coercive control is now considered a criminal offence. In the US, coercive control is not currently illegal unless it escalates to physical violence, as assault or rape. However, coercive control is not a specific action. It is a pattern of behaviours. Some argue that criminalizing coercive control is not a complete solution to domestic abuse because many criminal justice systems are not equipped to make judgments on it. Most justice systems rely on physical evidence to charge people with specific criminal acts. One of the difficulties lies in that coercive control tends to leave less physical evidence than violence. It is more subtle than outright physical abuse and, therefore, more difficult to prosecute. However, the traumatic effects are extremely detrimental and long-lasting in the psychological health of its victims.

Children may also become targets of a vengeful father because of the anger a dad continues to feel toward their mother in his inability to control her desire to end the relationship or to attempt to continue to exert control over her once she has left.

The importance of educating others as to the tenets of coercive control cannot be overstated. Judges and lawyers, as a part of the legal system, as well as the general public, must be made aware of the symptoms and debilitating effects of such behaviours and the necessity of following the lead of the United Kingdom in having these behaviour patterns classified as criminal offences in the interest of the safety of women and children. It is an issue that needs the attention of all those interested in decreasing incidents of domestic violence and filicide.

***

Tracy and I shared a counselling session in my meditation room a few weeks later. In a former session, we had discussed the power of gratitude in changing brain pathways in a positive manner. I decided to challenge her by changing up my first question. "So … my friend. What are three things you are grateful for today?"

She laughed. "Here I am, ready with my 'What's going well?' answer, and you change it up!"

I laughed. "Just like to keep you ever ready for challenges, my friend!"

She replied: "Hmm. Three things. Well ... I am grateful for all those people who have helped put together the **R&R** Memorial Foundation website, which is now up and running! I am grateful that we are going to Toronto and Montreal to watch the Leafs and Canadians play next week, and ... I am grateful that I am here!"

"Wow!" I say. "Good job! Why are you grateful that you are here today, Tracy? What's on your mind?"

She breathed in. "What has been swirling over and over in my head is my frustration with Child Services, Sandra. I contacted Child Services with my concerns on December 3, 2016, sixteen days before my kids were killed. I begged them to help me! You read my letter, Sandra, and they did nothing to assist me in removing the boys from their dad's home. I did not need a cheerleader that day. I needed actual help in removing them. I felt abandoned after speaking with the woman at Child Services as if I were a burden to her and asking for help in removing the boys was ridiculous and outside the scope of her department. She did not understand the seriousness of my request. But then," she paused, "but then, I guess even I didn't fully realize the magnitude of it ... either."

She began tearing up early but we continued to engage, me working to ground her as she continued to share what was on her mind. "I was always wanting to ensure the boys were safe on Corry's watch but sometimes I felt so powerless because of the laws regarding the rights of biological parents and the lack of enforcement of court orders. I do continually remind myself that what has happened has happened and I need to move forward and I don't have to worry anymore about my boys!" We took our time as she sensed into her frustration and her resolution.

She grabbed a tissue and continued. "I am very proud of my boys, Sandra. I want to take their memory and I will find ways to immortalize them with their story being the push behind my work to change policies that, in my humble opinion as a mom, were factors in why my kids died."

We processed what she shared and gradually she settled as she continued emptying that trauma cup as she sat and noticed the sensations telling us she was letting go of the activation in her nervous system. So brave. So strong. Facing each day with our mantra: Today is a Good Day to Have a Good Day!

Chapter 65

ON THE WORLD STAGE

HOCKEY CONTINUED TO BE AN IMPORTANT PART OF THE LIFE OF BRENT AND Tracy Stark. In the early summer of 2019, Brent was in meetings with other Alberta Junior A Hockey Team owners and management. After Brent returned home, I received the following email from Tracy.

> TRS to SYK: Brent was talking to Ryan Bartoshyk, the Commissioner of the AJHL (Alberta Junior Hockey League), as a team was being put together to represent Alberta in the Junior Club World Cup in Sochi, Russia, in August. Brent who was on the AJHL Board wanted to put the **R&R** heart patch on the Alberta team jerseys. Ryan agreed and called me to ask where we would want the heart placed. Of course, I opted for over their hearts. However, due to the "C" captain and "A" assistant captain having to wear the letters on the left-hand side, they decided to put the symbol on the right-hand side of the jerseys. This thoughtful man then had two AJHL jerseys made up with Ryder and Radek's names and numbers on them. My boys were a part of the team! Then, when the Alberta team members were presented with their silver medals at the end of the tournament, there were two silver medals for my boys.

Ryder & Radek play for Team Alberta.

Chapter 66

CONFESSIONS OF A
BROKEN MAMA

by
Sandra Young Kolbuc, Counselling Therapist

IN LATE SEPTEMBER 2019, I WAS TOTALLY ENGAGED IN A CANADIAN Foundation of Trauma Research and Education (CFTRE) course in Kelowna, BC, where I was learning more about the impact of childhood trauma on subsequent adult behaviours. On a break, I checked into Facebook on my phone and glanced at Tracy's latest post. It was a few days before Radek's birthday. We had not been through a major anniversary regarding the boys since we had begun to collaborate on the book in April. I had concerns because we were reviewing events in our writing and Tracy was detailing the trauma that she had not revisited at length for a long while. I wanted her in my chair regularly as she wrote the details of her experiences. Revisiting her story without a therapeutic session where we could titrate the experience and help bring her internal resources into play was a part of the process I wanted in place. This was my greatest concern as a therapist.

Preparations for the new school year that fall were well underway. September frenzy had brought up feeling of loss for Tracy as other parents prepared their kids for the upcoming school year. It was also Ryder's year to be eligible for try outs with the Whitecourt Wolverines, which again was overwhelming for the Mama Wolverine. I was continually attempting to get her in the blue chair to no avail. It wasn't working. She was busy. So was I. Then, I read her post.

Facebook Post

by

Tracy Stark

Confessions of THIS Broken Mama: OCTOBER 2, 2019 10:30 p.m.

*You don't know how you got through "that day," let alone every day past.

*You wonder how you failed to see the signs of danger before it was too late.

*You wonder how their father could pull the trigger on your beautiful boys.

*You wonder if your son screamed for you as he was being shot at.

*You wonder what made Child Services ignore your case. Why were my boys not worth saving … ? I did my part. I just needed help from the justice system.

*You wonder who the justice system helps.

*You wonder how people defend the person who murdered his own kids.

*You wonder what the hell mental illness is.

*You're thankful for the man who raised these boys like they were his own, and is strong enough to pick you up also.

*You know the meaning of true friendship and are beyond thankful for it as well.

*You also have people who think "you should get over it", "move on" …. ummm … guaranteed these people haven't felt the loss of a child nor do you ever wish this upon them.

*You become very protective of and develop a strong bond with other "broken mamas."

*You wonder who your kids would be today.

*You look at kids in passing, thinking one looks like your boy.

*You watch all their friends grow older, getting learner's permits and driver's licences, drinking beer, having girlfriends, playing hockey. Although it kills you inside, you are proud of these kids. Proud to know them.

*You are envious of those parents who get to continue making memories with their kids and resent those parents who take it for granted.

*You wonder who said "time heals." It doesn't heal. It only makes it worse.

*Anniversaries are the worst days. Birthdays … ugggggg … birthdays … I have to do this twice a year and it almost kills me!

*You hide in the bathroom to avoid sharing your emotion in front of people.

*You can't stop living your life! You live for them now.

*You love hearing their names.

*You love hearing and telling stories about them.

*You miss the sound of their voices.

*You run out of pictures.

*You miss holding their hands.

*You miss hugging them.

*You miss spending time with them.

*You are stuck on the last moments you had with them.

*You read the news articles of the tragedy over and over again.

*You are angry!

*You get a lump in your throat when people ask you if you have kids ... "I did ..." No one knows how to take this. "I had two beautiful sons whose father chose to murder them." It is harsh but it's the truth ...

*You never forget the letter you wrote to Child Services and the phone call from the lady who called you back. I can guarantee this woman isn't a mother because if she was, she would have had some compassion. And if she went home to children ...

*You post pictures and people comment and say, "It's nice to see you happy. It's nice to see you smile" ... Well thanks ... but if you could feel what's behind this smile, you would take back your words.

*You see so many are broken from the loss of my boys ... but .... you aren't their mama. There will never be a level in you where you will feel my pain.

*You realize this type of thing doesn't just happen to other people ... It happened to me!

*You think maybe your life was just a dream ... dreaming I had these two amazing sons but when I awaken, I no longer do!

*You have this feeling inside from the day you had to pick outfits for your children to wear to be cremated in. There are no words in this world to describe it.

That day, December 19, 2016, I lived a nightmare from which I cannot awaken. But what I know for sure is ... I am not afraid to die.

***

SYK: As I read of her despair, I felt helpless except to add a heart emoji, like many others wishing to ease her pain. Once I finished the course that day, I went for another brief foray into Facebook before I opened the manuscript to continue working on the story. Within seconds, Tracy's post of October 2 came up and I reread it. Big mistake! I felt sick to my stomach as I fully acknowledged the deep pain coming from the words she had written. Just writing about the trauma on Facebook had to be reactivating. Without an immediate counselling session to quell the activation in her system, I felt powerless. I called to arrange a virtual session but could not reach her as she too was on the move. As I read the post again, my breath felt heavy. Heavier than it had felt through all our work together. To me, the post was worrisome. She and I had talked a lot about grief bursts, but this was an obvious flood. I too needed a break from the words in Tracy's post. My head was spinning. It did not stop. I closed my computer, telling myself I had to leave the manuscript.

I quickly changed into my workout gear, grabbed my walking poles and headed out into the warmth of the Kelowna sunshine, the left-right left of the poles providing a rhythm to the thoughts coursing through my brain. My sadness and compassion for my client reflected in the intensity of my walk along the shores of Okanagan Lake. Gradually I settled into a pattern that calmed me. I walked and walked, returning to my hotel room more settled. I showered and changed and grabbed some supper before returning to Tracy's post on my laptop. I instinctively knew this post would have to be in the book. I reviewed the hundreds of responses that followed it, all filled with loving kindness and supportive messages. In my head, I commended the sweetness and concern of the many, many individuals sending heartfelt love to my client in response to her in her moments of profound grief, all obviously wanting to provide Tracy with a degree of comfort. We were one and the same in feeling her sorrow as our empathy created an energy that each one of us hoped would be helpful to the "Broken Mama."

The next morning I took a flight back to Alberta. It was late afternoon when I arrived at the Kolbuc Quarters. The CFTRE[24] training had once again been excellent but I didn't even take the time to unpack before heading to Whitecourt to retrieve the package filled with Tracy's manuscript revisions that she had left at the AIM office the previous week before she had left on another adventure. That evening I tore open the package to view her input into what had been

---

24   CFTRE: Canadian Foundation of Trauma Research & Education

written thus far. She had done some excellent editing of a confusing and dis-combobulated disorganized first draft. She had broken it down page by page. I texted her, commending her for the detail and the rewrites she had completed. I told her I wanted to meet and go over changes she had suggested. Mostly, I just wanted to ensure she was okay after her concentrated work with the draft as well as my concern regarding her post on Facebook. I emailed her.

> SYK to TRS: Hey Little Mama. Your post of October 2 tipped me off to how hard this writing may have been for you and how much you need the heart-warming support of your many followers as you write this story. It is wonderful to read the posts of the many there for you! Before we do any more work on the book, I want to do an SRT[25] session with you if that is ok. I worry that even though you are f'ing tough, this is very difficult work and I do not want to see you retraumatized! Please book in with me asap. Thanks!

I received her reply the following morning.

> TRS to SYK: I just emailed you additional corrections. Let me know if it worked. I'm just running into the city right now to get balloons for Radek's birthday tomorrow. I have definitely struggled a bit going through the manuscript, but in a good way. I promise I won't drown doing this. It's just a hard reality to see where I am today. Kidless. I do want to meet with you as well. Just busy right now.

---

25   SRT - Self Regulation Therapy

Chapter 66

EASING THE SORROW

Sandra Young Kolbuc, Counselling Therapist

AS TRACY PREPARED TO REMEMBER RADEK THE NEXT DAY, ON WHAT WOULD have been his fourteenth birthday, I contemplated what I could possibly do to ease the dejection I read in her text. I fell fast asleep that night still unclear of what I could say or do to ease her sorrow. I awakened early, dressed warmly that brisk October day, laced up my hiking boots, grabbed my hiking poles and my bear spray, put on my backpack, and headed outside into the sleet wanting to walk off my distress at that word "kidless" that had appeared in her recent email. It just sounded so raw. So callous. So devastating.

Gradually, as the numbers on the step count increased on the face of my Fitbit, I was focused on the wonder of the women who continued to gather around my client; those who took the time out of their day to support her with their words, their emojis, and their warm thoughts each time she posted. Women who got it. Women who had lost their babies and those who had not, all wanting to fill her heart with their love so as to shelter her from her own grievous thoughts. What a wonderful community of so many whose empathy was intense and real, all simply wanting to do whatever they could to help her make it through those particularly challenging days, hours, and minutes. Moms with her in their thoughts, as each year brought forward the most painful dates once more. I walked the trails, needing to clear my head and settle the angst of the compassion I felt for my client, my writing companion.

It seemed as I trudged along the trails in the falling sleet, the sounds of nature helped me to settle as I worked at being fully present to the crunch of the dead leaves beneath my boots and the sound of the sleet hitting the ground. I meandered through the forest, attempting to activate all my five senses to bring myself to the present moment. What did I hear, see, smell, taste and feel? It was cold and my golden retrievers were busy chasing a spruce hen that seemed to be accompanying us or was sending us her cousins along the route.

When I arrived at the "Bear Cabin" in the secluded woods, I grabbed the Pendleton blanket from one of the beds inside, wrapped it snugly around me, and sat in the rocking chair on the covered deck, knowing I was carrying too much of Tracy's sadness. Vicarious trauma, I suppose it would be called therapeutically, as I was writing and rewriting pages and pages of the story. Again, I worked at mindfully bringing myself to the present moment, breathing in and feeling the rocking chair under me. I sat in silence, rocking. Back and forth. Back and forth. The patterned rhythm calmed me. I returned to thoughts of Tracy, wondering if there was anything I could do or say to ease her pain.

Gradually it came to me in the tranquility of the moment, in the rhythmic motion of the chair. So often, as I shared with Tracy, it was in those moments of silence when the answers I was looking for would come to me. I breathed in deeply. There it was....I would write Radek a birthday wish and send it via his Mama. I reached into my pocket, retrieving my iPhone, clicked on Notes, and began to formulate some key messages for this young man who would be just a little younger than my grandson, his former teammate, on Radek's special day tomorrow. It was too cold for my fingers to punch much in on the screen, so after a bit, I returned the blanket to the bed inside and again took up my poles and began the walk back to my home, calmer now with what had transpired in my brain as I continued to think about what I wanted to say in a birthday letter to Radek. As I did so, I looked up and across the sky, sending the lady picking up balloons, many miles away, strength and love as she planned Radek's birthday celebration.

I was pensively composing my message in my head as I followed another winding trail back home. I warmed up briefly with a cup of mint tea, took out my phone again, and expanded upon the ideas that had begun to resonate with me. My iPhone and I flowed seamlessly with the words as I wrote to Radek. Funny how that happens ... I revisited the damn autocorrects that continually made me insane, especially with the stiffness of my fingers, and then laid my phone aside. That evening I reread my text ... and then ... I pressed SEND.

HELLO # 8

SYK: Hey Little Mama. This message is for the Birthday Boy!

*Hello #8 and a very Happy Birthday to you Radek! I hope your mama has the balloons flying high to celebrate such a beautiful boy! You two have made such amazing memories of so many great adventures. I know she is holding you close to her heart today remembering all the giggles you shared, your "Where's the Stark Spirit!!!" rant and your always hoping for a big win in scratching your lottery tickets. Your mama made a big win when she got you and Ryder and ... I think you did too! She is a cool mom and I know you would be proud of all she is doing to make things better for kids in your and Ryder's name. And ... **R&R** stickers???? They are all over the place and you boys are always going here there and everywhere! Seeing the world. It is really interesting to hear how much thought goes into where those stickers are placed! Everyone lucky enough to position a sticker just wants to give you guys the best view! At a STOP sign in Whitecourt, I saw one on the back window of a flashy, dark-blue pick up truck and of course I thought of you and your beautiful grin, which I remember well from when you played for Coach Joe and with my grandson, Gavin. I hope you have a great day Radek because Today is a Good Day to Have a Good Day. Let your mama feel your hugs today. Hug her hard! She needs your spirit and Ryder's drive because she and I are writing an incredible story about two amazing boys and their mama! You make sure she is looking up at the stars tonight and remembering she holds you and Ryder and the times you shared together forever in her precious heart and nobody, nobody can ever steal you away from her! Gotta go and work on the book.*

Lots of Love from Gavin Kolbuc Stark's Old Granny!

Within minutes I received the following:

TRS to SYK: Aw Sandra. I've never had anyone send me a message for my boys. This is amazing! I love you! Lol and ... Granny's Kisses are the best!

Chapter 67

THE 3RD MEMORIAL GAME

December 21, 2019

I ASKED MY TWO OLDEST GRANDDAUGHTERS TO ACCOMPANY ME TO THE **R&R** Memorial Game. I had never been. Nor had they. I planned that we would stay for the first two periods. There were few people at the arena when we arrived and we quickly found some seats. Foolishly, without thinking like a hockey fan, I selected seats in the opposing Saints side of the arena!

On each seat in the arena was a small black nylon bag containing the following items: a candy cane, a chocolate, an **R&R** waterless tattoo, an **R&R** wrist band and decal, and a small businesslike card asking the recipient to perform an act of kindness on behalf of Ryder and Radek. The bags were beautifully put together and I thought of the time and dedication it must have taken to create and place on each seat in the arena such a lovely keepsake for each person attending the game.

My nine-year-old granddaughter was not from Whitecourt and did not quite understand what the evening was all about and had many questions. Why were those boys' pictures on the screen 'Gaga'? Why was there writing on the ice? What's a Memorial Game? How did they die? My Whitecourt granddaughter, aged eleven, quickly filled her in. I saw the shock in my smaller granddaughter's eyes.

"Why would a daddy do that, 'Gaga'? she asked as had many young children three years prior when they had learned of the death of the boys. It was a difficult question and I felt sad and conflicted as I attempted to explain to the younger girl in the least possible words, how each year Radek and Ryder were celebrated with a game of hockey to remember what amazing young boys they were. She started to tear up as I put my arm around her and changing the focus pointed out some of the messages that had been painted all over the ice surface by friends and family earlier in the day.

We Play for You
We Miss You Boys
'Til We Meet Again

This would be the last year messages would be written on the ice, so the messages were particularly special. I pointed out to what Ryder and Radek's mom, Tracy and the boys' stepdad, Brent, had painted on the ice earlier in the day.

Always in Our Hearts
Ryder & Radek
You are My Reason
Love you and Miss You
♥Mom & Brent
4Ever

I sent the girls to get themselves a treat from the Overtime Lounge while I sat in the silence of the arena, just looking around, feeling the energy of the venue, watching as the boys' pictures came up on the screen beneath the scoreboard. I thought of how challenging this event was for Tracy as she had indicated that this is still one of the very hardest days of her year. I had sent a text that morning to wish her courage on this day of days.

People began to filter into the seats. The Zamboni proceeded to circle the ice surface, adding a shine to the messages on the ice as people began to file into the seats. The stage was set. The lights darkened and soon there were beautiful red hearts flashing on the ice as the evening began. It was extremely cold outside the arena but inside the building there was a warm sense of community and connection amongst the hockey family.

The crowd cheered and clapped and a video began to play on the screen situated above the ice. Spectators had an opportunity to witness places around the globe where **R&R** stickers had been sighted: the United Kingdom, Switzerland, Cuba, Mexico, Arizona, Las Vegas, Whitecourt, Germany, Newfoundland, Australia, and so many more. It was dynamic and impressive. The video ended with Tracy coming on screen, thanking all those who had supported her and her family, and informing people how to access stickers and apply for support from the **R&R** Memorial Foundation. She had told me the previous Monday how nervous she was having her speech presented on the video screen in front of the crowd in the arena. I looked up. She was poised and spoke well. The sound system in the arena did not do her words justice, but her speech reflected the undying love of a mother for her sons and the determination of a woman to create a kinder and more just world in memory of her boys.

As the video ended, my mind was drawn back to January 2017, when I first got to know Tracy Stark on a more personal level, a month after the death of her boys when her friend, my niece, Trish, lost her husband, Trevor. My little grandnephew, Trevor's five-year-old son, had sparked that idea of using a hockey theme for his dad's celebration of life when he asked if we could start the service by singing "O Canada" just like at a hockey game. In the mind of the fanatic little hockey player, singing our national anthem would make everything better in the craziness of the untimely death of his dad.

Here now, almost three years later, I sat in the Scott Safety Arena in Whitecourt at the Memorial Game for Radek and Ryder with my young grand-daughters beside me, honouring Tracy's boys. In typical hockey tradition, the crowd stood and joined the soloist in the singing of "O Canada" before the game between the Spruce Grove Saints and the Whitecourt Wolverines began. I regarded the pictures of Radek and Ryder beneath the score clock. If only, as my grandnephew believed, the magic of singing "O Canada, our home and native land" could really heal the broken hearts of so many fans here mourning the loss that night of the two beautiful young hockey-playing boys.

Between the second and third periods, the girls and I descended the stairs to meet my daughter and son-in-law, who waited outside in their vehicle, ready to take the girls on a tour of the Christmas lights in our small community before heading home for the night. As my granddaughters put on their coats to exit the venue, I saw they were both sporting the **R&R** bracelets from their gift bags on their wrists, honouring the boys they never knew. Gone ... but not forgotten. Forever Wolverines.

As we left the arena, the street lights themselves shone brightly on the Scott Safety Arena where memories of Radek and Ryder still lived inside the venue, strong and free.

TRS to SYK: December 22/19. Good day my woman. I heard you were at the game last night. I wish I would have seen you. That day was probably the busiest day of my life. Glad it is over. I am exhausted physically and emotionally. I hate to do this but I can't make it to our meeting tomorrow. I have to run into the city as I have a million things to do before Christmas.

SYK to TRS: No problem Tracy. I totally understand. It is a crazy time. Just wanted to begin 2020 on a positive note for things to come next year. You looked poised on the screen last night. Calm and collected. Sounds like you still have a lot on your plate, so simply take care of a very special woman aka YOU!

Chapter 68

THE END OF THE BEGINNING

LONG AFTER MY FAMILY WAS ASLEEP ON CHRISTMAS EVE 2019, I CRUISED
Facebook sand saw the following post:

Christmas Eve

December 24, 2019
Tracy Stark

As I spend this Christmas Eve reminiscing the past … the past month, the past year, the past three years and then … before … when life was perfect and Radek and Ryder were nestled all snug in their beds … I am remembering their love of Christmas and all the fun of being a part of their excitement.

I never knew December 16, 2015, would be the last family picture we would take with our kids and my family

I never knew Ryder's hockey tournament in the spring of 2016 in Los Angeles, California, would be our last family vacation.

I never knew letting my boys experience a year with their father would be the worst decision of my life.

The Last "Ross" Family Picture December 2015

I never knew I would be standing on a snow-covered street, as if I were part of a *Dateline* episode, on that fateful day.

I never knew three years ago would feel like yesterday.

And I never knew that the power of love and support from our friends, family, community and even total strangers would get our family past the worst experience we could ever live through.

It is true Christmas will never be the same without my beautiful boys, Ryder and Radek, but here we are, living and loving this holiday season simply because of the compassion and caring showered on us these past three seasons of love and peace by so many kind and caring people.

Thank you to all my Facebook family and friends for all your prayers and messages not only during this month but every day.

You are my STRENGTH and my boys are my REASON.

TRACY

SYK to TRS: Good Christmas Eve 2019 Tracy Stark. May you walk tall as you continue your journey to make a difference in the lives of women and children. May you never stop shouting from the highest set of bleachers of every arena with the messages we have continually repeated in our writing together. That the power of women and men who love them cannot be denied if we band together as one to stop the reprehensible abuse of women and children.

All change begins with reflection in silence where ideas are born. Then, in conversations, where ideas are shared. May many conversations take place amongst people after the reading of this book and the changes that need action be enacted into law and into the hearts of those committing such abuse in order to make our communities safer for children and women of separation and divorce and for those who continue to be in unhealthy relationships.

May you also remember, Tracy, that trying to change systems is extremely challenging. But, once you start with that single step, all kinds of unseen forces will come together to impact the hearts and minds of many who hear the powerful message in your effort to make sure that Radek and Ryder's lives make that profound difference in the lives of other children … and their mamas. The walk began on Day 1 with the initiation of the **R&R** sticker and has blossomed with your many initiatives. The book, with its written words and pictures, will bring it all together. I am very proud of us!

My gift to you to begin 2020 is simply my recommitment to our work together in releasing our book. Thank you for sharing the kindness and the beauty I have seen in you and that you have found in yourself as you have risen to the challenge of not only grieving your children but of bringing forward the best in you to make a far-reaching difference in the lives of many who will read your story. You are truly a shining star of hope for a safer world for kids and their mamas. MERRY CHRISTMAS LITTLE MAMA! See you in 2020! *Sandra*

Chapter 69

WHITECOURT WOLVERINE LADIES' NIGHT

January 10, 2020

SYK to TRS: Hello Cinderella. I know you will soon be dressing for the ball! Take a mindful moment tonight to take note of the many women excited to be sharing tables and drinks and living the themes they have chosen to personify for this wonderful fun-filled occasion! Hear the laughter! Look around and witness the energy and the joy you see amongst your many friends, old and new, and remember … Tonight you and your little cluster of organizers are dropping little sparkles of light into the lives of two hundred and eighty women!

The radiance of the event reflects the power of a small group of women committed to making things happen and the energy and power of such a committee. Cheers to your dynamite first-class organizers.

It is actually an updating of the scene in ancient times of women gathering at the well in the centre of each village. Yes in ancient times it was women working rather than playing together but the event also represents the women toiling together during harvest to feed the thrashing crews. It displays women volunteers making things happen in our communities. On this night the women will not be cooking, getting water, or scrubbing clothes, but the power of the feminine energy in that one room will be real just as it was in former times when women did gather at the well or in the fields … and the connector tonight in bringing women together? The Mama Wolverine, smiling her brilliant smile and wearing the gorgeous blue diamond glistening on the fourth finger of her right hand, raising money for the **R&R** Memorial Foundation and the Whitecourt Wolverines Hockey Club. It is a reminder of the potential of women gathering together to make things happen! Have a beautiful night!

Chapter 70

HAPPY 17TH BIRTHDAY, RYDER PATRYK!

I PUNCHED INTO MY FACEBOOK APP, KNOWING THAT TRACY WAS PREPARING to celebrate Ryder's seventeenth birthday on March 1, 2020. Prefacing her writing was the most beautiful picture of Tracy and Ryder when Ryder was probably about four or five. He had the most peaceful smile emanating from his lips. Almost that "Just me and my sweet mama," the picture capturing the son-to-mother connection. Yes, the relationship between Tracy and the boys had definitely changed but guaranteed, it would never be broken.

Ryder hugging and kissing his Mama

My mind was immersed in the essence of the love in the pictures of Ryder and his Mom that sustained and displayed the incredible connection between Tracy and her boys then ... and now. Then I read her post:

FACEBOOK POST

Tracy Stark, March 1, 2020

What does 17 look like?

What did 14, 15, and 16 look like?! It looks like this ...

Writing a message on a balloon and hoping it reaches Heaven so you can read it.

It's writing a stupid Facebook post or hash tagging #missingyou as I am looking through the same pictures I've looked at for 1168 days.

It's wondering what you would look like. Wondering what you would be like? Wondering what you would want to do for your birthday ...

It's living your best life FOR YOU but not with you

It's wishing I was with you today and every day

> Today is your day my boy.
> I hate that this is our life.
> I hate that you're so far away and I can't hold you.
> You are so loved and so missed down here

But as you requested, we will celebrate today with you...

You wanted drinks. So, drinks will be had ...

Love you to the moon and back, Ryder!

Cheers, my angel!

Tracy and Ryder's friends celebrate Ryder's 17th birthday

Chapter 71

OUR LIGHT *
OUR COMFORT *
OUR STRENGTH *

BRENT AND TRACY STARK HAVE HAD MANY SUPPORTIVE FRIENDS WHO HAVE walked beside them, never missing a step, through the agony of the death of Radek and Ryder. Two of those friends, Joey and Jenneka Bouchard, had been close friends since Joey commanded the position of head coach of the Junior A Whitecourt Wolverines during the 2012–2014 seasons. The alliance remained solid even after the Bouchards moved to a community two hours away in 2015. They were there with the Starks on the last night that Tracy and Brent were with their boys. They were there when the news of the murder of Ryder and Radek hit the airwaves. They were there with dear friends, Brett and Carla Evasiuk, forming a circle of love and strength around the devastated couple outside the Stony Pain RCMP Station on that fateful December day. They were there and have continued to share their love and compassion for their dear friends.

In 2019 I asked Tracy if she could have Jenneka share her thoughts regarding the tragedy. I received the following:

GROSS MISCONDUCT

December 21st: a strange number comes across my call display, reluctantly, I answer the phone...

Me: "Hello"

Voice: "Hi there, I am calling to follow up with you about the house that you viewed the other day, are you still interested in renting it?"

I freeze.

Voice: "are you still there?"

I hang up.

How is it possible that just a few short weeks earlier we were house shopping with the boys, and now...we were planning their funeral. From picking out which bedrooms they each liked best, to watching Tracy struggle with what clothes they would be cremated in. This was not supposed to happen, we had a plan...it was going to be perfect...the Bouchards and the Starks, reunited again. We dreamt of the days that we would get to pick up Radek after school, drop Ryder off at hockey practice, or share joint family dinners. I closed my eyes on December 18th without a care in the world, and when I opened them the next morning, life as we knew it would never be the same. Oftentimes I can't decipher what hurts more, the thought of what has happened, or the reality of what never will.

They say that one day... there is a last time for everything. One day, your child will crawl into your bed for the last time. They hold your hand to cross the street for the last time. You read them a bedtime story for the last time. We never get the privilege of knowing which time will be the final one. These things just happen again and again, day after day...until one day they don't. We never could have known that the goodbye hugs in the parking lot were going to be the last, or that the memory of Ryder glancing back at us in the stands would become permanently etched in our memories... We never could have known.

I used to believe that "everything happens for a reason". I think we use this as a personal mantra to shelter and protect ourselves from the array of disappointments and heartaches in life. We reassure ourselves, that regardless of what happens, it must be the result of some divine intervention. We find comfort in telling ourselves that there is a greater purpose or a bigger plan, that is just beyond our comprehension. I now know this to be untrue... There is no "reason" under the sun that could explain the horrific murder of those two precious boys. And searching for a "why" felt as if I was somehow trying to justify the tragedy. To say that this happened to teach us a lesson about life, or to serve as some sort of a reminder for everyone, seemed to cruel to accept. Instead I came to decide that sometimes....thing's just happen. Unimaginable, gut wrenching, and life stopping things happen. And they happen to good people, for no good reason at all. I believe that the long-term result of these happenings, is a matter of our own choice and intervention. Whether it causes us to pause and count our blessings, to squeeze our loved ones a little tighter, or to appreciate the life we have...those are by products of tragedy, but they do not give us a why. Sometimes, there just isn't one to be found, and there is no comfort in trying to construct one. The death of Ryder and Radek has proven to me that pain does not have a predetermined purpose, but it can be a catalyst for change, and for choice.

You see, the boys' story is one of devasting loss and unbearable heartbreak; it is a nightmare that I can never wake up from, and a reality that continues to steal the breath from my chest. <u>But there is another</u>

<u>story to tell here</u>... one of profound perseverance, super-human strength, and extraordinary grace. I also used to believe that the death of a child is too painful to endure and is something that a parent just couldn't survive. But for the past 3 years, I have had the immense privilege of watching my best friends not only, survive, but THRIVE through something that would have destroyed most. Everyday, I witness as Brent and Tracy <u>choose</u> life over loss, light over dark, connection over isolation, and strength over surrender. Everyday they make the conscious decision to rise and fight, and it is because of their unwavering courage, that so many of us have found the strength to carry on. There are somethings in life that cannot be fixed...they can only be carried; Brent and Tracy have demonstrated how to carry life's heaviest weight with grace and humility. While losing Ryder and Radek has taught me profound life lessons, it is in watching my friends navigate through loss, that I have gained the inspiration to fully live. **On the darkest days, they are our light. In the loneliest nights, they are our comfort. And in our weakest moments, they are our strength.**

My prayer is that the true Ryder and Radek "story" is not lost in the horrific tragedy of what happened on the night of December 19th. But rather that the memory of the boys and the perseverance of their parents, serves as an inspiration and a reminder for us all, that we each have a choice to make. Everyday, and every moment, presents an opportunity – I pray that you choose light, love and hope. I pray that you choose <u>life.</u> And if the weight of your life is heavy or you can not find a light...then I pray that you remember Brent and Tracy and BECOME the light.

Ryder and Radek, I love you...and I am sorry <3

Jenneka

Tracy and Jenneka

Chapter 72

THE DIVINE SPARK

TRACY AND I ARRANGED TO MEET TO GO OVER THE MANUSCRIPT AND MAKE some final decisions on the content of the book. She shared her challenges of again celebrating a birthday for one of her absent sons. We talked of the relationships that she maintained with Ryder and Radek's friends. I, of course, added a little gem of therapeutic wisdom regarding the importance of such.

I began: "Dr. Daniel Siegel in his book, _Brainstorm: The Power and Purpose of The Teenage Brain,_ states that the developmental goal of young people transitioning through the teen years is ultimately to separate from their own parents. Having other safe, caring adults in their lives who can offer their own sage wisdom can assist with this transitional phase in helping kids make good decisions when they are vehemently separating from the parental influence. Their brains are still growing until they are about twenty-five years of age, so there are times when they, with their underdeveloped brains, will not be making good choices. How great to have someone like you Tracy in their lives to be there when they need another perspective and, how lucky for their parents!"

She smiled. "I feel I am the lucky one to continue to have these kids in my life!"

I shuffled through some pages of our manuscript where I needed clarification. "Tracy," I asked, "What did you mean when you say you feel you have become a better person since dealing with the death of your boys?"

She pondered this for a moment before she spoke. "I believe I am a far more compassionate and empathetic person. You know, Sandra, so many people have given me so much love and support that I have become far more conscious of doing the same to others. I am braver now in stepping forward and opening my heart when others are suffering because I have been there and know what has helped and continues to help me make it through my grief and sorrow."

She shifted in the chair and began to manipulate the blue diamond on her fourth finger. I pointed out to her what I was observing.

She responded, "It has taken so little time for my blue diamond to become a part of me. It truly is my touchstone with my boys when I am deeply in thought about my life or theirs. I was so lucky to have been so loved by my boys even though our time together was far shorter than I ever thought would be our story. I will always continue to live my life on behalf of them and work to continue their legacy. Today I am in a good place. I do not feel guilty about finding joy in my days for all the little things for which I am grateful I am loving who I continue to become."

There was power in her voice as she continued. "Now tomorrow I do not know where I will be. But right now … in this moment, I am OK! There is more of that in my life now, that being in the moment and being OK. I know there will still be tough days but right now, I am OK."

We reviewed our work together, and then, our session was almost over. She sat in my meditation room, gathering herself to head back into her world.

She looked at me and said, "My dream since the boys died has been to immortalize Ryder and Radek by getting their story out there, and here we are about to finish our first draft, make revisions, find an editor, and get it published! You will never know how much this means to me, Sandra!"

I breathed in as Tracy shared her appreciation.

"It has been an incredible journey, Tracy, with you and your boys." I motioned to the candle shining brightly on the sideboard. "It has been very special to have shared so many moments in our quest to tell your story."

She smiled. "And after I drafted you onto my team, honestly, I never ever even tried to trade you! Honest!"

I started to laugh and said, "Well, Tracy, there were times I was left sitting on the bench when you were flitting off to the rinks in Vegas or Phoenix or Toronto or Kelowna or were somewhere in Mexico dipping into those sun-kissed waters. There were times when you didn't answer my texts or took forever to rebook an appointment with me and I was left wondering if you had changed your mind about the book or if I had overwhelmed your nervous system with homework assignments or ….if you were looking for another head coach! Then, after I had decided you must have had a change of mind, out of the dressing room you would sashay into my world wearing your Wolverine jersey and your high stilettos or caressing the floor with your bare feet or texting me your whereabouts, smiling brightly with your emojis and filling your texts and emails with more of the story."

She looked at me. "I know that there will be people who will not see the way you and I do. Perhaps there will be those who will not like what we have put together in the telling of my story but never once did I want to abandon our game plan of telling this story together. You have truly been "my woman" in sharing your perspective on my healing journey and the lives of Radek and Ryder. As well, you have been my therapist, attempting to keep me safe in revisiting extremely difficult scenes from the past. Thank you for taking all I have shared and putting it together into this manuscript." I could feel the tears beginning in my own eyes as I observed my client as she continued. "Thank you for walking beside me on this rocky road and sharing the essence of my story through your eyes as my therapist. I will be forever indebted to you."

I paused. "Thank you for trusting me with your story, Tracy." I met her gaze and said, "If it's okay, I want to share with you a message to carry in that Wolverine sport duffel bag of yours for the rest of your life."

My tear-filled eyes held fast with hers. "You are truly an amazing woman, Tracy Stark. I feel privileged to have coached you, my star centre, in this critical second period of your game of life!"

She smiled through her own tears and nodded as I continued sharing my perspective on the title of the book.

"You know, Tracy, I love how the title *Gross Misconduct* Hitting from Behind * A Mother's Love Story* found its way into my brain. Sometimes I just like to roll it around in my mouth. It sounds right and has ever since it first came to me after I agreed to work together. A gross misconduct is the worst penalty a player can receive in the game of hockey and yet mixed into all the devastation, trauma, and grief, this narrative is still a beautiful, cherished love story of a devoted mother and her beautiful sons, a wife and her husband, a woman and her friends, a mom and her Facebook, Twitter, and Instagram followers, and an involved community member and her community. As well, it is a love story between you and all those who simply want to be a part of the **R&R** team and make a difference in the lives of women and children."

She smiled. "Thank you, Sandra. I have learned a lot about love this past while. It truly is a mother's love story."

I looked down at the paper in my hand and then up at Tracy and said, "The following passage has provided guidance for many of my clients throughout my years as a therapist."

Tracy settled back in the chair to listen. I cleared my throat and began the message of hope.

My Prayer for You

by
Dr. Alan D. Wolfelt[26]

May you continue to discover hope – an expectation of a good that is yet to be. May you continue to find new ways to renew your divine spark and to believe that meaning, purpose, and love will come back into your life. No, you did not go in search of this loss but it has come to you and you have discovered the importance of sitting in your wound on the pathway to your healing. If you give up, the essence of who you are will die or be muted for the rest of your life. Hope can and will keep this from happening.

May you never give up and may you consciously choose life! May you turn your face to the radiance of joy every day. May you live in the continued awareness that you are being cradled in love by a caring presence that never deserts you. May you keep your heart open wide and receptive to what life brings you, both happy and sad. And may you walk a pathway to living your life fully and on purpose until you die. Blessings to you as you befriend hope and choose to celebrate life. May your Divine Spark shine brightly as you share your gifts and your love with the universe.

I looked up and saw the glistening eyes of my client—the Warrior Goddess, Cinderella, the Queen of the Laundry Room, the bright Starkshine, the Mama Wolverine. Then I knew, without reservation, that I had chosen the perfect

---

26   Dr. Alan D. Wolfelt, *The Mourner's Book of Hope: 30 Days of Inspiration* (Fort Collins, CO: Companion Press, 2010). Dr. Wolfelt is an internationally noted author, teacher, and grief counsellor who serves as Director of the Center for Loss and Life Transition in Fort Collins, Colorado.

passage to share with a woman who, through her words and actions on this grieving journey, has chosen LIFE. A woman who has focused on making for a safer, kinder place for all those in need of such in our corner of the universe and beyond.

May your blue diamond continue to sparkle for always and forever, Tracy Stark. 💍 You have truly won the "Heart" trophy in the telling of your story!

Sandra

Chapter 73

HAPPY EIGHTEENTH BIRTHDAY RYDER

THEN ... IT WAS FEBRUARY 2021. HOW TRACY WOULD NEED DR. WOLFELT'S words regarding the divine spark in the coming days, weeks and months. We had had our first edit and were in the ups and downs of a real editor evaluating what had been written. I incorporated the necessary changes. I had not heard from Tracy for some time. My texts went unanswered. I knew December was always a difficult month. It had been hard to pin her down. COVID wasn't helping our cause either! She was always busy, but I felt it was more than that. Then, on Facebook, I read her post.

Tracy's Facebook Post
February 2021

The year 2021 has already been full of many emotions. The two months into this year have been the most trying time since my boys died. Ryder's birthday on March 1, 2021 was a day I was dreading. Having a child officially become an adult is such a special milestone in a parent's life as your child is launched into the big bad world and that, that wasn't happening for me and my son Ryder.

In a later email following Ryder's birthday, Tracy shared the following:

TRS to SYK: One Sunday in February, two of Ryder's friends landed on my doorstep wearing their Grad 2021 hoodies and graciously handed me one as well. On the back of the hoodie was the **R&R** symbol. It was so kind of them to remember my Ryder as 2021 would have been his graduation year as well. Having the **R&R** logo embroidered on their sweatshirt was an option that many of Ryder's classmates chose.

Two of Ryder's team of Hilltop High School graduates

The boys told me they wanted to include Ryder in their grad and they were having masks with the **R&R** symbol made as well. Kids who were graduating in Spruce Grove who had been Ryder's last hockey teammates were also having the **R&R** logo emblazed on their graduation hoodies. I was deeply touched by the gesture of these boys and their parents. However, just the thought of Ryder's graduation day pulled me even deeper into the darkness.

As March 1st came closer, I found myself just wanting to be alone. I didn't want to hang out with my friends as much because when I did, they seemed only to talk about their kids, and what they were doing, from drinking beers with their boys in the garage, to texting their boys' cute girlfriends, to who they would get to be the designated driver for Grad night if they got to gather during

COVID, to their kids' teenager attitudes and upcoming skiing trips with other grad families. Although I know this was no one's intention, every part of this hurt my heart even more. I found myself not having anything in common with my closest friends. I had nothing to add to any conversation, so, to avoid the hurt, it was easier to be alone. You wanted me to call you but I knew you would want me to come and see you and I did not want to see or talk to anyone.

I found I was sinking deeper and deeper into that hole by the day. The week before Ryder's birthday, I was drowning. I could not breathe. My whole body ached. I was filled with rage and underneath it all was such a profound hurt that my boy was not here to celebrate becoming an adult.

Friends reached out to see what I was planning on doing for Ryder's big day! I was thinking, *How the hell do I know what to do for an eighteen-year-old who isn't here in the physical world? 'Frick. I'd lost him as a thirteen-year-old when he was barely a teenager. I didn't even know how eighteen-year-olds act. I didn't know what his friends were into, what they drank, what games they would want to play at a party where the guest of honour was not physically present.*

The more I asked myself these questions, the more despondent I became. I felt I had aged twenty years in less than a month. I found myself struggling with the idea of watching all of Ryder's friends in Ryder's home, doing the things Ryder should be doing.

I read your email, Sandra, asking me to set up a meeting to discuss the book. I knew that was a cover for your concern about my state of mind.

So... I replied.

TRS to SYK: Date: February 26, 2021. Good day my woman. Sorry I was in the city all day yesterday and today my mom is coming up so I can't come out. It's been a hard few weeks to be honest. Ryder's 18th birthday is coming up on Monday. But this is my life. I will be going through the book this weekend. So sometime next week?

SYK to TRS: You name the date and time, Tracy. I have clients Monday from 9 am -12:00 Noon. Other than that, I am free ... and easy! Have a good day with your mom and remember that **R&R** are walking with you on this journey every single day. And, Ryder and his little brother would want to see their Mama rocking Ryder's birthday. Remember we are building a sensational heartfelt book Starkshine! Write about the actions of some of the members of Ryder's Grad Class and how they are making their Grad Ryder's Grad as well. I was tearing up as I saw the picture of you and the boys in the grad hoodies. This is absolutely fantastic that your boy is being so honoured by his friends. Let YOUR team and HIS lift you up when you feel down.

After Ryder's birthday Tracy shared the following:

TRS to SYK: 02 March 2021. On Ryder's birthday so many friends reached out with empathy and their forever love. It took me days to read all the beautiful messages and acknowledge the acts of kindness by so many. Actually, an email from my therapist aka YOU started my day. Here it is as it too should be a part of the book.

SYK to TRS: 01 March 6:00 A.M. MST **Today is a good day** *… .. to remember not why he left but why he came, Little Mama. Not that you cannot see him but that you can feel him. Not that his life was short but that it was long enough to impact many and maybe … even change laws and procedures and the mind of another distressed father or mother … thru our writings. Tracy – celebrate that boy today with great joy in your heart more than sad tears in your eyes because, of all the other mothers on the planet … HE CHOSE YOU! And … You … You chose me … to help share his story and give the world a chance to know his and his brother's name. Take the time to remember the wonder of a young man turning 18. I want to hug you tightly for your courage and tenacity. Damn COVID! Just an elbow bump I guess!*

Take a minute and imagine holding Ryder tightly in your arms, whispering a love song in his ear and hearing his laughter as he pushes you away for being such a … mother! **Today is a good day** *to celebrate Ryder Patryk as well as your privilege of birthing two boys whose story can change the world … one child at a time. Thank him for choosing you to be his mom as you celebrate not his short life but his long influence on his friends and family and everyone who hears the beautiful name you chose for him 18 years ago … Ryder Patryk. And … for his little brother, Radek Stryker. The world will know* **R&R.** *Stand tall. Look good! And Dance, Dance, Dance to the music of Ryder's soul and … Tomorrow? Remember my number!* Your Coach.

Her email continued.

TRS to SYK: I had decided to have a few of Ryder's closest friends come over and do the things eighteen-year-olds do, whatever that is. Well, they drank the drinks. They played the games. Most importantly, they talked about their friend Ryder and wanted to be with Brent and me on his day. That was what made March 01, 2021 a very special day.

Friends had also been absolutely wonderful, making videos, sending beautiful caring messages, responding to my post. But Ryder's birthday took everything out of me. I found myself still sad and still angry. As I thought about the next few months ahead, my stomach was in knots just thinking about watching Ryder's friends mount the stage and receive their high school diplomas without my boy in the queue in June of 2021. It all just seemed so emotionally overwhelming.

March 1, 2021 Today is your day, Ryder!

Chapter 74

HILLTOP HIGH SCHOOL GRADUATION 2021

TRS to SYK: As graduation day crept closer, I became more and more saddened by what was never going to be for my boys. I'd been to numerous high school graduations. As I documented previously, I had even attended one as an escort, but none came with the despair that overtook me when I thought about what should have been Ryder's graduation year. The idea of seeing all the handsome young men and beautiful young ladies that I had watched grow up with my boy since preschool days all dressed up and experiencing one of the best days of their lives truly killed me. Ryder should have been crossing that stage to receive his diploma. I knew that there would be a virtual tribute for my boy during the ceremony and the anticipation of that also took my breath away ... the same way it did that cold December morning in 2016.

Don't get me wrong. I was beyond grateful for all the love and support from so many who worked to have my boy included in what would have been his potential graduation day. It was just so hard to accept that Ryder would not be among the graduates.

I hadn't connected with my therapist/writer aka you for some time. Sorry but I was so low, far beyond what you might have even labelled as a grief burst. I did not want to talk to anyone! I knew I should be calling you but even pressing the buttons on my phone seemed like too much effort.

In early April, Brent and I headed to Arizona. We would be able to get both of our COVID vaccinations more quickly in the USA and God did I need the Arizona sunshine to warm my soul and ease the pain of what would never be. We headed south for a month. Gradually, the crushing wave of depression began to lift. I began to think about Ryder's classmates who would be a part of the Hilltop High School Class of 2021. As I sat in the healing energy of the Arizona sun, an idea began to fester as I thought about the group of kids who were beautifully remembering Ryder bent on honouring my son at their high school graduation.

Across the nation, COVID was not co-operating with many 2021 graduation celebrations. At the Hilltop virtual ceremony each graduate was to cross the stage and receive his/her high school diploma, shake hands with school administration with but two guests physically accompanying the graduate into the school to bear witness to the success of their graduate. We as spectators were directed to watch the ceremony virtually on devices in our vehicles in the school parking.

In Arizona, I had made the decision to construct a message to the Hilltop Class of 2021 and put it on YouTube for Grad Day 2021. You encouraged me. However, no matter how hard I tried, I was unsuccessful. Each time I attempted to record my message, it proved beyond my emotional capacity to do so. Try as I might, it was too much. The tears just kept interrupting my message time and time again. So … I relented and went with the backup plan you had suggested if I felt overwhelmed. I would put the text of the message in the book. So here it is.

Message to the Hilltop High School Graduates of 2021

GOOD DAY GRADUATES. Even with COVID interfering with the pageantry of a normal high school graduation, today is a good day to have a good day. I am so proud of each of you as you reach this milestone of your youth. I wish every one of you the gift of finding a future that truly makes you excited to have the privileges and responsibilities of being an adult. But first, I would like to thank those of you who were friends of my son Ryder for including him in your celebrations. For including him in your graduation day and for having Ryder in your thoughts. I cannot fully express how much your many acts of kindness have meant to me and Brent and our girls.

You know there are many paths that you might take as you begin the journey of adulthood as a high school graduate. If Ryder were alive today, I think, like all parents, I would want to give my son some special gems of wisdom to carry in his pocket as he negotiated the adult world. I often think of what I would have said to Ryder today as my graduate flashed me that beautiful smile of his if he were among us. I hope he is listening as I share my words with all those he called friends and classmates. The last hockey number Ryder wore was with the Spruce Grove Saints. His number was #3. Today I choose to be the fairy godmother of your class and wave my magic wand and give you my three wishes to carry in your pocket or purse for the rest of your life.

Number 1: **Find your passion.** May you find a path through life that rocks you and excites and brings you great happiness midst all its challenges as well as the focus required to find work that ignites you because ... when that happens there is no difference between work and play. My work with the **R&R** Memorial Foundation created in Ryder and Radek's memory does just that for me.

Number 2: **Be a good person** filled with compassion and kindness for those who walk a less privileged road that you will as a high school graduate. May you reach out with a hand up for those needing your grasp. May you find your voice and join others in matters of social justice to prevent further instances of injustice for children and mothers so that all those at risk of violence have a team that lifts them up. That now is my goal.

Number 3: **Live in gratitude** for what you have rather than anger for what you do not. Live each moment in thankfulness for the opportunities that lie before you as a high school graduate, knowing that every moment you live in anger or negativity takes away one moment for potential happiness. If you decide to change your negative thoughts and adopt more positive ones, you can actually change the trajectory of your life.

That said ... most people live in the past or the future when what is real is only this moment. May you savour every second of right now as you breathe in memories of this incredible day of victory and celebration. When Ryder died, someone sent me a card that read: He died much too young so I guess we better do some living for him! I hope you will safely do that tonight and throughout your life when you think of my boy.

On this June 25, 2021, I am honoured to watch classmates of Ryder Patryk exit Hilltop High School as high school graduates. Of course, I wish with all my heart that Ryder too was shaking the hand of the Hilltop's Principal, holding his diploma high in his other hand and, in Ryder style, probably doing a flip off the stage.

However, although Ryder's life was short, it was filled with many incredible moments of love and laughter with his many friends. Thank you all for being a part of his TEAM. Here's to the Class of 2021.

Tracy Stark
June 25, 2021

Here's to the Class of 2021!

Epilogue

by
Tracy Stark, Mother

AFTER READING THIS BOOK, YOU, THE READER, MAY OR MAY NOT HAVE A DIF-
ferent outlook on me and my situation than that portrayed by the news and others
who judged Brent and me on social media in 2016. When tragedy strikes, you can't
help but read online what people have to say about you and your circumstances.
Ninety percent of people were extremely sympathetic for what we were going
through. Although, like with all social media, there are those who had nothing
nice to say, blaming me or Brent for what had happened to my kids. Some actually
pointed the finger at us, insinuating that we were the ones who had committed
this horrible crime and made what happened to my boys and their father look like
a murder-suicide. Let's just say, I hope none of those individuals ever have to live
through what we have, or read such judgmental comments directed at them.

I have read the manuscript of the book numerous times as it evolved, wondering if I wanted to put myself out there to be bashed again as some people did
to me when my kids were murdered. However, I expect the same response from
our readers—the good, the bad, and the ugly. The difference now? I am much
stronger. I don't care what people have to say. This is my story and I am telling it.
I don't put myself out there to be the victim or the innocent. It's been almost five
years since my boys died and Corry Gene MacDougall was guilty of the most
horrendous crime a parent could possibly commit.

I have reread the texts Corry and I exchanged the day before my boys
lost their lives and wondered, *Is this the reason Corry did what he did?* Then I
shake my head and think ... *No Way. NO F*#KING WAY! That to punish their
mother, a man could actually take a loaded shotgun and destroy his children as they
slept defenselessly in their beds and in Radek's case, in his father's bed, is beyond
my comprehension.*

I think, I truly think, this was not a random act nor a spur of the moment decision. I believe my ex-husband had this final act planned out for a while. The evidence? The writing on the mirror in his bathroom. The pictures in his closet. The "family" pictures on my kids' bedside tables. This was a man who was never going to get over my leaving him. The fact that the kids wanted to be back with me was never going to be an option with which he could or would live and I believe he was supremely afraid of what the boys would share with me.

After Corry's home was "released," meaning after the carpet, soaked with my children's blood was removed, and the other evidence from Corry's night of terror was confiscated by the law enforcement officers, I received a text from Corry's brother. He told me we could go in and grab the boys' things from Corry's home. Obviously, I was not about to step foot in that hell, but Brent said he would go and it was through him that I learned of the Post-It Notes on his bathroom mirror, the gun casings in his bedside night stand, the shrine of my life with Corry in his closet, and all the pictures of me and Corry and the kids when they were little. This to me was far from normal!

Corry and I had had a very conflictual divorce, as stated in the numerous court orders that became available to the media and were publicized just days after the murder/suicide. Many readers have already read about our "issues," which seem to become public knowledge when a mother finds her children murdered.

The sad reality is that the issues of which I have spoken are the norm for far too many separated and divorced couples. I'm sure some, living this same hell, will read this book and think, *This is MY LIFE.*! Others may instead hug or shake the hands of their ex-partners and thank them for working together to manage tough issues as separated parents raising their children in two homes with the best interests and safety of the children being their primary purpose.

I have shared my story with my therapist-writer as it happened. We have included letters, scans, emails, texts, and Facebook posts as written. I have shared information from my counselling sessions as I struggled with the reality of losing my sons. In this book, I am putting my whole life out there to be sifted through and judged. Almost five years ago, the media did just that. However, they had only part of the story. Within these pages, my therapist and I have shared much of the rest.

It is not my purpose to bash Corry MacDougall or his family. In fact, I feel deeply for his family. As I grieve my sons, they grieve a son and brother. However, their grief is different from mine. I grieve for my children and their unlived lives.

I hate Corry for what he has done. However, Corry is loved and missed by his family and friends. To them, I extend my sympathies.

Forgiveness????

Facebook Post
Tracy Stark
October 21, 2021

The day I finally got Radek's cell phone back from the Police station…I brought it home. I plugged it in to charge…thinking the next day I would try to get into it. But at 4:00 a.m. his phone started blasting the song Unsteady by X Ambassadors.

> Hold, hold on, hold onto me
> 'Cause I'm a little unsteady
> A little unsteady
> Hold, hold on, hold onto me
> 'Cause I'm a little unsteady
> A little unsteady.[27]

It was set as an alarm EVERYDAY…to go off at the same time. A Reminder? What happened at 4:00 a.m.? I will tell you what happened at 4:00 a.m. My kids were shot to death starting at that time.

My question 'til this day is …WHY was Radek's phone found in the monster's pick-up truck and why was this song set as an alarm to remind me of the time my child took his last breath? I have listened to this song on repeat numerous times reading between the lines, trying to find a message…But I get nothing… … … … …..!

So you ask me about forgiveness? My therapist and I have spoken on this topic. She is gentle in her approach as she knows how difficult this dialogue is for me. With great tenderness, she calls me on the fact that I have said I will never forgive Corry. She wonders how holding on to my inability to forgive him impacts me. She wonders if I might be able to let go of the angst and rage that are still a part of my energy field whenever I heard his name; if holding on to those feelings might be affecting my ability to move even more powerfully forward in

---

27   X-Ambassadors - Unsteady - YouTube Source Musixmatch.com

my own life. She says I could become a "free agent" and reclaim my life if I were able to let go of the negative feelings that occasionally lock me in their low vibrational energy. She says I will be far more powerful in doing what I am doing out of my incredible love for my boys rather than any hate I harbour in my being for Corry. By being in such negative energy, she says I am hurting myself because such negativity blocked my ability to let go of the pain of losing my boys—that forgiveness is not for Corry. It is for me and my own well-being.

I have given a lot of thought to the words of my therapist. However, there are times when this aching in my heart is still so deep that I have great difficulty with letting go of the hate and anger I feel for what Corry did, although I know that such emotions do not serve me well. I know Corry loved his boys as best he knew how to love. He was really funny and a joker and fun to be around when he was up. However, I know that wherever his soul has come to rest he will be sitting in his own pain for what he did for all eternity. He destroyed his own legacy by taking away the goals and dreams of Radek and Ryder and their opportunity to shine fully on this earth. Such selfishness still leaves me sitting in great sorrow. Forgiveness???? I'm working on it.

But, may the reader know that this book has been written not to seek revenge for the inconceivable act of injustice that was performed by my ex-husband. Rather it has been written to create awareness in all who take the time to read the story in order to create justice in my boys' names. This book asks others who live the same life I lived with Corry to find their courage and their voices and ultimately join with me in creating a full roster of people who will no longer accept the actions of entitled men who practice coercive control to the detriment of both women and children. I want the justice system to step up and stop giving biological parents rights they do not warrant. I want the justice system to protect innocent children.

To be brutally honest, I hold lawyers, judges, law enforcement, the justice system, Child Services and the hockey community complicit in Corry's action by allowing a vengeful father to put his ideas to destroy me in place through their inaction or by those in roles following inadequate procedures and protocols. I call upon others who simply turned the other way because of the belief that one must not get involved in other people's business. We all must awaken when our guts tell us that some sort of action needs to be taken when an individual bullies any child or other vulnerable individual.

For years, I was on the other end of a tug-of-war rope with Corry MacDougall.

Unfortunately, Corry won that tug-of-war but the ultimate victims were my children. He could not have hurt me more. The justice system also won. There was no need for an expensive trial. No need for a prosecutor or a jury to determine guilt or innocence and to my knowledge, no laws or procedures changed after the death of my sons regarding the enforcement of court orders. Maybe the losers were also the lawyers who Corry would have had to hire to defend his actions if he had not taken his own life.

I was never contacted or involved in any investigation by Child Services concerning the desperate cry of a mother worried about the safety of her children. There was no hearing or review involving me as a mother or Brent as a stepfather to determine our concerns. There was nothing asked of us regarding our thoughts on more effective policies and procedures to change things for other mothers finding themselves seeking help in difficult situations with ex-partners, which unfortunately, are none too rare. All this at the expense of my innocent sleeping children.

My hope? That the book _Gross Misconduct: Hitting From Behind_ is a wakeup call to action to those in positions of power or authority who read my narrative and have the determination and courage to gather all the evidence to examine and fight to change inadequate laws and procedures that do not justly protect women and their children. It is well past time for justice to be done. The answer is not solely in building more women's shelters. Domestic abuse and family violence must end in all homes in our supposed civilized society.

You can be sure as a Mama Wolverine I will tenaciously continue to dig the "puck" out of the corners to ensure such **R&R** legislation makes it through the "Blue Paint" rather than the "Red Tape" and slides unencumbered across the goal line in the making of this world a kinder and safer place for women and children. Such would be but a small reckoning for the deaths of my two precious sons, Ryder Patryk and Radek Stryker.

Facebook Post

Tracy Stark, Mother

Some nights I sit alone. I listen to music and just reflect ...
A song came on tonight ... "Build Me a Daddy" by Luke Bryan. Ugggg.
It's about a child who lost his dad ... and wants a man to rebuild him ...
So many things this "Daddy did not do with him" ... "Build him strong

as superman …"

I wish more than anything that my boys' dad had been built better ... I wish he had loved my kids more than he hated me.

I wish my kids got to live their lives.

I wish they got to date pretty girls, drive fast cars, make bad decisions, Do a keg stand (lol) ...

If I could have built their "dad," he would be me

I would build ME twice …

Because …

I loved my boys more than my own life ...

I wanted nothing but happiness and success for them.

I miss you more than words Ryder and Radek

LOVE MOM

Tracy and her angels

RYDER AND RADEK
JUST WANT YOU TO KNOW….
YOUR MAMA IS DOIN' OK

Appendix

R & R Memorial Foundation

(rnrmemorialfund.com)

Excerpt
by Tracy Stark

On December 19, 2016, my world was changed forever. My two beautiful sons, thirteen-year-old Ryder and eleven-year-old Radek, were tragically and selfishly taken from this world far too soon. Through this unthinkable tragedy, I have not only seen my family and friends come together to support me but also witnessed my entire community of Whitecourt, Alberta, and the hockey community do so as well.

My two boys loved—perhaps that's not a strong-enough word—obsessed over the game of hockey. Whether it was playing in the basement, out on the street, on an outdoor rink, or at the arena, they were unbelievably passionate about the sport. While they were fierce competitors with their opponents, they were even more known for being incredible team players, always the first to support their teammates in their successes or failures. That's just who they were.

With all the support my community has given to me in this time, I, on behalf of my two sons and myself, would like to give something back.

The (Ryder and Radek) *R&R* Memorial Foundation will give children in Whitecourt who otherwise wouldn't have the opportunity to do so the chance to play hockey. I think this is a perfect way to keep Radek and Ryder's memory alive as it reflects their love of sport as well as our family's connection to our community.

When my boys left this earth, it created a hole, not just in my life but in that of our entire Whitecourt community. I truly believe this scholarship will not only help fill that void but will also keep the memory of my boys alive and thriving.

I think this is a perfect way to honour their love of sport as well as give back to those families in our area in need of a hand up.

TO CONTRIBUTE TO OR UTILIZE THE SCHOLARSHIP PROGRAM OF THE **R&R MEMORIAL FOUNDATION**, GO TO:

RnR memorialfund.com.

***

Resources

1. The Canadian Foundation for Trauma Research & Education, Inc. with Dr. Ed Josephs and Dr. Lynne Zettl. http://www.cftre.com
2. Coaching Association of Canada. https://coach.ca/
3. Sheryl Sandberg & Adam Grant, *Option B: Facing Adversity, Building Resilience and Finding Joy* (New York, NY: Alfred A. Knopf, 2017).
4. Laura Markham, PhD, *Aha! Parenting.* https://www.ahaparenting.com/
5. Bruce D. Perry, PhD & Oprah Winfrey, *What Happened to You?* (New York, NY: Flatiron Books, 2021).
6. *Women's Aid: Until Women and Children Are Safe,* https://www.womensaid.org.uk/
7. Ian Mulgrew, "Ian Mulgrew: Andrew Berry's Convictions Raise Child-Protection Issues," *The Vancouver Sun,* October 18, 2019, https://vancouversun.com/news/crime/ian-mulgrew-andrew-berrys-convictions-raise-child-protection-issues
8. "Dr. Peter Jaffe, a psychologist and Professor in the Faculty of Education at Western University and the Academic Director of the Centre for Research and Education on Violence Against Women & Children. He is the Director Emeritus for the London Family Court Clinic, which is a children's mental health centre specializing in issues that bring children and families into the justice system in London, Ontario. He has co-authored ten books, 29 chapters and over 80 articles related to domestic violence, the impact of domestic violence on children, homicide prevention and the role of the criminal and family justice systems." https://www.edu.uwo.ca/faculty-profiles/peter-jaffe.html
9. Alberta Council of Women's Shelters (acws.ca)
10. Ending Violence Association of Canada.org
11. Wellspring Family Resource and Crisis Centre -Whitecourt, Alberta Canada 780-778-6209 or 24/7 Crisis Line: 1 800 467 4049
12. Leading change@acws.ca – A call to action to men
13. A comprehensive list of resources on family violence can be found at https://www.alberta.ca/family-violence-prevention-resources.aspx

A Back Story

Words from the author of the poem, "Heaven's Team" – Lisa Kovacs
December 2021

THIS WEEK BRINGS ME AGAIN TO A TIME IN MY LIFE THAT A "STORY ON THE news" in December 2016 became so much more. The depth of emotion that ran through me was immeasurable. I watched with my mouth agape as the news announced the deaths of two young brothers that I had never met ... Ryder and Radek. Killed by someone who should have loved them ... their obsessive, abusive father. A horrible tragedy, the news said, but it was so much more than that.

As many who have read my poems know, when moments of extreme pain and loss are experienced by others, I feel a need to write even if I personally don't know them. I do believe that much of my poetry is "written" by the souls that have passed. Messages sent ... last words spoken. It's more of a "push" through an invisible veil ... a whisper to my fingertips. This was no different. I felt I needed to write ...

I had felt the urges or whispers of "angels" before, but this was two ... I felt that "push" and the words couldn't be written fast enough. My fingers flew across the keyboard. Within minutes I was reading these words as if I was seeing them for the first time ... tears streaming down my face.

I posted the poem to my profile and a page in Spruce Grove, and from there it went in so many directions. Hundreds and hundreds of shares and likes and even a few edits. I never knew who would read it and what they would think ... until one day I received a message. This message was from a friend of Ryder and Radek's family, asking if she could share it with Tracy, the mother of these two very precious angels. Of course, I was touched that my words had meant so much to others ... and more so that they had reached the person the message was for. Usually, this is where most of my connections end, but not this time.

Christmas Day 2016, just days after she lost her sons, I received a message from Tracy. She will NEVER understand what a gift she gave me when she told me how much she knew these words were from her boys and to the deepest depth of my inner core, I knew it too. It has been read at a candlelight vigil and placed beneath the ice at a memorial hockey game. Tracy then told me words from the poem had been written on each of her sons' urns. There are still no words for how this makes me feel.

I recently received a new message from Tracy, asking permission to have my poem in the book she and her therapist were writing. Those words have always been hers and I told her that ... written in the ink of her pain. Now I look forward to words written by Tracy and Sandra.

The news story that brought me to her is not over for her. It's a continuing nightmare of loss, grief, and anger and every emotion in between. One could NEVER imagine the magnitude it took and still must take to even breathe. Writing the book must have taken everything Tracy had when she barely felt she had anything left. May her words be carried to everyone on the wings of her angels.

Lisa

EVERY DECEMBER
WE REMEMBER

Acknowledgements

WE FEEL TREMENDOUS GRATITUDE FOR ALL THOSE AT FRIESENPRESS WHO have been instrumental in assisting us in the editing and publishing of the book,

Gross Misconduct: Hitting from Behind
A Mother's Love Story.

***To our excellent editor, Rhonda Hayter, whose skill and honesty flipped our first edition of the manuscript on its head, reminding us always that this is a mother's story told through the eyes of her therapist. Rhonda's many brilliant insights and knowledge of the correctness of the written word have made for a superior telling of the story.

***To our publishing specialist, Jess Feser, whose knowledge and leadership with such ever-present calmness in forging through the storms of the writing process and helping us find solutions, we thank you for your professionalism and your kindness. You truly inspired our efforts to keep going forward despite the challenges of writing such a heartfelt book.

***To Teresita Hernandez-Quesada for her expertise in book design and format and to Kiana Karimkhani for her excellent assistance in getting this book in front of the eyes and into the hearts and minds of our readers.

Tracy & Sandra

TRACY STARK:
I extend my sincere thanks to the
all-star players of TEAM TRS

***To my husband, Brent. He is my person. He makes me laugh. He makes me cry. Most of all, he makes my life worth living again. Ryder and Radek were his boys too and we both lost a piece of us that December day. Although he fights with his feelings of anger and complete heartbreak, he still manages to pick me up, brush me off, and give me the confidence to continue on this writing journey. He gives me everything I need to make this happens. He sits countless nights watching me work on the manuscript, feeling helpless but still encouraging me. He is my safe place, my protector and my biggest fan. I could not do this life without him.

***To my beautiful stepdaughters, Alesha and Shelbey. Thank you for accepting me and my boys in your world, loving Ryder and Radek and me and making our family complete. So many cherished moments!

***To the Whitecourt Wolverines. It is not every day you have a whole team behind you and your mission. Brent created a hockey community with our team to ensure Ryder and Radek are never forgotten. What a great team!

***To our staff – Nathalie Beaudoin, Shawn Martin, Troy Ryan, Malcolm Heaven, Wendy Poirier, and our players from past and present. Thank you for "playing" for our boys.

***To all volunteers and the great Whitecourt community who were there for the Whitecourt Wolverine Hockey Club. Thank you to all who supported us as we struggled.

***To Stacy Crossland, Andrew Peard, and Joey and Jenneka Bouchard for speaking on our behalf when we had no words.

***To my incredible support team of friends and family. The list is so very long. They are still the reason we are able to do what we do today – live our lives for our boys. Since the day Ryder and Radek were taken from us, we have been shown so much love and support from around the world. Friends, family, strangers, and communities have all come together to show us that we are not alone.

That we have not been the only ones who have lost these beautiful boys. The world did too. Our heartbreak has been felt by so very many.

***To everyone who stood by us, who sat with us, who organized and attended vigils, who dropped off home-cooked meals, who kept our liquor cabinet full, who kept our home clean and prepared snacks for visitors, who just came to give a hug at the door or sent texts, emails and Facebook messages. Thank you for sharing your love with our family and most of all for showing us your love for our boys.

***To those who continue to send messages of support when the dark days come.

***To the men who loaded up a trailer and packed up my duplex in Spruce Grove and went into that dark dark house of Corry's one last time to grab the boy's belongings ... Forever Grateful.

***To everyone who made the beautiful gifts which are cherished and displayed in the boys' converted bedrooms, aptly named the Zen Den and filled with such love for **R&R.**

***To Rodney Koscielney and Miles Valiquette for your kind words at the boy's funeral.

***To Ryder and Radek's friends who continue to come and hang out and call us randomly, keeping our boys alive.

***To Melissa Baker, artist and photographer, whose creative work has resulted in our amazing front cover.

***To Chad & Laurie Trigg and family of the amazing Backwoods Buffalo Ranch who allowed us the privilege of taking our author photos in the majesty of the buffalo. What an incredible experience!

***To Mackenzie Cortes of Kinderwolf Photography whose gentle spirit and artistic excellence captured our author photos in the midst of the buffalo! You nailed the final touches of *Gross Misconduct: Hitting from Behind* with originality and class.

And finally, to my woman, Sandra Young Kolbuc. When someone comes into your life and gives you her time. Gives you a chair. Gives you her ear…. You sit. You cry. You connect and most of all, you feel the love in the room. Sandra has given me exactly that and most importantly she has given me a voice and the confidence to share my story. She has pushed me to step out of my box and here I am with her beside me … a TEAM to be reckoned with! Thank you Sandra for believing in me and having the patience to work together to get our book out into the world. I can't wait to see where this road takes us next!

LOVE TRACY

SANDRA YONG KOLBUC
"I extend my sincere thanks to the all-star players of TEAM SYK"

***To all those who attempted to read the tragic story but could not because it was so very sad.

***To my sweet man, my husband David, for his continued interest in and support of my passion for writing Tracy's story despite my disappearing for hours upstairs at my desk locked in the writing process. I am forever grateful for his insights, encouragement, male perspective, and deep understanding of the importance of the telling of this story. Fifty years on a winning team with such an incredible man. Not bad….

***To my incredible son, Joseph Kolbuc, former hockey coach of both Ryder and Radek whose love for **R&R** shone through in his inability to put the manuscript down as he read through his tears for two days straight to provide me with his excellent feedback and some great hockey metaphors!

***To my beautifully strong Calgary daughters Meisha and Zoe who in their very busy lives as mothers and professional women still inquired about our progress on the book and continually encouraged my involvement in the writing. Their backing of my foray into authorship was undeniably a tremendous asset.

***To my precious niece Trish who with loving kindness allowed her love story and the incredible painful loss of her late husband Trevor Hayter to be a part of sharing of the 'inside' story. For this, both Tracy and I are sincerely grateful.

***To my dear, dear women friends, aka beta readers, who listened to my concerns as a neophyte writer and found time to read and share their perspectives.

    a.   Connie Braithwaite, my first beta editor, whose sincere loving evaluations of what I had initially written made me a much better teller of the story.

    b.   Donna Vansant & Patricia Wilson, excellent writers in their own right, whose initial input gave me direction on issues with which I was struggling.

    c.   Juliana DeWinetz, Kathleen Nelson & Lesia Hleck who were continually outstanding supporters & cheerleaders in my overcoming the trials and tribulations of this amazing and challenging writing experience.

***To My Technical Support People – Bryan Ritchie and Malcolm Heaven whose expertise was invaluable. I would still be trying to send in Chapter 1 to the publisher without you!

***To My Professional Colleagues:

    a.   Kristin Kolbuc LeCoure, M.A., R. Psych, my excellent AIM counselling colleague & most importantly my oldest daughter, whose many insights were invaluable in understanding Tracy's perspective & who was instrumental in eliminating my long-winded dissertations, which had no place in the dynamics of the telling of the story. Love you!

    b.   Dr. Edward Josephs and Dr Lynne Zettl of the Canadian Foundation of Trauma Research and Education whose wise counsel in working with trauma since beginning my training as an SRT therapist in 2005 has been one of the greatest gifts I have been given in my role as therapist, wife, mother, grandmother, friend, and now author as I learned about CHANGING THE WORLD – ONE NERVOUS SYSTEM AT A TIME.

***And lastly to my beautiful Co-writer – my first-line centre, Tracy Stark. What can I say about such a courageous woman willing to share the intimate details of her life to make for a safer and kinder place for all women and children? Strong. Feisty. Empathetic. Resilient and Caring and filled with the ever-present goal of making sure that the lives of Radek and Ryder, her **R&R,** made a difference in the circumstances of other children. So proud of our work together, Tracy Stark, and of the privilege of sharing in the writing of your story and that of the boys. A scintillating combination of love and tenacity – a winning combination as we set our sights on an incredible goal and scored – TOP SHELF!

LOVE SANDRA

The Writing Team

AUTHOR PHOTOSHOOT

By
Tracy Stark

SINCE THE BOYS DIED, IT WAS SOMETHING I HAD ALWAYS WANTED TO DO. A
Photo Shoot I mean. With a real live buffalo. But somehow it never worked out.
Then as synchronicity would have it, it happened tenfold! I wanted something
unique for our author photo as Sandra and I finished the writing component of
the book. Writing had had many incredible moments of joy as well as a million
tears as we revisited scenes from my life and now, we were finally done with
the content of the script. It had been challenging emotionally, physically and
technically for both me and my therapist-turned writer. But now...now we were
through the most difficult part. The book was almost ready to go into layout
when Sandra called and said "How about a Buffalo Shoot for our picture?" She
knew how I pondered as to why I felt so connected with my boys when I even
saw a buffalo picture or statute. It seemed every single day the picture of the
buffalo in my sitting room gave me strength as I walked by it. As Sandra spoke
about this photo opportunity, I began to think about my first encounter with the
Sturgis buffalo and the connection I felt with Ryder and Radek that moment I
had looked into its eyes. And now...What the hell? She was suggesting a buffalo
photoshoot at the Backwoods Buffalo Ranch. She had already talked to the
owners about such a possibility. This was unbelievable! I followed up immediately and on a perfect September evening it happened and was, without a doubt,
one of the very best experiences of my life.

About the Authors

SANDRA YOUNG KOLBUC, BPE, MSC, RMFT, CCC, IS A COUNSELLING THERAPIST well-trained in working with trauma through the Canadian Foundation of Trauma Research and Education (cftre.com). She is the mother of four adult children and the grandmother of nine and lives with her husband David in the beauty of the boreal forest near Whitecourt, Alberta, Canada, with their two golden retrievers, Sage and Sugah, their two outdoor cats Puff the Magic Dragon and Ghostbuster and the moose, deer, bear and cougar. Sandra continues to influence and champion those needing courage in finding their voices about important matters and the tenacity to speak truth to power.

TRACY STARK and her husband, Brent, are the former co-owners of the Whitecourt Wolverines Junior A Hockey Club. Tracy also heads up The R♥R Memorial Foundation (rnrmemorial foundation.com), established in Ryder and Radek's memory, to provide financial assistance to families needing a hand up in supporting children's participation in sport. She continues to keep the beautiful legacy of her boys alive through the R&R sticker campaign. Tracy is the stepmother of two adult daughters. She and Brent live in Whitecourt, Alberta, Canada, where Tracy continues to advocate for women and children in the name of her sons, Ryder Patryk & Radek Stryker.